Islam, Islamic Law, and the Turn to Violence

by Sam S. Souryal, Ph.D.
The College of Criminal Justice
Sam Houston State University
Huntsville, Texas

Office of International Criminal Justice (OICJ),
Sam Houston State University, Criminal Justice Center
Box 1819, Huntsville, TX 77342-1819, USA
Telephone: (936) 294-3173 — Fax: (936) 294-4053
e-mail: books@oicj.org — www.oicj.org

Printed in the United States of America

ISBN: 0-942511-47-6 Paperbound
Library of Congress Control Number: 2004106544

This book is dedicated to Tom S. Shelly, Lamya Souryal Shelly, Catherine Grace Shelly, and Claire Ellen Shelly.

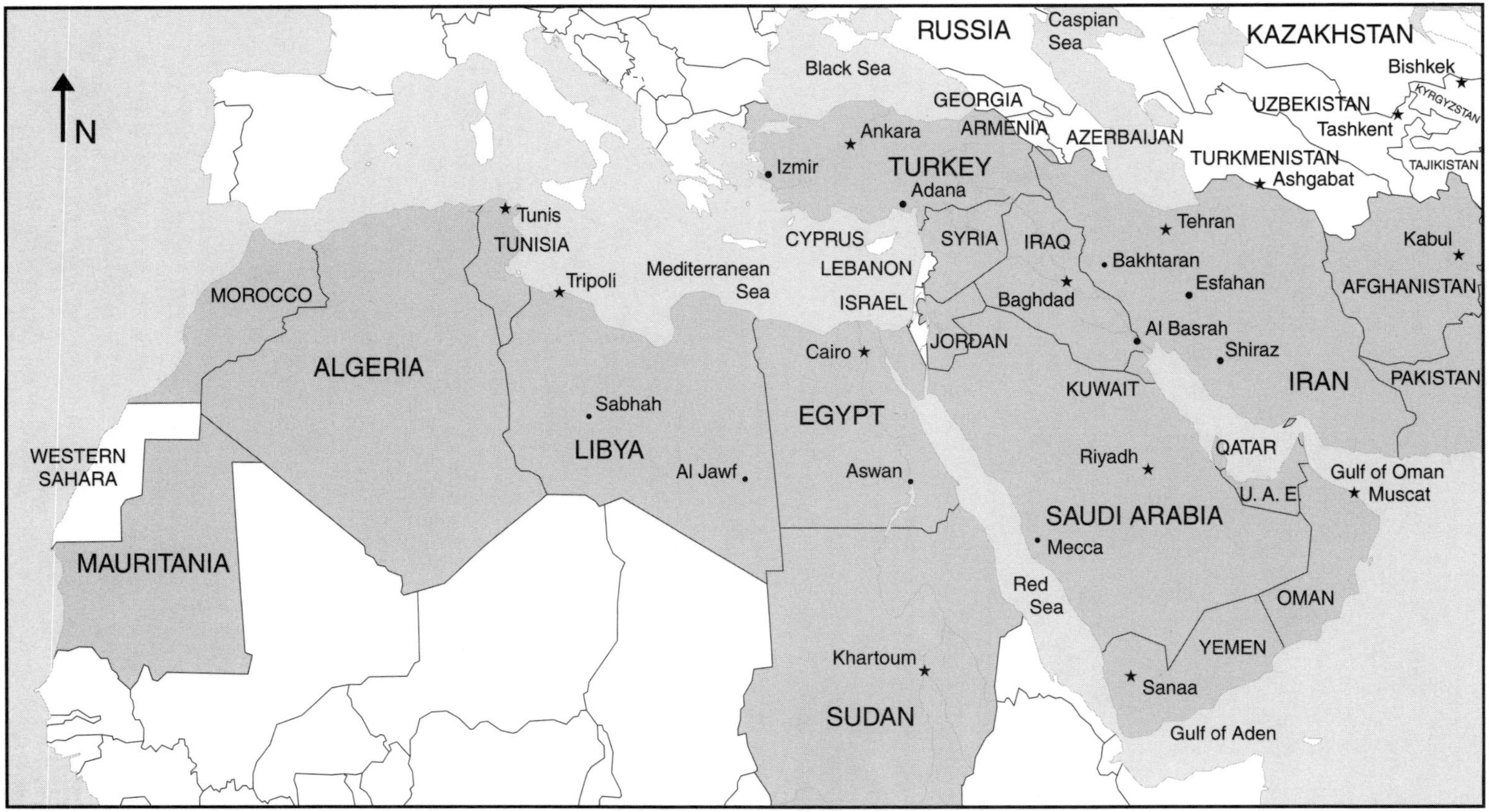
N
RUSSIA
Caspian Sea
KAZAKHSTAN
Bishkek
KYRGYZSTAN
UZBEKISTAN
Tashkent
TAJIKISTAN
TURKMENISTAN
Ashgabat
Black Sea
GEORGIA
ARMENIA
AZERBAIJAN
Ankara
Izmir
TURKEY
Adana
Tunis
TUNISIA
Tripoli
Mediterranean Sea
CYPRUS
LEBANON
ISRAEL
SYRIA
IRAQ
Baghdad
JORDAN
Tehran
Bakhtaran
Esfahan
Al Basrah
Shiraz
IRAN
Kabul
AFGHANISTAN
PAKISTAN
MOROCCO
ALGERIA
LIBYA
Sabhah
Al Jawf
Cairo
EGYPT
Aswan
KUWAIT
Riyadh
QATAR
U. A. E.
Gulf of Oman
Muscat
SAUDI ARABIA
Mecca
WESTERN SAHARA
MAURITANIA
Red Sea
OMAN
YEMEN
Sanaa
Gulf of Aden
Khartoum
SUDAN

Table of Contents

Acknowledgements 11

Prologue 13

Part I
The Nature of Islam **17**

1 Origins of Islam: The Markings of Benevolence 19

2 Mohammed's Footprints: The Sira of Islam 33

3 The Empire That Was Islam: Unintended Consequences 53

Part II
Islamic Law **63**

4 Overview of Islamic Government and Penal Laws 65

5 Crime, Justice, and Punishment in Islamic Jurisprudence 81

6 The Classification of Crime in Islamic Penal Law 101

7 Fundamentals of Islamic Penal Law 119

8 Criminal Responsibility in Islamic Criminal Law 133

9 The System of Proof in Islamic Law 147

Part III
Islamic Fundamentalism and the Turn to Violence **155**

10 From the Book to the Kalashnikov: Islam, Fundamentalism, and Terrorism 157

11 The Crusades: The Ghost Behind All Ghosts 169

12 The Humiliation Due to Military Defeats by Israel 175

13 The Islamic Revolution: Khomeini's New Export 189

14 The Fury of Islam: Bin Laden and Beyond 199

15 Beyond Bin Laden: The Future of the Islamic State 209

Epilogue 225

Glossary 229

Index 241

List of Tables

Table 1
Total Numbers of Offenses for 5 Years (1996 – 2000) 109

Table 2
Total Numbers of Offenses by Population and Rate per 100,000 (2000) 110

Table 3
Total Numbers of Murders by Population and Rate per 100,000 (2000) 110

Table 4
Total Numbers of Thefts by Population and Rate per 100,000 (2000) 111

Acknowledgements

The author acknowledges the previous work by Nagaty Sanad. Professor Sanad is a profound scholar of Islamic Jurisprudence and a well-published student of the Quran. While his views were certainly enlightening, this manuscript goes far beyond the scope of his analysis, especially in elucidating the natures of comparative religion; the geopolitical history of Islam; the foundations of the Islamic faith; the theory of fundamentalism, in general, and in Islam, in particular; as well as the reasons why Islamic fundamentalist groups have turned to violence.

The author also acknowledges assistance by James Blair, a doctoral student at the Criminal Justice Center, Sam Houston State University. Mr. Blair, an ardent student of comparative religion, assisted me in "filling the theological gaps" that I thought unnecessary to mention and helped in editing the manuscript—all when he was totally unfamiliar with the Arabic language frequently used in the manuscript. Having done exactly what he promised to do, James' contribution to the clarity and flow of this manuscript is nothing short of remarkable. This was in no way surprising, since his profound knowledge in so many scholarly areas and his modest temperament in presenting his views have made him the young scholar that each doctoral program must have or produce.

I would also like to acknowledge the valiant work by Harriet Brewster and Christopher Fisher. They have been instrumental in streamlining the manuscript, meticulously editing each chapter and assisting in the general flow of the book.

Finally, I acknowledge the encouraging role of Dr. Richard Ward, dean and director of the Criminal Justice Center, Sam Houston State

University, and the head of the Office of International Criminal Justice. He encouraged me to write this book when a considerable number of books have already been published on the same subject. He offered me valuable guidance when I needed it. His continuing support will always be appreciated.

Sam S. Souryal, Ph.D.
Sam Houston State University

Prologue

The author is Christian, a member of the Coptic Orthodox Church of Egypt. The Copts (whom the Greeks called Gypts, hence the name Egypt) established the first Christian church in Alexandria under the tutelage of the Apostle Mark. After the ascension of Christ, Mark, being one of the least experienced of the disciples, traveled from Jerusalem to Alexandria. There, in 57 A.D., he began his ministry before the Apostles Peter and Paul began theirs in Rome. Ironically, while Egypt at the time of the Greeks was known as "land of the Christians," a few centuries later it was known as a Moslem country. In the 1940's, the Moslems of Egypt, perhaps because of the intellectual prominence of the Al-Azhar University, began the Moslem Brotherhood movement which later dominated Islamic thought in the Middle East and beyond. Some of its younger leaders at the time are now chief architects of the Al-Qaeda movement in Afghanistan and throughout the world.

The reason for this brief commentary is two-fold. First, in the comparative method, especially when a specific religion is being studied, reliance on homegrown authors has been questionable, and at times dangerous. Their cultural and spiritual proximity to the faith being examined, even with the best of their intentions, can blur their objectivity, making them either unable or unwilling (or both) to argue logically or to see points of incoherence which outsiders could so easily see. Second, religion, perhaps the predominant social factor, can alter the political identity of countries as effectively as the political identity of countries can alter the religion being practiced. For instance, while Egypt was pagan under the pharaohs, it became Christian under the Apostle Mark and later converted to Islam after Amr-ibn-al-As, Mohammed's most energetic general, smashed his way toward the Atlantic Ocean. By the same token, Rome was pagan until Emperor Constantine turned it to Christianity; England was Catholic until 1534 when Henry the VIII quarreled with the Pope; and Pakistan was Hindu until 711 when the Moslem General Ibn-Qasim conquered Al-Sind.

As a teenager, this author grew up with Moslem and Jewish friends, classmates, and neighbors who never even asked what the other's religion was. He later joined the police constabulary under the British rule and bonded well with Moslem and Jewish police officers. Together they ate "fool" (brown beans) for breakfast, "falafel" (vegetarian patties) for lunch, played soccer in the afternoons, and went to the cinema in the evenings. They laughed, grieved, and always kept each other's secrets. They respected all of the three faiths and treated religion as a minor issue that mattered not in "the grand scheme of brotherhood." At the time, the Egyptians (i.e., Jews, Copts, and Moslems) had only one common enemy—the British. These were seen as both political "enemies" and religious "infidels," labels that were used interchangeably. As such, fighting the British by whatever means was a "jihad," a blustering word that, as youngsters, resounded in their "bones" before they could understand what the word really meant. As they grew in knowledge, they were exposed to many of the other "isms" in the political lexicon—imperialism, colonialism, socialism, communism, and Zionism. Under these highly charged clichés, the British were seen as the Neo-Crusaders who returned to finish off what the original Crusaders had failed to accomplish a thousand years earlier.

In 1948, the Egyptian social bubble burst and with it the bonding between members of the three religions. As soon as the State of Israel was declared in 1948, the Jewish "boys" were the first to leave with their families, rabbis, Torahs, and their huge financial assets. In 1956, a few of them briefly flew over Egypt as Israeli pilots and demolished the entire Egyptian Air Force on the ground. Furthermore, having been aroused by the establishment of the Israeli State and the news that the Palestinians had been dispossessed of their lands, the Moslem clerics called upon the Moslem nation to begin a Jihad against the Zionist "gangs." In 1967 the Moslem countries were again humiliated in the Six Day War. As a direct result, perhaps, Moslem fundamentalism flourished throughout the region inspiring an extremist ideology, one that could redeem the Arabs' wounded honor. The fundamentalists blamed the Christian West for the military defeat, began a Pan-Islamic culture, and launched a "fidayeen" (martyrs) campaign that spanned across the entire Moslem world.

In the early 1970s, it was the turn for the Coptic minority to leave Egypt. They had been made so politically and socially uncomfortable, they had to begin their own Diaspora, the first since the Apostle Mark hailed from the East. Much like the Jews of the Middle Ages, the Copts assimilated into the cultures of the New World and their children and grandchildren became patriotic Americans, Canadians, British, and Australians. Also, not unlike the Jews before them, the Copts built Coptic churches everywhere they settled. Yet, throughout their Diaspora, they kept asking one of the most solemn questions: "whatever happened to the Moslems we left behind?" For more than four decades, the question was considered rhetorical until the howling sound of extremism became so audible and terrorist groups such as "Ikhwan Moslemeen," "Islamic Jihad," and "Jammaat Islamiyah," became threateningly active. Iyman al-Zawahiri and Mohammed Atef, two of the fiery leaders of the Ikhwan movement became Bin-Laden's top assistants (Atef was later killed in the war in Afghanistan). On September 11, 2001, the rhetorical question raised by Egyptian Copts ceased to be rhetorical, and the answer was calamitous. Not unlike the story of Samson, the Islamic fundamentalists seemed bent on destroying the world as well as themselves. Ironically, the descendents of "Egalitarian Islam" that, for a thousand years, enriched civilization in Byzantine, Persia, South East Asia, North Africa, Spain, and Southern Europe were literally destroying their own civilization while the descendents of the "Crusaders" were hugely strengthening their own. The events of September 11th changed the old assumptions about the world. If for no other reason, they forced social scientists to re-think the symbiotic relationship between religion, technology, and geo-politics.

This manuscript will address these issues not only from the Western perspective, but more so from the Moslem perspective—what went wrong and why are the Moslems now acting this way? To accomplish that, two promising signs are in place, one is personal and the other prophetical. The personal sign is the author himself; a Coptic Christian by birth, a police officer by training, a political scientist by education, a criminal justician by vocation, and a student of comparative religion by necessity. When an Egyptian, he suffered professionally under Moslem rule, yet as an American social scientist, he maintains an objective view that can distinguish between "the religion of Islam" and "the geo-politics of Islam." With this intellectual divide in mind, the author has no reason to make Islam look any better or worse than it inherently is. The prophetic sign, on the other hand, is already visible to all those who have "eyes to see": the terroristic acts in Beirut, Nairobi, Dar-al-Salam, New York, Bali, Mombasa, Al-khobor, Algiers, Istanbul, and currently in Afghanistan, Iraq, and Palestine. While it is infinitely true that terrorism has no religion, the manner in which radical Islamic groups have recently practiced terrorism gave Islam a repugnant reputation that offends the conscience of the world.

One would hope this book could, at least to a small measure, raise national and international awareness to the background of religious extremism and minimize, if not halt, the madness of national and international terrorism.

Sam S. Souryal
Huntsville, Texas
2004

Part I

The Nature of Islam

1

Origins of Islam: The Markings of Benevolence

Writing on religion has been a challenge to social scientists since the subject matter is shrouded in faith, a domain perfectly situated in the realm of metaphysics. As a result, investigating religion cannot be subjected to the logic of science, sociology, psychology, or even to the "logic of logic." Before anything else, all religions presuppose the axiom of "thus Spake the Lord," and whatever the Lord is believed to have said—for whatever reason—is considered beyond the human capacity to reason or explain. It is no wonder that the purpose of all universities in medieval Europe was not to teach philosophy, as most students mistakenly believe, but to use philosophy to coherently reconcile the words of God with what the human mind can understand and accept. Hence, that was the genesis of Oxford, Cambridge, Harvard, Princeton, Yale, and many other old universities. Subsequently, perhaps, the safest (if not the only) way to examine religion is through the comparative method by which one can compare one religion to another and deduce the cultural and social reasons for similarities and differences. By this method, social researchers can intelligently discern the origins, tenets, and principles of any specific religion. The only caveat in this method, however, is for the researcher to maintain a high level of objectivity in the process. This can best be done by genuinely suppressing collective and personal beliefs and by courageously accepting or rejecting arguments solely on the basis of their merits.

In its purist and simplest form, the message of Islam is relatively brief: instilling monotheism and social justice. Without the former, the latter is irrelevant, and without the latter, the former is illogical.

Toward achieving these two values, the philosophy of Islam assumes that, for a number of reasons, people are either unaware of these values, are misinformed, or are inherently opposed to them. Hence, the continual demand that God sends prophets to certain populations, at certain times, in certain locations, to reeducate His people. In Islamic theology, worshiping a monotheist God is the natural and most sacred duty of the created to glorify the Creator. Faithfully practicing this duty constitutes the essence of Islam—total surrender to God with "nothing" to hold back. Consequently, Moslem scholars believe that all God's prophets—regardless of their religious affiliation—were "virtual" Moslems teaching "virtual" Islam. Accordingly, all such prophets including Adam, Noah, Abraham, Isaac, Ishmael, Lot, Job, Jonah, Ezra, Elijah, Jacob, Joseph, Moses, David, Solomon, John (the Baptist), Jesus, and Mohammed, delivered the same message in their own time, culture, and tongue. As a result, one may intellectually appreciate the fact that, while Christianity, Judaism, and Islam seem distinctly separate, in the objective reality of serving a monotheist God, they may be much closer to each other than generally believed (Bahgat, 1993:16-20).

Nevertheless, when comparing these three monotheistic religions, it is evident that each religion is possessed by its own set of Scriptures. These are considered holy since they constitute the foundation of the faith. To followers of each religion, they represent the material transcription of divine revelation, one that is neither subject to negotiation nor doubt. Entertaining either of these sentiments (negotiation or doubt) constitutes a de facto sin that draws God's wrath. In the case of Judaism, Moses is believed to have directly received God's commandments etched on tablets of stone. In the case of Christianity, Jesus was reportedly speaking on behalf of the Father, and to prove it, he was endowed with the ability to perform miracles, including healing the sick and raising people from the dead. In the case of Mohammed, the teachings of Judaism and Christianity—and by implication everything associated with them—were already known and discounted since Judaism and Christianity were considered incremental toward the fulfillment of Islam. Therefore, early Moslems reasoned that what was true in Judaism and Christianity was already incorporated in Islam, and what was not, was false (Lewis, 2002: 36).

Yet, it should come as no surprise that the fundamental tenets of the Jewish and the Islamic faiths are qualitatively even more similar: an observation which members of either faith wouldn't care to appreciate or admit. Both of these religions originated at the time of Abraham when Isaac and Ishmael grew up as half brothers. Isaac remained with his mother Sarah in the land of Canaan, giving rise to Judaism, while Ishmael had to move with his mother, Hagar, to the Arabian land of Mecca, laying the foundation for another prophet and another religion—Mohammed and Islam. Both of these religions are theocratic in the sense that they rest on the concept of a divine law revealed to a prophet in a holy scripture. For the Jews, the scripture is the Torah, given to Moses, and for the Moslems, it is the Quran (literally, Reading), given to Mohammed by Angel Gabriel. The Jewish laws were developed during the first five centuries B.C., culminating in the editing of the Talmud in the sixth century. By contrast, Islamic laws were given to the Prophet Mohammed in an exact and full form during his life, culminating in the classical theory of Islamic jurisprudence (Wegner, 1982: 26-30). Wegner, who brilliantly compared each of the four roots of Islamic law with their Talmudic counterparts, discovered striking parallels between Islamic and Talmudic jurisprudence (Wegner, 1982: 28). By contrast, Christianity is neither theocratic nor does it possess a God-revealed scripture. The Christian scriptures have been a compilation of testimonials by individuals who lived during the time of Christ or after his death. It is also possible that many of these writers never met Jesus nor heard him speak.

Not only do Judaism and Islam share a common theocratic framework, the application of this framework requires similarly prescribed rules of exegesis (Wegner, 1982:28). Mainly for that reason, perhaps, Wegner suggests there is strong circumstantial evidence of Islamic borrowing of fundamental Talmudic concepts. For instance, there are more similarities in the family and social behaviors exhibited by Moslems and Jews than between either group and any other religious group. Most noted among these similarities are the circumcision of boys, the role of women, the passion for rearing children, and dietary laws that prohibit certain foods or the mixing of different kinds of food (i.e., religiously permitted foods in Judaism are called kosher while in Islam they are called Qashar). To underscore similarities between the Quran and the Torah, Wegner calls attention to the Quranic verse "Behold, we have sent it down an Arabic Quran that ye may understand" (Wegner, 1982: 32). The emphasis in Wegner's view is so clearly made by the adjective "Arabic" which, in this context, means an indigenous scripture with equal legitimacy to that of its mother faith (the Torah) or its sister faith (the Bible). Correspondingly, Wegner points out that the textual analysis of the Quran shows that Mohammed equated the Moslem Book with the Jewish Torah and the Christian Gospel (Wegner, 1982: 29-32). Nevertheless, because the new faith had to appeal to more simple and unlettered people, Islamic teachings had to be simple, stern, and uncompromising. Interestingly, not totally unlike Moses, opposition by the powerful Qurayshite clan may have made Mohammed a harsher leader and the Islamic state a more austere culture.

Epistemologically, the word Islam is a noun that stems from the Arabic/ Hebrew root "Salam/Shalom." While some sources suggest that this root was mentioned in the Psalms, Wegner dismisses that view as rhetorical since the name does not actually appear in the Book of Psalms (Wegner, 1982: 29). The word Islam, however, can have two meanings: "peace" as in the term "peace be with you," or "submission" as in one's wholehearted "submission to God." Both meanings identify a behavior that seeks peace under the tutelage of a divine sovereign. The second interpretation may have caused ambivalence in understanding the socio-political behavior of Moslems, since, if taken to an extreme, it may give the impression of fatalism, a behavior generally associated with people who may be irrational, incapable of making appropriate choices, or deeply attached to astrological events. This interpretation may have mistakenly contributed to the formulation of controversial comments about the role and mission of Islam.

From the root Islam, three adjectives are begotten: "Moslem," "Muslim," and "Mohammedan." Traditionally, the first adjective distinguishes the original Moslems from the Middle East region as well as from different parts of the world other than the United States. The second has been used to identify converts to Islam, especially in the United States (i.e., the Nation of Islam). The third is considered objectionable to both Moslems and Muslims, since the Quran explicitly forbad worshiping Mohammed who, despite his great eminence, was considered a man and a mortal. Unlike Jesus, Mohammed never performed miracles, healed the sick, walked on water, or raised anyone from the dead. Moslems regularly call the attention of non-Moslems to the error of calling them Mohammedans, since, if the same error were to be applied to Christians and Jews, they would be called Jesusites or Mosesites. Out of religious respect, however, when the name Mohammed is mentioned, it is incumbent upon Moslems to show reverence by uttering the refrain "May God's Peace be Upon Him." Failure to make this affirmation can reveal a character imperfection on the part of a Moslem.

Wegner elaborates on how the Quran came to reflect such strong Jewish and Christian influences. She suggests that when the Quran was first revealed to Mohammed, Jewish and Christian tribes lived peacefully alongside the population of Mecca. It was only natural then that Mohammed exhort his new converts to learn from them (Jews and Christians), since they too were "ahl-il-Kitab," people who believed in a holy scripture (Wegner, 1982: 29). In 622 A.D., however, Mohammed was forced by his own Qurayshite clan into Hijrah to Medina about 300 miles north of Mecca. In Medina, the new Moslems came into closer contacts with more advanced Jewish and Christian tribes which were more political and less doctrinal than the Jews and Christians of Mecca. Accordingly, despite the fact the Quran is believed to be divinely revealed, it reflected on two subcultures; a Mecca-based culture and a Medina-based culture. The first 90 surats (a Quranic chapter) highlighted the doctrinal influence on Mohammed by the relatively primitive Jews and Christians of Mecca. These surats are mostly short, incisive, impassionate, and replete with prophetic fervor. The remaining 24 surats (the Quran has a total of 114 surats) reflected more deeply on matters of governance and statesmanship as learned from the more sophisticated Medina Jews. These surats are mostly long, verbose, and rich in legislative context. This should not come as a surprise since the Medina Jews had already had a more integrated body of theocratic law, one that regulated all aspects of life both sacred and secular (Wegner, 1982: 29-30).

Yet, during the early Islamic period, Mohammed also had to address the old "Jahiliyah" questions—matters of idolatry, ignorance, and character rottenness that permeated the ancient Arabian culture. This *gemeinschaft* culture continued to exist until it was countermanded by the newly revealed Quran. That might have caused the new religion to develop gradually and cautiously. For example, the Islamic prohibition on drinking alcohol had to be implemented in three stages over 20 years, before it finally became a full-fledged commandment. The first stage was to command Moslems to abstain from drinking alcohol because drinking made people vulnerable to physical and religious sins; the second stage was to command Moslems to abstain from drinking in preparation for prayers; and the third stage was to command Moslems to abstain totally.

Jewish and Christian traditions are thought to have reached Mohammed through tales told by Jewish and Christian merchants traveling the southern trade routs of Arabia. As a trader and convoy leader himself, Mohammed and his trading parties reportedly camped each night at Jewish and Christian monasteries where Mohammed was able to hear chanting monks and arguing Rabbis. This is probably one reason, perhaps, why Islam, Judaism, and Christianity entertain similar views on life, worship, monasticism, and social ethics. For example, they all believe that God created Adam and Eve, placed them in the Garden of Eden, and instructed them not to submit to Satan by eating of the forbidden tree. The punishment for violating God's commandment was death. According to all three religions, when Adam and Eve ate of the tree, they discovered their nakedness, were expelled out of Eden, and their descendents were forever doomed to toil. As a result, God sent prophets to convey in their own tongues a message that elaborates on God's commandments and instructs people how to worship God. Over time, new prophets were sent to complete the messages of the previous ones. That is thought to be the origin of prophets like Adam, Noah, Moses, Abraham, and Mohammed. According to Islamic teachings, Mohammed was the last prophet and was designated "Khatim al-Anbyia," the completer of all religions (Hykal, 1976:72). Arguably, no other prophet of his stature has since appeared.

Following in the Jewish tradition, Islam used the name Allah for God, a name not too different from Elohim, the name ancient rabbis used for God. Islam also required keeping a Sabbath day (in Arabic *Sabt*) to be set apart for group worshipping. However, to distinguish the new religion, Friday was the Moslem Sabbath. Furthermore, and also in the Jewish tradition, Islam did not recognize any separation between religion and law (church and state). In this context, it may not be coincidental that the Hebrew word din, which means "law", also means "religion" in Arabic (Wegner, 1982: 27). Wegner further points out that the "five pillars" of Islam (affirmation of monotheistic faith, prayer, fasting, almsgiving, and pilgrimage) were not indigenous to Islam; they were derived from Hebrew/Aramaic terminology (Wegner, 1982: 27). Indeed, the Hebrew word for almsgiving is Izedaka, while in Arabic it is Sadaka. Furthermore, Islamic teachings are taught to youngsters in Madrassas (religious schools for children), a derivation of the Jewish word Midrash which means the same kind of teaching institution. Furthermore, it may be especially interesting to note that despite the long period of time that lapsed between Moses and Mohammed, they reportedly used the same reply when God commanded each of them individually to "read" His divine scripture. Moses reportedly replied, "I am not a man of words" (Exodus 4:10), while Mohammed replied, "I am not a reciter" (Wegner, 1982: 27).

From a ritualistic perspective, some of the more common features which Islam borrows from Judaism and Christianity include reciting the rosary, growing beards, wearing turbans, sacrificing animals on "adha" (day of atonement), and making the pilgrimage to Mecca. To increase the Moslem population, especially in the beginning when new converts were necessary, and not unlike Jewish and Christian traditions of the time, Islam allowed polygamy (although limiting it to no more than four wives at a time). To make this practice work, Islam allowed husbands to divorce their wives with considerable ease. Yet to maintain the integrity of the "Ummah" (Islamic society), it also made slandering the chastity of women a Hadd crime, a serious offense. Furthermore, unlike Judaism or Christianity, conversion to Islam was made simpler. All that was necessary to convert was to publicly utter the Shehada, a one line article of faith that proclaims, "Allah is the only God and Mohammed is His messenger." Moreover, when the early Moslems needed an Islamic calendar commemorating the Prophet's Hijrah to Medina, they naturally adopted the Jewish lunar calendar that is 11 days shorter than the Gregorian calendar (accordingly, every 34 Hijri years would equal 33 Gregorian years). All in all, Mohammed, not unlike Moses, assumed both roles as prophet and chief executive of the faith. In Christianity, Jesus assumed only the former role rejecting the latter, which he left to Caesar. In time, Saint Augustine (345-430 A.D.) provided Christian doctrines that indirectly articulated the role of popes as the chief executives of the Catholic Church.

From a practical perspective, however, Mohammed had to distinguish the new religion from its predecessors. Before Mohammed's days, the Jews and the Christians were accustomed to reading their scriptures publicly and invariably aloud. The Jews called their scriptures Miqra (from the root *qaraa* meaning reading) while the Christians called their scripture *qeryana* (possibly from the same root). Mohammed used the word Quran (also from the same root). Although the word Quran is morphologically close to the word *qeryana*, using the name Quran demonstrated an attempt to distance the new faith from Judaism; the more dominant religion in pre-Islamic Arabia. Furthermore, while the Jews and Christians used to read their scriptures within the confines of their synagogues and churches, Islam assigned a special reader (Mua'zzen) to proclaim the scriptures five times a day from the rooftop of mosques. Also, while the Jews were commanded to pray at least three times a day, Islam increased the number to five. Such distinctions were thought necessary to educate the converts to Islam who were mostly illiterate (including Mohammed himself), as opposed to the more literate Jews and Christians of the time. These distinctions were necessary to remind the Moslem worshippers of keeping their ferud (plural of fard, meaning a scriptural obligation), especially the fard of salat (prayer).

Having said all of that, the influence of Judaism and Christianity on Islam can hardly be overstated. This may also have given rise to the misguided belief by many medieval European and Oriental Christians that Islam was indeed another heretic Christian sect. Many non-Moslem groups attacked the person of Mohammed and attributed some of the most unbecoming epithets to him. Pope Innocent III, for example, considered Mohammed an Antichrist and the Quran a "tissue of absurdities" while Dante (1224-1274) in The Divine Comedy consigned Mohammed to one of the lowest Hells with all the sowers of scandals and schism (Hykal, 1993:x1iv). While such attacks were more likely motivated by ignorance, they often revealed sentiments of resentment and contempt, sentiments repeatedly endorsed by the Christian Crusaders of the 11th and 13th centuries. Gradually, however, Islam grew into a more mature and egalitarian faith. Unsurprisingly, perhaps due to cultural transcendence and intellectual awareness, many Christian scholars including Saint Thomas Aquinas (1224-1274 A.D.) began communicating with Islamic philosophers (i.e., Ibn-Rushd, known in the West as Avernos) extending to them a generous hand of tolerance. Along the same pursuit, Pope John Paul II made it customary to meet with Moslem scholars in the Vatican and even to visit Moslem lands.

Unlike Christianity, Moslems believe in a direct prophethood, the kind through which God speaks directly to His prophets, conveying to them a timely message or correcting their speech or acts when they err. In this tradition, Moslems believe that the Quran was dictated to Mohammed (who was illiterate) by the Angel Gabriel and, as such, the Quranic teachings are divine, precise, and universal. Unlike Christian scriptures, which were edited and adjusted several times after the time of Christ, Moslems believe that the Quran spoke authoritatively to all people of the world regardless of religion, race, ethnicity, or gender.

They believe the Quranic scriptures address the essence, unity, and attributes of worship as well as support the institutions of family, city, government, and state. Consequently, the Moslems firmly believe that Mohammed was the ruler of an Ummah (nation), the commander of its armies, and its permanent teacher, organizer, and developer. Arguably, this belief may explain why the Moslems have been accused of unduly "essentializing" their faith and believing in its perpetuity.

Of greater significance, perhaps, is that the Quran explicitly forbids Moslems from attacking the person of Jesus or the Holy Mother Meriam (Mary). The Quran teaches that Jesus was a servant of God, was endowed with a scripture, and was assigned to prophethood by God. It also holds that Jesus was divinely blessed on the day of his birth since his mother (who has a special Surat in the Quran in her name) bore him as a virgin, reaffirming the divinity of both of them. Not only does the Quran honor Jesus and Mary, it presents them in such a light that the reader cannot help but feel a fraternal feeling toward Christianity when certain Quranic verses are read (Hykal, 1976:xxxix). In a famous story told by Al-Bukhari, Mohammed was once sitting in front of his house when a funeral procession passed. When the Prophet stood up as a sign of respect, one of his companions alerted him that the deceased was a Christian. Mohammed reportedly kept standing, responding, "Isn't he a human and an equal?" (Bebawy, 2003: 80). Yet, the Quran advises Moslems to expect less support from the Jews than from the Christians because the latter "have monks and priests among them and do not take to false pride" (Haykal, 1976: 64).

From the Moslem perspective, Mohammed was a greater prophet than his predecessors because, while not claiming to be a son of God, he accomplished more than Moses and Jesus combined as evidenced by the vast Moslem empire that so soon ensued. Moslems believe that their dramatic victories, especially between the 7th and the 17th centuries, were due before anything else to the influential message of Islam. During that period, the Moslems militarily vanquished paganism in Arabia, conquered Egypt, Persia, Byzantine, Yemen, India, and parts of China, and were instrumental in spreading Islam in Spain and the southern European region. Given these successes, Moslems, rather emotionally, believed that God was on their side because Mohammed, being the last prophet, was the most favored by Him. Subsequently, while Moslems do not dispute the divinity of Jesus, they believe Mohammed brought about a more perfect religion, one that transcended the weaknesses in both Judaism and Christianity. Consequently, while some German scholars have recently recommended Islam as an alternative to Judaism and Christianity (Hoffman, 2001: 10-13), other European thinkers accuse Moslems of "essentializing" their faith by creating a hegemonic self-image specifically to appeal to the illiterate masses of the world (Senghass; 1988).

To further contrast Islam with Christianity and Judaism, one should acknowledge the existence of three fundamental theological doctrines that are foundational to each faith. These doctrines are: (1) the Christian belief that Jesus is the Son of God; (2) the Jewish belief that Jews are God's only chosen people; and (3) the Islamic belief that the Quran is God's literal word that physically descended "unzil" upon Mohammed. In a comparative sense, these theological doctrines establish the immovable nature of Christ as the essence of Christianity; God's irrevocable will that the Jews are His chosen people for all times; and the Quran as God's final testament given to Mohammed. While these doctrines may not be philosophically rational or lend themselves to logical arguments, they stubbornly form the theological domain of each religion—without them, the faith cannot stand and anyone who doubts them is a heretic.

Despite these foundational doctrines, Moslem theologians argue that while Islam acknowledges the prophethood of Jesus, Christians do not acknowledge the prophethood of Mohammed. They believe that is due in part to five reasons. First, many Christian leaders, especially those who are unable or unwilling to understand the universal nature of God, could not accept the idea of a subsequent prophet to Jesus since such acceptance can threaten the integrity of their faith. Second, while Christianity upholds trinitarianism, Islam rejects anything but strictest monotheism. In Islamic theology, the idea of a trinity represents utter kufr (blasphemy) since God, in Islamic belief, is an absolute One. Moslem theologians argue that God could not have had children (even in the metaphorical sense) since such an assumption would fundamentally alter the nature of His deity. They also ask "if God indeed had children, why do Christians assume Jesus is the only child?" Third, Christianity is fundamentally based of the doctrine of the original sin, while Moslem theologians reject that view. They argue that if the doctrine were true, then God has failed in creating people in his image (as he promised). Furthermore, punishing people for the sins of their forefathers is grossly unjust. Fourth, Christianity teaches that for believers to get to Heaven, they must be saved by the blood of Jesus. Moslems consider this obligation unnecessary since God must, in his omniscient nature, be able to save His people without making them go through such a terrible ritual. Included in this view is the belief that Christ was neither crucified nor ascended to Heaven. Fifth, while Christianity upholds a hierarchy of popes, cardinals, and bishops serving as intermediaries between God and man, Islam rejects the need for such a hierarchy and considers such a practice idolatrous—one that is conducive to religious corruption.

As to the self-propagated image of Islam, many non-Moslem critics characterize Islam as a self-inflated and theonomous faith (Senghaas, 1998: 35-37). They argue that when compared to other religions, it can teach intolerance (i.e., Islam is the only religion that condemns to death those Moslems who convert to other religions); absolutism (i.e., Shariah law applies beheading and hand amputation as punishment for seemingly minor crimes); inflexibility (i.e., requiring a specific number of prayers with specific physical rituals to be performed every day); harshness (i.e., requiring fasting during the entire month of Ramadan, prohibiting food and drink and all other pleasures throughout the month); segregationism (i.e., requires total separation between the sexes until marriage); and sexism (i.e., treats males better than females, especially in matters of inheritance and individual freedom). This hegemonic image, critics argue, may have created a state of irrational submission to a hypostatized "reason of Islam" and its wide-ranging consequences. They further argue that, consistent with this glorified image of the faith, Islam may have contributed to the "dimming of the Moslem mind" by requiring its adherents to: (1) think in terms of a closed society; (2) live collectively rather than enjoying individual freedom; (3) develop an unrealistic sense of religiosity rather than a liberal concern for individuals; (4) lose sight of pluralism as a social value and democracy as a beneficial political instrument; and (5) totally submit their lives to the sovereignty of God at the cost of denying human reason and choice. In essence, the critics argue that the hegemonic "reason of Islam" may have led Moslems to reject plurality, forbid dissension, endanger the life and limb of sinners, and create a condition of mental and physical persecution (Senghaas, 1998: 37).

In direct opposition to Senghaas, however, Lewis (2002: 82), an eminent scholar in both Judaic and Islamic studies presents a considerably different view of Islam. Lewis states:

It is often said that Islam is an egalitarian religion. There is much truth in this assertion. If we compare Islam at the time of its advent with the societies that surrounded it—the stratified feudalism of Iran and the caste system of India to the East, the privileged aristocracies of both Byzantine and Latin Europe to the West—the Islamic dispensation does indeed bring a message of equality. Not only does Islam not endorse such systems of social differentiation; it explicitly and resolutely rejects them. The actions and utterances of the Prophet, the honored precedents of the early rulers of Islam as preserved by tradition, are overwhelming against privilege by descent, by birth, by status, by wealth, or even by race, and insist that rank and honor are determined by piety and merit in Islam.

In the Jewish Journal (2004), Nir Rosen echoes Lewis's evaluation of Islam. He states:

Although the Quran frequently condemns Jews, it mandates a modus vivendi with them, relegating them to an inferior but protected status. Historically, the Moslem attitude toward Jews lacked the racial element of European anti-Semitism, holding that if a Jew converted, he was to be treated like any other Moslem. But the conflict over Palestine, the creation of Israel and its defeat of Arabs and occupation of their land, intensified anti-Jewish feeling. Arab and Moslem authors began to adopt European racist and anti-Semitic theories about Jewish conspiracies to explain Israel's existence, strength, and American support. Those seeking to give these theories religious legitimacy have little trouble finding support in the Quran, a sprawling work with many passages that are open to interpretation.

In the following chapters, the reader will be made more closely familiar with the history and culture of Islam; where did it come from, what does it mean, and how did it evolve into what it is now?

Sources

Bahgat, A. (1993). *The Prophets of God.* Cairo: Dar-al-Shorouk.

Bebawy, N. (2003). *Terrorism: a non-Islamic Industry*. Cairo: Alahram Publishers.

Bucaille, M. (1979). *The Bible, The Quran and Science*. Indianapolis: American Trust Publications.

Haykal, M. H. (1976). *The Life of Muhammed.* USA: North American Trust Publications.

Hoffman, M. (2001). *Islam as an Alternative*. Bavaria: Bavaria Verlag & Handel.

Lewis, B. (2002). *What Went Wrong? Western Impact and Middle Eastern Response.* New York: Oxford.

Rosen, N. (2004). "Hostility to Jews Permeate New Iraq," The Jewish Journal of Los Angeles. Los Angeles, March 12-18: 22-23.

Senghass, D. (1998). *The Clash within Civilizations: Coming to Terms with Cultural Conflicts*. New York: Routledge.

Wegner, J. R. (1982). *Islamic and Talmudic jurisprudence: The four roots of Islamic law and their Talmudic counterparts*. The American Journal of Legal History, 26, 25-71.

2

Mohammed's Footprints: The Sira of Islam

Mohammed is the only prophet of Islam. He is its messenger, advocate, doctrinarian, and, during his life, the head of the Islamic state. To understand Islam, the reader should first be familiar with Mohammed's biography and his life philosophy. For a better understanding of these matters, one should also read the Hadith (i.e., acts and sayings of the Prophet, a sub-discipline of Islam that will not be examined in this book). Without a good familiarity with Mohammed's acts and sayings, one's knowledge of Islam would more likely be inaccurate, incomplete, or both.

While there are numerous references to the Prophet in the Quran, numerous biographies by trustworthy narrators and intellectuals exist. Prominent among these biographies are Hykal's *The Life of Mohammed* (1976) and Armajani's *Middle East: Past and Present* (1970). Hykal treats the biography of Mohammed with extraordinary precision and logic that resembles modern-day scientific method. Armajani, on the other hand, chronicles the Prophet's life from a humanistic and anecdotal perspective. Nevertheless, the reader should be aware that Mohammed's life, like the life of other prophets, was most likely fictionalized by his adoring followers who began writing his biography almost a century after his death. Interestingly, and not unlike the life of Jesus, there is no record of Mohammed's life between the ages of 12 and 24 (Armajani, 1970).

Mohammed was born in 570 A.D. during the Year of the Elephant when Abyssinian tribes using elephants reportedly invaded Mecca to destroy the temple of Kabba (Hykal, 1976). He belonged to the Quraysh family, one of the less influential tribes of the Hashim clan (the ancestors of the Hashimit monarchies that existed in Iraq and continue to exist in Jordan). Mohammed's father, Abdullah (literally, the slave of God) died before Mohammed was born, and his mother died when he was about five years old. Consequently, young Mohammed was raised by his granduncle, Abdul Muttalib, and after his granduncle died, he was raised by his uncle Abu Talib. When Mohammed was 12 years old, he accompanied his uncle Abu Talib to al-Sham (now Syria and Lebanon) where they reportedly encountered a Christian monk by the name of Bahira. The monk recognized in Mohammed the signs of prophethood and advised the uncle not to take the child too far away from al-Sham since, if the sign were to be recognized, Mohammed could be harmed by pagan tribes (Hykal, 1976: 54).

At the age of 24, Mohammed was known for his handsome features, uprightness, intelligence, charity, and his knowledge of the environment surrounding him. He was employed by a commercial enterprise run by the Quraysh family. Because he showed knowledge in the direction and movement of the stars, he was assigned to travel with camel caravans that criss-crossed the Arab peninsula and beyond (perhaps to Persia). As a caravan leader (most likely only a guide), he frequently had the opportunity to listen to conversations between his masters and the Christian and Jewish merchants. Armajani (1970: 30) suggests that Mohammed was probably curious, and possibly frustrated, when the conversations kept referring to one holy book or another. Mohammed reportedly wondered why his own people had no book to quote as well. If Armajani is correct, these conversations might have been the impetus of the idea of an Arabic holy book and an Arabian-based religion.

As Mohammed became more familiar with aspects of the trade and the traditional camel routes (including the main locations where caravans usually camped in the desert), his role became more important to Khadija, the rich female owner of the business. Since Mohammed was known to be fair, honest, and reflective (Armajani, 1970: 31), Khadija, who had lost her husband and decided to run the business herself, promoted Mohammed to the position of business manager and offered herself to him in marriage. This event may demonstrate that the role of women in ancient Islam could not have been as dismal as today's critics believe. Khadija's role contradicts the critics' view, since she held property and was self-supporting. The matrimony between Khadija and Mohammed was a milestone; it made Mohammed rich and gained him a higher social status. For that, Mohammed (who was 25 and Khadija 40) rewarded Khadija by not taking another wife (a common practice in both pre-Islamic and Islamic Arabia) besides her for the rest of her life. During their married life, the couple had two sons and four daughters. His sons died in their infancy while his daughters lived to marry influential compatriots in Mohammed's campaign for prophethood.

Like other reflective men of the Quraysh family, and in the hope of someday receiving prophethood, Mohammed acquired and furnished one of the many volcanic caves outside Mecca (he called the cave Hiraa') to be used as a resting place when he wanted to escape the desert heat or to meditate. There, he began to see visions in his dreams of the truth he sought. While he reportedly saw some truth in the teachings of Christians and Jews, he also saw a fair amount of falsehood and illusion that verged on paganism. At the time, he was also convinced that his people had gone astray and that their spiritual lives had been corrupted by the idols they falsely worshipped. The only truth he reportedly embraced was that God was One, Compassionate, and Merciful, and that all men would be held responsible for their deeds (Hykal, 1976:72). At Hiraa', Mohammed developed the habit of praying continuously and fasting for long periods of time. His fast regularly included the Jewish day of Tisha B'AV (the ninth day of the Jewish month of AV, known in Arabic as Ashura) that commemorated the victory of Moses over his Egyptian oppressors (Khalid, 1986: 80). Mohammed's custom of fasting Ashura continued until, later in the Quran, God designated the month of Ramadan as the only Moslem fast.

In the month of Ramadan, 610 A.D., Mohammed began hearing voices that he later described as the "ringing of bells" (Armajani, 1970: 31). Mohammed felt like an angel was approaching him, commanding him to read. Mohammed, illiterate as he was, replied "What shall I read?" The Angel said "iqra bism rabbika alathi khalaq… khalaq al- insan min alaq" [recite in the name of God who created man from a blood clot] (Hykal, 1976:73). Mohammed reportedly recited these words while trembling with fear and awe. According to Islamic stories, he thought he was "possessed" like many of the Jahiliyah (pre-Islamic ignorance) cult members. He reportedly was puzzled and even thought of committing suicide (Armajani, 1970:31). From that day on, Mohammed began seeing "visions of the truth dawning upon him [and] filling his conscience with great light" (Hykal, 1976:31). Fulfilled by what he had seen and heard, Mohammed returned to his home in Mecca (Hykal, 1976: 32).

Upon returning, Mohammed asked Khadija to wrap him in blankets because he was shivering as if he was struck with fever. He explained to her his experience, intimating his fear that his mind might have betrayed him, and that he had become mad. Khadija stood firm by her husband, devoid of any doubt of his sanity. Respectfully, even reverently, she said, "Joy to my cousin who dominates Khadija's soul, I pray and hope that you will be the Prophet of this nation. He will not let you down. You will be kind to your kin, your speech will all be true, you will rescue the weary, entertain the guest and help the truth prevail" (Hykal, 1976:32). The night that Mohammed received his call to prophethood became later known as the "Night of Power" (Armajani, 1970: 31).

Mohammed's discovery of Allah (the totality of all essences) symbolized God's tradition of revealing Himself to successive prophets as believed by the adherents of both the Jewish and Christian faiths (Hykal, 1976: 12). In the same sense, it was only natural that Mohammed assumed the prophethood as commanded. As a prophet, he began reiterating the stories of Adam, Noah, Abraham, the Children of Israel, and more frequently those preaching the oneness of God—the Creator of all matter, the Knower of all things, the Master of all destiny, yet the Compassionate and the Merciful. He preached that Allah is not only the God of Christians and Jews, but of the al-alameen (all people). He took advantage of the months of the pilgrimage when thousands of people traveled to Mecca to advocate his mission as a divine messenger. He reminded his audiences that he had been sent by Allah to dissuade them from practicing idolatry and to prepare them for the Day of Judgment and the punishment or reward that awaits them. Not unlike Isaiah's message, he predicted that "the trumpet shall sound one blast and the earth with its mountains shall be lifted up and crushed with one crash…on that day, the event [shall] befall…on that day all will be exposed; not a single secret will be hidden" (Armajani, 1970: 32).

In the beginning of his prophethood, not too many people took Mohammed seriously. His first believers were his wife, Khadiga, and his servant, Zayd. Among the first group he converted were Abu Bakr, who later became Mohammed's son-in-law and his successor, the Caliph of Islam. Yet it was the conversion of the next man, Omar ibn-al-Khattab, that was crucial to Mohammed's early successes. Omar, who later succeeded Abu Bakr as the second Caliph, brought with him to Islam the loyalty of other tribes which before had fought against Islam. Unlike other early believers, Omar did not conceal his conversion to Islam but proclaimed it everywhere. He also quarreled with the Qurayshites over disallowing the Moslems to make the pilgrimage to Mecca until they finally agreed to allowing them to pray only in the vicinity of the Kabba (Hykal, 1976: 115).

As Mohammed's influence increased, the Qurayshite control diminished. Although Mohammed's uncle Abu-Talib did not support his nephew's claim to prophethood, as an influential Qurayshite he protected him. Although many of the Qurayshite clan begged Mohammed to include in his faith some of their old gods and goddesses (in particular, Al-Lat, Al-Uzza, and Manah who were considered the daughters of Allah) in return for their support, Mohammed refused. As a result, the Qurayshites continued to ignore him, denigrate his prophethood, and persecute his followers. By the same token, many of Mohammed's fellow businessmen saw in his preaching the economic ruin of Mecca. They thought that preaching a new religion could destroy the pantheon around the Kaaba and possibly the Kaaba itself. As a result, the pilgrimage itself could be interrupted, and without it the significance of Mecca would be reduced and the Qurayshites would lose their economic prominence. Indeed, until 1936, when oil was discovered in Saudi Arabia, the greatest source of income for the Arab tribes came from the pilgrimage to Mecca.

The continuing hostility to Islam by the Qurayshites further spread the influence of Islam and its followers' determination to resist defamation. Indeed, a propaganda war began when the Qurayshites ridiculed Mohammed, insulted his mission, attempted to bribe him, and inflicted harm on his followers. Nevertheless (and perhaps because of the continuing war of words), Mohammed's mission became even better known in the outer environs of Mecca, as well as among the other tribes in the Arab peninsula. As a result, the Qurayshites threatened Mohammed and his followers. He responded by intensifying his preaching to them and refuting their arguments with what became known as Mohammed's "magical eloquence" (Hykal, 1976: 119). Not unlike the cases of Peter and Paul, Mohammed's mission began by preaching and reciting the Quran (from memory) at night in his house. Many of the antagonistic Qurayshites went secretly to hear him, wondering if he was really calling unto a religion of truth (Hykal, 1976: 120). During that period of time, Mohammed reportedly received a reinforcing call from God: the dramatic isra', a nocturnal journey to heaven and back. Mohammed was miraculously transported from al-Kaaba to Jerusalem where he ascended to the seventh heaven on a white horse with wings. And since Jerusalem served as the terrestrial station for Mohammed's memorable journey, the city—already sacred to Jews and Christians—also became sacred to the Moslems. They now consider Jerusalem the third holiest city after Mecca and Medina; the latter is where Mohammed later resided until his death.

Threatened by Mohammed's rising popularity, the Qurayshite resentment to his prophethood increased. Furthermore, Mohammed had to face one of his darkest years when, in 619 A.D., two of his major supporters died; his uncle Abu Talib and his wife Khadija. The Qurayshites, nevertheless, decided to put an end to Mohammed's prophethood by assassinating him. To avoid tribal blame for killing the first Arabian prophet, however, the Qurayshites devised a uniquely intriguing scheme by which one member of each tribe, armed with a sword, would enter Mohammed's house and simultaneously hit him with a single blow so as to hide the identity of the killer. The conspiracy was revealed to Mohammed beforehand, and, to avoid more bloodshed among the tribes, he decided to emigrate to Yathrib, a predominantly Jewish town about 300 miles north of Mecca. On July 16, 622 A.D. Mohammed and his followers secretly began their Hijrah (emigration), and, to commemorate that act, that day became the first day of the Moslem calendar.

The people of Yathrib (a city known in the Torah as the Beloved or the Virgin City, where King David was also rumored to have settled) were more supportive of Mohammed and his followers (Khalid, 1986: 27). They physically and economically protected him, ensuring the preservation of his prophethood. The town was later renamed al-Medina al-Munawara (the Enlightened City) because it gave refuge to Mohammed. The people of Medina also received a new identity. They became "Ansar Al-Islam" (supporters of Islam), a term that is presently used by some radical Islamic groups fighting in Afghanistan and Iraq. At the time of the Hijrah, the residents of al-Medina consisted of three groups: (1) al-Muhajirin, the emigrants who came with Mohammed from Mecca; (2) al-Ansar, the local residents who supported Mohammed and his Muhajirin; and (3) the Jewish tribes which initially moved to Yathrib from their homeland in Canaan to escape enslavement by Nebuchadnezzar, the king of Babylon (now Iraq). These Jewish tribes supported Mohammed at first. They later fought him, and eventually they were forced to leave town.

In Medina, Mohammed noted that, unlike the Jews and the Christians, the Moslems had no "sacred house of worship" similar to the Kabba in Mecca. Furthermore, to defend themselves, the Christian and Jewish tribes relied primarily on building fortresses. For instance, Khalid reports that the Jewish tribes alone erected 59 fortresses (Khalid, 1978: 26). Faced with these unfamiliar conditions in Medina, Mohammed had to make fundamental changes regarding the identity of his religion. First, he required that the Moslems build a mosque and, when they pray, they face in the direction of Mecca, where the Islamic faith originally began, instead of Jerusalem as was the custom of the Jewish tribes. The direction which the Moslems face during prayer is known as "Qibla" and is considered a significant theological symbol of Islam. Second, Mohammed established the first Moslem constitution, a peace covenant with the peoples of Medina known as the "Sahifa Accord." The Accord became known as the Islamic "rule of law charter." It included a general section applicable to the treatment of all people—in a sense, a universal statement of equality. While this section is rather simplistic (compared to modern day declarations), its essence was not too different from the 1784 declaration of The Rights of Man or the 1948 United Nations Universal Declaration of Human Rights (Khalid, 1986: 75-94). The Charter also included a more detailed section requiring the benevolent treatment of Jews.

Some of the general rules of the Accord were: (1) all Moslems regardless of tribe or family form an ummah, a community of believers; (2) Moslem tribes treat each other with justice and fairness; (3) Moslem elders treat their people with "Maaruf" (decency); (4) all believers are considered equal before God; (5) Moslems must avoid acts of oppression, corruption, or evil; (6) all believers must apply justice, both in times of war or peace; (7) murderers must be killed as punishment for their crimes unless the victim's family forgives the murderer; (8) believers must not entertain unbelievers in their homes; and (9) when believers disagree, they must ask God for spiritual guidance (Bebawy, 2003). Among the Accord's specific rules regarding the treatment of Jews were: (1) the Jews are to be considered a community with the believers; (2) a Jew is equally free to practice his faith as a Moslem; (3) all Jewish tribes are equal, none is any higher or lower than another; (4) Jewish people are free to practice their religion in their own ways at their own temples; (5) Jewish wealth and assets belong to the Jews and cannot be taken away from them; (6) Jews can freely and easily join Islam, and, if they so do, must be treated the same as other believers; (7) Jews are equal to believers before God; and (8) the only difference between a Moslem and a Jew is the extent of his or her piety (Bebawy, 2003).

The Islamic state Mohammed created in Medina was basically a federation of Arab tribes. Primary among these tribes were those that believed in God and followed the commands of His rasul (prophet). In time, many Arab tribes from outside Medina joined the federation and allied themselves with the new religion and its community of believers. In the beginning, Mohammed did not require conversion to Islam as a condition for admission into the Arab tribal federation. Later, however, conversion became a condition and Mohammed assumed the role of both the spiritual and the secular leader of the Moslem state. Instead of being only a preacher in the fashion of Jesus and most other prophets, Mohammed, more in the tradition of Moses, established the rules of worship and personally administered the affairs of the Islamic state. In the latter capacity, Mohammed had to defend the state, wage war, make peace, establish justice, mete out penalties, and to always protect the rights of the Moslem Ummah.

Once Mohammed's role was more clearly defined, and given the poor economic conditions in Medina, Mohammed had to provide for the welfare of both his followers from Mecca and his "Ansar" of Medina. The only practical method at the time, and one that Mohammed was better acquainted with, was raiding rich Meccan caravans. During the month of Ramadan in 623 Hijri, Mohammed personally led a raid against a caravan he learned was worth 50,000 Dinars (the equivalent of $200,000 U.S. in 2004) headed to Mecca under the leadership of Abu Sufyan, a famous Qurayshite figure. The Moslem raiders had two objectives: (1) to seize the Qurayshite caravan and take possession of the goods it carried, and (2) to cut off the Qurayshite caravan routes to Al-Sham (Syria and Lebanon) to undermine the economic status of the Qurayshite clan. The latter objective was to be achieved by concluding covenants with the various tribes settled along these routes. When Abu Sufyan heard of Mohammed's plan to attack the caravan at the location of "Badr," he asked the Meccan leaders for military assistance. When the battle lines were finally drawn, there were about 1000 Meccans and 313 Moslems (Armajani, 1970: 37). The battle was short and desperate. At the end, the Moslems were victorious. Their triumph reaffirmed Mohammed's belief that God was on their side. How else could a small number of poorly armed and trained believers defeat an army three times their size? The victory at Badr established the reputation of the Moslems as a powerful fighting force.

It is especially interesting to note how the Moslem victory at Badr was perceived. While the Western historians considered it an insignificant engagement between two crude groups of fighters, Moslem historians consider it a divinely orchestrated victory. They argue that the battle was crucial for the survival of Mohammed and Islam. Without victory, the emerging religion would have been totally destroyed. Nevertheless, the news of the Moslem victory traveled across the Arab peninsula, confirming the power of the Moslems and validating the prophethood of Mohammed. From an economic perspective, the victory at Badr was also instrumental in establishing the Moslem institution of bait al-Mal (the state treasury). According to post-Badr Quranic verses, Moslem believers had to donate 20% of the assets they accumulate from war or trade to a central pool that supports the poor, the widows, the handicapped, and the families of the soldiers killed in battle. On the Qurayshite side, the defeat at Badr was so humiliating that the tribe's leaders pledged 50,000 Dinars to defeat Mohammed's army and to put an end to Islam once and for all (Bebawy, 2003: 49).

After Badr, Mohammed fought six more battles. Of these, two were particularly significant: Uhud (the name of a hill), which the Moslems lost, and the Khandaq (the trench), which they won. Both battles were fought against the infidels (a generic group of people who rejected Islam). In Uhud, the infidels were the same Qurayshites whom Mohammed had defeated earlier at Badr. At Khandaq, the infidels were a generic group of tribes organized and supported by the Jewish tribes (Bebawy, 2003: 50). At Uhud, Mohammed chose to fight at the foothills of Mount Uhud. He personally led about 700 fighters against a well-organized army of Qurayshites that included 3,000 men, 3,000 camels, and 200 cavalrymen. While Mohammed's forces were at first victorious, they were later defeated when he, against his better judgement, followed his companions' poor advice. As a result, the Moslems lost 70 Shaheeds (martyrs) and the Prophet was injured while the Meccans lost only 23 fighters (Bebawy, 2003: 52). Of particular interest in the Uhud battle was the role of the Qurayshite women. Seventeen women, including the commanding general's wife reportedly accompanied the troops and served as support auxiliaries. In this context, one could safely infer that women at the time did not wear veils (which were not required by Islam) and that they served with the fighting men on an equal footing. If that were the case, one may wonder why the Arabian women, even before Islam, were treated in a far more humane manner than the way the Afghani women were treated by the Talibans or the Saudi women are currently treated by the Wahhabi fundamentalists in Saudi Arabia.

In the Battle of Khandaq (trench), the Prophet again had to fight for his own survival, as well as the survival of his new religion. In the battle (basically a rematch of Uhud), Mohammed reversed his Uhud strategy choosing to fight inside Medina where his warriors would be better protected and better able to exploit their advantage as a guerrilla force. The opposing Meccans were about 10,000 fighters including a considerable number of Jewish fighters (Bebawy, 2003: 53). To maximize the chances of victory, the Prophet ordered the Moslems to dig a trench across the northern edge of Medina (hence the name of the battle). The trench was about 5 kilometers long, 6 meters wide, and 5 meters deep (Bebawy, 2003: 53). The trench, which was dug in 4 weeks by primitive tools, served as an effective crevasse that stopped the attackers and their cavalry from reaching the town. As the battle progressed, the defenders remained in town effectively blunting the invasion. The attacking Meccans then changed their strategy and laid siege to Medina for several weeks. However, the siege was later disrupted by a severe sandstorm that was followed by a drenching rain, forcing the attackers to abandon their positions and return to Mecca (Bebawy, 2003: 55). The news of the Moslem victory at Khandaq resounded across the land of Arabia, affirming these convictions: (1) the steadily surging military prowess of the new Moslem state; (2) God's clear intervention on the side of the believers by sending the sandstorm and the rain to end the siege of Medina; (3) Mohammed's role as God's Commander-in-Chief; and (4) the end of the Qurayshite hegemony, since the tribe had to accept a truce with the Moslem believers.

In the year 627 Hijri, Mohammed returned to Mecca for the first time since his emigration to Medina. He was accompanied by 1400 Moslem believers who, expecting victory, brought along a large number of sheep for the victory sacrifice. Upon hearing of the march, the Qurayshites again confronted the Moslems outside Mecca at a place called Hudybeyah. Instead of fighting the Meccans, Mohammed preached to them assuring them that he did not want to conquer Mecca. As a result, the opposing parties agreed to sign a peace treaty known as the "Hudybeyah Treaty." The treaty required: (1) peace to be kept between the parties for at least 10 years; (2) the Moslems to abstain from accepting Qurayshite converts without their family's approval; (3) the Moslems to accept converts from other Arab tribes without permission; and (4) the Moslems to return to Mecca the following year for the pilgrimage (Bebawy, 2003: 58). The Hudybeyah treaty accomplished what Mohammed wanted without having to fight his former clan, a matter that would have caused a major upheaval among the Arab tribes. The treaty also spared the Arabs the humiliation of having to fight inside the sacred city of Mecca. Furthermore, by signing the treaty, Mohammed demonstrated to the Arab tribes that he was a compassionate and tolerant statesman who sought peace even when his pilgrimage was unfulfilled and he was fully capable of taking the city by force. By avoiding war, Mohammed also demonstrated to the Arab tribes that the Qurayshites were the aggressors and could not be trusted as custodians of the Kaaba.

In 628 Hijri, in accordance with the Hudybeyah Treaty, Mohammed journeyed back to Mecca for the pilgrimage. His pilgrimage was planned to last for three days, during which time the local inhabitants were to leave the city, making room for Mohammed's party to worship freely. As the ritual progressed, Mohammed and his compatriots made the pilgrimage in an impressive and pious fashion. They toured the Kaaba in clean garments, chanted the Quran, prayed in public, and exhibited reverent respect and dignity. The Moslem's behavior immensely impressed the Qurayshites who watched the believers from a distance. As a result, many Qurayshites chose to convert to Islam. Two of the most famous of these were Omar ibn-al-Khatab and Amr ibn-al-As. Both were Qurayshite generals who later served Mohammed and Islam most loyally. They were those who later triumphantly led the Moslem armies into Syria, Egypt, and Persia.

In 629 Hijri, the Qurayshites broke the Hudybeyah Treaty when one of their influential tribes (Bani Bakr) raided the Moslem tribe of Khuzaa, which had asked the Prophet for protection (Bebawy, 2003: 79). Troubled by this unjustified aggression, Mohammed decided to return and take Mecca by force. In the month of Ramadan of the same year, he marched into Mecca ahead of 3,900 Moslem fighters and a large number of non-Moslems who joined him along the way. Unable to protect their own capital, the Qurayshites surrendered Mecca without a fight. As a statesman, however, Mohammed wanted his followers to share in the glory of capturing Mecca. He divided his forces into four groups, each of which would simultaneously enter the city from a different direction. Mohammed offered peace and safety to all Meccans. He toured the Kaaba seven times, and, standing at its door, he preached Islam to the multitudes. When the fearful Qurayshite leaders asked him: "Now that you have taken Mecca, what will you do to us?" the Prophet, offering a general amnesty, replied: "I am your brother and nephew; go, you are all free" (Bebawy, 2003: 81). One of Mohammed's first functions in Mecca was to destroy the stone gods and goddesses inside the Kaaba and to wash it with rose water, thus announcing the beginning of the Islamic state.

In late 631 Hijri, Mohammed made his last pilgrimage to Mecca. Feeling that his death was soon approaching, he wanted to institute the procedures of the pilgrimage. He took his wives and more than 10,000 Moslems who had come from all over Arabia to walk with him for the last time. In Mecca, he gave what was considered his farewell speech. He implored the Moslems to obey God, to uphold the Quran as their constitution, to observe the daily ferud (obligations), to treat each other with tolerance and mercy, to forgive others in order to be forgiven, to give away part of their wealth to the poor and orphans, and to fear God in whatever they do until they have to face their Maker.

Upon his return to Medina in early 632 Hijri, Mohammed caught a fever and was ill for 12 days. On a Sunday morning, he was able to pray in the mosque with Abu-Bakr (who would soon be his successor). He also gave away all the money he owned (a total of seven dinars a sum equal to $20 in 2004), his white mule, and his sword. Of especial interest is the report that, at the time of his death, Mohammed had pawned his body armor with a Jewish companion he trusted for an amount of money equal to the price of a one hundred pounds of barley (possibly $1.00 at the time). The next day, Mohammed died. It has been said that on his last hour, he was visited by two angels; Archangel Gabriel and Asrael, the Angel of Death. The first angel invited him to "come home," and the latter apologetically asked for his permission to "take him home," a gesture no angel ever before made for a prophet. In the Moslem tradition, Mohammed was buried in an unmarked grave in Medina (Bebawy: 2003: 95; Bahgat, 1993: 472).

Having chronicled the biography of Mohammed, the adversaries of Islam have been known to criticize Mohammed on two levels, personal and categorical. On the personal level, Western critics accused Mohammed of being lascivious and a womanizer—having had 11 wives at once. Moslem historians respond to this accusation by explaining that the Prophet was only married to one wife (Khadija) for 25 years and that upon her death, and him being over 50 years old, he "took in other wives" basically to reinforce peaceful relations among the warring Arab tribes—a practice that was not too different from Jewish or Christian prophets before him (Bebawy, 2003: 103). On the categorical level, Western critics accused Islam of being a particularly violent faith. Moslem historians respond to this accusation by stating that all religions have, at one time or another, resorted to violence for different reasons, including: (1) misinterpretation of the faith by misguided clerics and religious interpreters; (2) the normal tendency of irreverent believers to engage in unjustified violence to enhance their own prestige; (3) having to live under unjust or oppressive conditions that could potentially foster violent reactions; and (4) the failure of some Moslem rulers to develop their communities in such a way as to promote a decent level of civility. Subsequently, Moslem scholars argue that no religion should be blamed for violent behaviors committed by its believers who, under hard social or geopolitical conditions, may find such conditions unbearable (e.g., the Crusades, the Spanish Inquisition, Hitler's *Libensraum*, the Holocaust, as well as acts of violence by Irish, Italian, and German terrorists). These same scholars also emphasize the state's role in spreading justice, promoting social tolerance, advocating democracy, and, when necessary, crushing terrorism and prosecuting all those who advocate religious violence.

Moslem scholars further suggest that there are four reasons why Westerners have been particularly critical of the Islamic faith. First, they do not have enough knowledge of the true tenets of Islam or possess the philosophical capacity to objectively examine Quranic principles. Moslem scholars question, for example, whether the leading Crusaders like Richard the Lion-Hearted and Baldwin the Count of Edessa (1096-1128 A.D.) were sufficiently familiar with Islamic principles or even cared to know when they so recklessly devastated Jerusalem and slaughtered its inhabitants in 1099. Arguably, a considerable number of Westerners were indoctrinated into believing that Islam was a counter-conversion movement against Christianity and that Mohammed was a renegade Catholic cardinal (Hoffman, 2001:10). Second, few Westerners had an appreciation for Arab culture or harbored unbiased respect for a "bedouin religion" that came out of a distant desert land. Understandably, some may have thought that the Arab region was so backward (as it most likely was) that God, in His wisdom, could not have chosen to bring a prophet from among its inhabitants. Third, the rapid expansion of the Moslem forces into Europe during the 7th century must have astounded the Westerners at the time, leaving them with a bitter memory that was hard to overcome. Only 40 years after Mohammed's death, the "primitive" Arabs were able to subdue the entire Spanish peninsula and most of southern Europe. Maalouf (1984) suggests that this sudden expansion stunned the Western kings and Visigoths as well as their entire populations. To soften the impact of the Moslem onslaught, Western historians found it more convenient to characterize the Moslems as barbarians, not too different from those who subdued Europe two hundred years earlier (Maalouf, 1984: xiv). Fourth, the fact that the Moslems captured the Holy city of Jerusalem only four years after the death of Mohammed must have outraged the Christians. Jerusalem, at the time, was the heart and crown of Christendom, and aggression against it (especially by the bedouin Arabs) must have insulted the Western sense of honor. Echoes of this view may still linger, frustrating the continuing attempts to resolve the Arab-Israeli conflict.

In defense of Islam, Moslem philosophers—especially Middle Eastern religious scholars—raise several issues. First, the main tenets of Islam are not substantially different from those of Judaism and Christianity. Except for the Christian concept of Trinity and Christ's resurrection from the dead (concepts with which the Jewish faith also disagrees), all other features are basically similar, if not invariably the same. All of the three religions recognize the oneness of God, honor the Virgin Mary, fear the Day of Judgment, keep a Sabbath day, fast, pray, worship, make the pilgrimage, and seek peace and justice on earth. If this comparison is accurate, they add, then Western resentment towards Islam must be illogical and unjustified.

Second, while both Moses and Jesus are revered in Islam, Mohammed was not only unrecognized by the other two religions, he was demonized and detested. By the same token, while Jerusalem has been recognized in Islam as a Holy City, Mecca and Medina have not been recognized by either of the other two religions. Islamic historians argue that such discrepancies are unnatural, and as such, reveal sentiments of cultural bias, social relativism, intolerance, or plain contempt of Islam.

Third, the popular image of Moslems as turbaned men in long garments and veiled women is both misleading and unfair. In most Islamic countries, this image is rare (e.g., Egypt, Lebanon, Tunisia, Morocco, Jordan, Indonesia, Malaysia, the Philippines), and, in Turkey, this style of dress is banned. Even in countries where this image is true (e.g., Saudi Arabia, Kuwait, UAE, Oman), this should not tarnish the image of the Moslem faith. Indeed, wearing a beard has traditionally been a sign of piety among the three religions and was the custom during the times of Moses and Jesus. Furthermore, covering one's head has long been a Jewish tradition (the story of Samson may have inspired that tradition), and for women to wear a long and loose outergarment, while not a Moslem requirement, has been a symbol of chastity, one that is not too different from what Christian nuns wear.

Fourth, the perception that Moslems (as a population) endorse Holy War is inaccurate. Moslem historians argue that it would be inconsistent (if not contradictory) to teach that Mohammed was not a holy man, on the one hand, and to claim that Moslems fight holy wars, on the other hand. On the contrary, they argue that the concept of a holy war was indeed the Crusaders' favorite "battle cry." It was used by popes and kings to mold peasants into an "army of God" and to reinforce their will to sacrifice their lives to liberate Jerusalem from the Moslem infidels (Hoffman, 2001: 15). Moslem historians further argue that the epistemological meaning of the word Jihad is non-threatening. It simply means "a pursuit," "an endeavor," or "an earnest attempt." As such, it can mean any kind of action conducted in pursuit of knowledge, wisdom, self-actualization, or even simple happiness. When used in a religious sense, the word could mean any effort "in support of religion," and—only when justifiable—"in the defense of religion." Even in this usage, Moslem historians point out that the word has been equally used by all religions including Judaism and Christianity (Hoffman, 2001: 15; Bebawy; 2003:78).

Fifth, while Moslem scholars uphold the holiness of the Quran and its teachings, they admit that many wrong interpretations of the Quran existed. Some of these evoke the sentiments of "extremism," "fundamentalism, or "radicalism." They further point out that original Islamic teachings neither condone nor tolerate such interpretations, since they entail the use of "unjustified violence" and the killing of innocent people. Moslem scholars add that such interpretations are anti-Quranic and violate the peaceful nature of Islam. Consequently, only those individuals and groups who endorse such interpretations should be held accountable. Any attempt to stigmatize an entire religion for the misdeeds of a few of its adherents is infinitely unjust.

Before concluding this chapter, it may be necessary to focus on one of the most critical questions in Islamic faith: was the Quran *munzal* (descended from above) upon Mohammed or was it created by man, Mohammed himself? While Judaic theology is thought to be literally written by God on a pair of tablets, and Christian theology written in epistles by those who had witnessed or heard of its practice, Islam offers neither eyewitnesses nor material evidence. And, since Mohammed was known to be illiterate, yet the Quran is so sublimely phrased to the extent that no human being could possibly have composed it, the vast majority of Moslems believe the Quran is unquestionably divine, and any argument to the contrary is heretical.

Yet raising this question was not entirely new in Islamic history. For instance, upon the death of Mohammed, many Moslem tribes subsequently seceded questioning the relevance of Islam and its divine origin. Several Moslems at the time claimed they too were prophets including individuals such as Abu-Selima from Yamama who claimed he was a co-prophet, and a woman called Sugah bint al-Hareth who claimed she was the only Arabian prophet (Bebawy, 2003:111). As a result, many Moslem tribes at the time refused to pay Zakah (religious tax) and even threatened to attack Medina to put an end to Islam altogether (Bebawy, 2003: 115). This compelled the first Caliph Abu-Bakr to raise a Moslem army that successfully ended the expanding apostasy. Yet, because many of the known Quran scribes were killed during the previous wars, Abu-Bakr commissioned a group of loyal Moslems to compile an official manuscript of the Quran. Later, in the time of the third Caliph, Othman, disparities appeared between the Qurans used in Egypt, Syria, and Iraq. That prompted Othman to commission another group of religious scholars that finally validated what is now recognized as the universal Quran (Bebawy, 2003:174). Yet, while all other versions of the Quran were put to the fire, the celebrated burning begged the original question of the divinity of the Quran.

During the Ummayad dynasty (660-750 A.D.), the issue of the divinity of the Quran was again raised. Damascus, at the time, was the capital of the Moslem empire, and Mu'awiyah (whose wife, poet, and physician were Christian) was the Caliph. During that period, several religious/philosophical movements emerged and shook Islam to its foundation. Among the more outspoken movements was the Mu'tazilah, whose ideology was strongly influenced by the Greek and Christian cultures prevalent in Baghdad and Basra at the time. In the Greek tradition, the Mu'tazilah group was bent on reconciling Islam and philosophy. Prominent among the Mu'tazilah views were: (1) God is neither born nor could He have given birth. He had neither names nor human attributes; (2) the world was not created, it simply existed without a beginning or an end; (3) the Quran was created by Mohammed to help govern a particular population during a particular time. As such, it is neither holy, nor universal, nor eternal; and (4) man is endowed with a free will, because without such a will, God can be neither just, nor merciful, nor compassionate. Based on these views, the Mu'tazilah ideology dominated Islamic thought during the Ummayad dynasty and was indeed adopted by the Ummayad Caliphs (Hoffman, 2001: 72; The Copts, 2000: 35-36).

In the 18th century, Islam again experienced a counter-revolutionary movement that advocated returning the faith to the puritanical times of Mohammed. The effects of this movement continue to resound throughout the Islamic world today and have been seen as a major cause of Islamic fundamentalism. The leader of this movement was a puritan Moslem by the name of Mohammed ibn Abd-al-Wahhab (hence the Wahhabi movement). Born in Al' Uyaynah in what is now Saudi Arabia, it was said that he had memorized the Quran at the age of 10 and traveled extensively to al-Kufa (now Iraq) as well as Kurdistan and Yemen. This fiery preacher advocated that Islam as practiced under the Caliphs and recently under Arab rulers had been polluted and had lost its theological integrity. Instead of a monotheistic faith, Islam had become polytheistic, much like the infidels' faiths. The Moslems, he argued, were worshiping saints, offering sacrifices, practicing sorcery, and doing magic in the name of Allah. Ibn-al-Wahhab went as far as to order his followers to "cut down the trees that lived on the [Arab] peninsula because they were worshiped by pagans" (Baer, 2003: 84).

To return Islam to its pure form, Ibn Abd-al-Wahhab offered strict prescriptions that extended to the intimate details of everyday life. He taught that there was a Wahhabi way to "sneeze, embrace, shake hands, yawn, kiss, dress, and so on" (Baer, 2003: 85). Yet, discouraged by the local Sheiks who disagreed with him, the young Wahhabi traveled to Dariya (near present day Riyadh) and took refuge with the powerful ruler Ibn-Saud. United in a new Moslem alliance, the Wahhabis and the Saudis waged tribal war against those who rejected Wahhabism as the new form of Islam. In the context of these wars, the Wahhabi Ikhwan (brothers) reportedly massacred five thousand Shiites and enabled the Saudis to conquer Mecca and Medina. Victorious, the powerful Saud united most of the Arab peninsula, naming it Saudi Arabia and establishing Wahhabisim as its state religion. The Ikhwan, nevertheless, continued to preach Wahhabism throughout the Moslem world. In particular, it flourished in Cairo, perhaps due to the Al-Azhar University, the only Moslem university at the time. The university provided a legitimate facade to the radical Islamic movement, and its graduates were the pioneers of what later became known as the Moslem Brotherhood.

As for a definite answer to the original question "Was the Quran *munzal* (past tense of *unzil*)?", the vast majority of Moslems would strongly agree, while the vast majority of non-Moslems would strongly disagree. As for the curious reader, given the factor of religious analogy, one cannot answer that question without answering the other two questions posted earlier: "Was Jesus the only Son of God?" and "Are the Jews the only chosen people of God?" The divinity of the Quran cannot be settled in isolation from the divinity of the other two faiths, since to doubt one, is to doubt all. Herein lies the infinite contradiction between two of the greatest mysteries of humanity: the mystery of "faith" and the mystery of "reason." In this context, the curious reader is left alone. He or she must rethink this contradiction, and the verdict must "intelligently and objectively" fit one's level of human awareness.

Sources

Ali, A. (1946). *The Holy Quran: Text, Translations and Commentary*. New York: Hafner Publishing Company.

Armajani, Y. (1970). *Middle East Past and Present*. Englewood Cliffs, NJ: Prentice-Hall.

Baer, R. (2003). *Sleeping With The Devil*. New York: Crown Publishers.

Bahgat, A. (1993). *The Prophets of God*. Cairo: Dar-al-Shorouk.

Bebawy, N. (2003). *Terrorism: a non-Islamic Industry*. Cairo: Alahram Publishers.

Haykal, M. H. (1976). *The Life of Muhammed.* USA: North American Trust Publications.

Hoffman, M. (2001). *Islam as an Alternative*. Bavaria: Bavaria Verlag & Handel.

Khalid, H. (1986). *Mugtama Al-Medina (The Society of Medina)*. Beirut, Dar-al-Nahda Al-Arabia.

Maalouf, A. (1984). *The Crusades Through Arab Eyes*. New York: Schocken Books.

The Copts (2000). Los Angeles: The Coptic Association of America.

3

The Empire That Was Islam: Unintended Consequences

Ten years after the death of Mohammed, the Moslems were able to amass a huge empire, one that is, perhaps, second only to the Roman Empire at its zenith. That empire included the entire Middle East region, North and Central Africa, most of the Iberian Peninsula and southern Europe, and most of south-eastern Asia including India, Indonesia, and parts of China. In Europe, the Moslem invasion continued northward until it was halted by Charles Martel in 732 A.D. (the hundredth anniversary of the death of Mohammed) at the celebrated battle of Poitiers. This point marked the north-western limit of the Arab empire.

The reader should note that all of the Moslem conquests took place after the death of Mohammed. The Prophet never thought his followers would need or want to conquer any lands beyond the immediate area of Hijaz in Arabia proper. Subsequently, the seemingly rapid expansion of Islam could hardly have been planned. Indeed, it was thought to be a natural extension of military skirmishes Mohammed's successors fought against neighboring non-Moslem Arab communities. Having accomplished that objective with relative ease, the emerging Islamic state recognized its political and military superiority and its ability to conquer other countries beyond its regional borders. The first targets were countries that either resented their brutal colonizers, or were too weak to stand against the battle-tested Moslem fighters. (Hitti, 1967: 139-142).

The inhabitants of this vast empire included peoples of all races and colors. For instance, people such as the Egyptians, Lebanese, Syrians,

Libyans, Turks, and Persians are Caucasian of the same general type as Greeks, Italians, and Spanish. People from Sudan, Somalia, and central Africa are Negroid. Those from China and south-eastern Asia are Mongoloid. Presently, most Moslems live outside the Middle East region. They are located in Indonesia (which has more Moslems than anywhere else in the world), Malaysia, Sri Lanka, and the southern rim of the former Soviet Union, as well as in Albania and the Balkans. One hundred years after the death of Mohammed, the Islamic empire extended from the Bay of Biscay to the Indus and from the borders of China to the lower cataracts of the Nile (Hitti, 1967: 139-152).

Yet as the subjects of the Islamic empire were distinguished by religion, they were divided into Moslems and non-Moslems. The non-Moslems were divided into two categories: ahl-al-kitab (people of the book) such as Christians and Jews, and the infidels who included pagans and members of cults (i.e., non-Islamic and non-Judeo-Christian faiths). The Moslems were divided as Sunnis and Shiites, with the majority of Moslems in the world being Sunnis. The Sunni population consider themselves the adherents of the Sunna, (practices of the Prophet) and as such, orthodox Moslems. The Shiites are adherents to the fourth Caliph Ali (Mohammed's son-in-law) who was murdered during a bloody struggle over succession in Karballa (now in Iraq) in the 40th year of Hijrah.

After the death of Mohammed, the Moslem community had to cope with two serious questions. First, the issue of riddah (apostasy), whereas many newly converted tribes denounced Islam and reverted to idolatry. Second, the issue of the caliphate (succession) that continues to shake the legitimacy of Islam today. This issue was indeed the central reason why the Moslem nation broke into Sunnis and Shiites, creating an untenable split among the Moslem believers. Because these two issues have been substantial to the development of modern Islam, they will be explained here in more detail.

The issue of apostasy was much more crucial to the integrity of Islam. It entailed the Moslem state's response to those Moslem tribes which, after the Prophet's death, renounced Islam and returned to Jahiliyah traditions, including following false prophets (Bebawy, 2003: 109). From an analytical perspective, however, the issue of riddah, especially by new converts to Islam, was not totally unexpected. Due to the lack of public communication at the time, the absence of organized missionary activities, and the relatively short time between the beginning of Islam and the death of Mohammed, no more than one third of the Arab tribes could have professed Islam during the Prophet's life. Furthermore, even in the Hijaz region where Mohammed first began his prophethood, the local tribesmen could not have converted to Islam until approximately a year or two before Mohammed's death. Moreover, for a tribe in those times to become Moslem required only the conversion of its chiefs. Subsequently, many tribes in the Hijaz—even during the life of Mohammed—were naturally reluctant to pay the Zakat (the annual payment to Bait al-Mal, the Islamic treasury in Medina. The death of Mohammed provided them with a legitimate rationale for active refusal. Allowing such a refusal (to pay Zakat) to occur was a serious issue; it could bankrupt the new Islamic state, destroy its legitimacy, and force it into oblivion.

The first Caliph, Abu-Bakr, insisted on fighting the "seceders" and forcing them to return to Islam. The hero of these campaigns was Khalid ibn-al-Walid, the same cavalry general who first fought against Mohammed at Uhud and later fought for him. It took Ibn al-Walid six months to subdue the tribes of central Arabia. One of the more stubborn fights took place against the tribes in Yamamah where the renegade Moslems had established their own religion around a Christian prophetess. Other riddah campaigns were conducted by other Moslem generals with varying degrees of success. Western historians cite the riddah wars as evidence Islam has been a brutal faith that always "got its way" by the sword. Arab historians oppose this view, stating that most of the riddah wars were directed not so much toward holding the secessionists by force as toward bringing over to Islam many who had until then been Moslems in name only (Bebawy, 2003:111). Having successfully accomplished that, Abu-Bakr moved his forces to subdue the rest of Arabia and penetrated deep into the Byzantine Empire.

The issue of succession erupted upon the assassination of Ali (the fourth Caliph) and, later, his sons over a major dispute over religious succession. The Shiites questioned who was then to be the legitimate Moslem Imam (religious leader). They believed that since Ali was Mohammed's nephew, as well as his son in law, he was the legitimate one. But since the Moslems killed him and his sons in favor of Muawiah, a Quraishite general and statesman unrelated to the Prophet, the followers of Ali formed their own Shiite sect of Islam. Shiism came into existence on the 10th of the month of Muhharam (680 Hijiri) after Ali's son Hussain was decapitated near Karbala, Iraq, by troops of the

Umayyad Caliph Yazid. In a sense, the institution of the Imamate was the Shiites' response to the perceived arrogance of Moslems who, at the time, fashioned their relationship with God as they saw politically fit. The continuing saga of Shiism became even more complicated when the first Imam selected by the Shiites was a Yamanite Jew. Throughout history, however, the Shiite Moslems continue to observe Ashura (the first ten days of the Hijri month of Muharram) as days of lamentations in memory of the "absent Imam." Currently, there are about 185 million Shiites, of whom about 61 million are in Iran, 11 million in Iraq, and 4 million in Yemen (where they are known as Zaydis). Some ultra Shiite sects are scattered in the Middle East and are known as Druzes, Yazidis, and Ismailites (http//:www.adherents.com, retrieved June 16, 2004).

With the Arab peninsula finally united under the second Caliph, Omar ibn-al-Khatab, the Moslems were anxious to move against the outer world. Their drive to conquer other lands was inspired by four geo-political sentiments: (1) under Islam, the Arabs were not allowed to fight each other nor "raid each other's tent," and since raiding was an old culture that could not be outgrown easily, new targets of raiding had to be found; (2) Caliph Omar encouraged his people to fight abroad, thereby ridding himself of Bedouin intransigence at home and affording his new government the prospects of seizing new wealth abroad; (3) it was not difficult to induce the Arab warriors to keep fighting because the wealth of the Persian and Roman empires was considered legendary; and (4) the Arab bedouins firmly believed that if they were killed in the conquest, they would go to paradise, and if they survived, they would share in the booty.

One should also realize that Caliph Omar and his successors must have been aware of the opportunity to extract a generous tribute from the new lands they conquered. As expected, this would enrich the Moslem treasury which, at the time of Omar, was near insolvency. While this view has been repeatedly mentioned by Western historians, Moslem historians disregard it, and instead emphasize the purely religious motivation for the conquests (Armajani, 1970: 52, Bebawy, 2003: 121). It should also be noted that in all of these conquests, the Moslem generals offered the Christian and Jewish populations "Aman Writs" (peace agreements) as long as they agreed to pay the tribute. Such writs allowed them to keep their faith and practice their rituals. In one such writ, the Moslem general Khalid allowed the conquered Christian population to "ring their church bells as often as they wished as long as they did not interrupt the Moslem's call for prayer" (Bebawy, 2003: 125). In the absence of such writs, the Moslem generals gave enemy populations three choices which became standard operational policy in the subsequent wars of Islam. These choices were to accept Islam, to pay the tribute, or to fight. The Moslem system of tribute, however, exempted the women, the young, the old, the blind, and the mentally retarded from having to pay. That basically left only the men who were young enough to carry weapons against the Moslems. Those who eventually had to pay the tribute were estimated as 70% of the conquered population (Bebawy, 2003: 126).

With Syria as a base, the Arab armies proceeded to conquer the regions of Armenia, Georgia, and southern Russia. In the meantime, Amr ibn-al-As (the second most famous Moslem general and the rival of Khalid ibn-al-Walid) moved on Egypt and North Africa. By 639 Hijrah, he reached the Egyptian border at Al-Irish and pushed on to Heliopolis and Aim-Shams—an old capital during the times of the Pharaohs (Hitti, 1967: 160). Al-As besieged the towns of Farma and Babylon as the Byzantine army was routed. He then offered the three standard choices to the Byzantines of Egypt. They chose to pay the tribute. Al-as then moved to finish off the conquest of Egypt by crossing the Nile and taking Alexandria. But because the Arabs were culturally afraid of crossing water barriers, the Caliph in Medina wanted Al-As to halt the conquest. He sent the general an order to stop if he had not already crossed the river. Al-As, who at the time had not crossed the river and was strongly desirous of outdoing his rival ibn-Al-Walid, ignored the order until his fighters had already made the crossing (Hitti, 1967:160).

In 641 Hijri, Alexandria fell to ibn-al-As. The Coptic population, which had been persecuted by the Byzantine ruler Cyrus, surrendered without a fight. As to the story that the invading Arabs burned the library of Alexandria, Moslem scholars argue that no evidence supports this story. They argue that there were actually two Alexandria libraries: a Ptolemaic Library that was burned about 48 A.D. by Julius Caesar and a "Daughter Library" that was later destroyed in 389 A.D. by Emperor Theodosius. As for the reason why these libraries were destroyed, history has been vague (Hitti, 1967: 166). With the conquest of Egypt completed, the Byzantine Empire in North Africa was laid defenseless. To exploit the situation, and certainly not to be outdone by Khalid, al-As swiftly moved westward taking Pentapolis and Barquah (both now in Libya) and forcing the surrender of the pagan Berber (possibly a derivation from German for barbarian) tribes in Tripoli and Carthage. These Berbers (also known as the Moors) later turned out to be instrumental to the success of the Moslem conquest of Spain.

In 711 Hijri, a Berber general by the name of Tariq ibn Ziad (hence Gibraltar, the "Mount of Tariq") led the conquest of Spain. The crossing of the Mediterranean isthmus (about 15 miles across) by the novice Moslem sailors progressed in three stages. They first sailed one quarter of the way and then returned in order to gain confidence. Then they went half the way across the isthmus and again returned to test their ability to ride the sea. Finally, they went all the way, where they reportedly burned their fleet behind them to force the troops to either conquer or die fighting. The conquest quickly led to the occupation of the Iberian Peninsula, lands the Moslems called al-Andalus. These lands constituted the farthest expansion by the Moslems in Southern Europe. By capturing Spain and the southern fringes of France and Italy, the Moslems became the masters of an empire greater than that of Rome at its zenith. The name of Allah, joined with the name of his prophet Mohammed, was being called five times a day in faraway lands where the franj (Franks) inhabitants never thought an Arabian religion could ever reach their lands (Hitti, 1967: 215). With these victories, the Ummayad Caliph Muawiah reigned in Damascus over a huge empire with unmatched wealth.

The Moslem expansion, barely 100 years after the death of Mohammed, was both stunning and dramatic. The Moslems, enjoying the newly acquired empire and associating with new cultures, began to experience a momentous intellectual awakening, one that later left its marks on the world today. Starting with very little science, philosophy, literature, or culture, the Moslems manifested a voracious appetite for learning and became the adopters of great classical cultures. From Syria, they adopted the Aramaic civilization, itself influenced by the Greeks; from Iraq they adopted a civilization strongly influenced by the Persians; from India, they learned the latest in Indian scientific work, especially in the field of mathematics; and from Cyprus and Malta, they came into possession of the chief philosophical works of Aristotle, the neo-Platonic commentaries, and the medical writings of Galen (Hitti, 1967: 307). By bringing this wealth of knowledge to their compatriots in the new region of al-Andalus, the Moslems ostensibly linked the cultures of Europe to those of Egypt, Persia, and India.

Among the more significant advancements introduced by the Moslems was the bureaucratic system of government. This system included, first, the position of wazir (vizir or minister,) whose office was influenced by the Persian tradition. The wazir acted as the Caliph's chief minister. He drafted and articulated public policy, appointing and deposing governors and judges, and even perpetuated his own influence by appointing his elder son in his place before he retired. This probably inspired the ministerial system of government that later flourished in Europe. Second was the administration of al-barid (the postal service) establishing postal routes between cities and towns utilizing hundreds of riders on mules and horses. Third was the diwan of Zimam (the finance bureau), charged with collecting, auditing, and dispensing the state revenue. This might have been the genesis of the office of the Chancellor of Exchequer now instrumental in most advanced states. Fourth was the diwan al-mazalim (court of appeals), charged with receiving and adjudicating grievances of miscarriage of justice in the entire realm. The Norman King Roger II (1130-54) reportedly later introduced this institution in his court (Hitti, 1967:322). And, fifth, was the institution of shurta (police departments), whose head served as chief of police, as well as head of the Caliph's bodyguard. In time, each city and town had its own police force including a detachment of *assas* (night detectives) whose function was to patrol the streets at night and to establish order within the community (Hitti, 1967: 319-330).

In the fields of philosophy, science, and the humanities, the Moslems seem to have left a firm imprint. For instance, the philosopher al-Kindi, who was known during the medieval period as "the Philosopher of the Arabs," single-handedly preserved the works of Aristotle and Plato which had been lost centuries before. Al-Farabi gained the title of "the second Teacher" (with Aristotle being the first). He logically explained the discrepancies between Greek and Moslem philosophies—the former favoring the philosopher king concept, while the latter only God. To the Greeks, law was a product of human reasoning; to the Moslems, it was the will of God. Later, Ibn Khaldon, the premiere Arab sociologist, examined the configurations of society, introduced social typologies, and discovered the rational/ethical basis for a virtuous society.

In the field of sciences, the most original medical works were completed by two Persian Moslems, al-Razi and ibn-Sina (Avicennia). Both were converts from Christianity. Al-Razi wrote on the seton in surgery, kidney stones, smallpox, and measles. His books (especially Al-Hawy) were translated into French, German, and English. Avicennia, a great philosopher in his own right, wrote on medicine, mathematics, logic, and art. This scholar, who wrote that medicine "was not a difficult science," completed an encyclopedia on medicine called the Qanun (the Rules). His Qanun continued to be the basic textbook on medicine in European medical schools well into the seventeenth century (Armajani, 1970: 112). In the fields of mathematics and astronomy, Moslem scholars drew from Greek and Indian sources. Two of the most significant contributions of the Moslems were the "Arabic numerals" and "algabr" (the origin of algebra). Other Arabic scientists, in Aristotle's tradition, wrote on chemistry, physics, biology, zoology, and botany. A few others wrote on geography and travel. Among these were Al-Estakhri (c. 980) and Al-Idrisi (1166 A.D.). Al-Estakhri produced the first map of the world, and Al-Idrisi taught that the earth was a complete sphere (Armajani, 1970: 108-110).

In the area of art and architecture, Islam took a peculiar stand; it forbade arts, especially the painting and drawing of persons. This kind of art was considered idolatry (Armajani, 1970:117). On the other hand, Moslems built mosques that displayed courtyards, pools, and fountains. The mosques created the need for beautiful minarets (from the Hebrew Minora). These were decorated with intricate geometric or floral designs and beautifully calligraphied verses from the Quran. Among the most artistically built mosques was the Dome of the Rock in Jerusalem and Aya-Sophia in Constantinople (Armajani, 1970: 118).

Finally, the true glory of Islam at the time can perhaps be seen in the influence of the Arabic culture on the daily life of individuals in non-Moslem lands. Especially among Europeans, it is rather surprising how Moslem culture and language has made lasting contributions to their lives and the betterment of their civilization. For example, a typical day in the life of a Westerner is enriched by so many articles of Islamic origin: "they wash themselves in a bath introduced to the world by the Turks...they dry themselves with a Turkish towel (Arabic tawla)...they may drink coffee (Arabic qahwa)...they may use algebra (Arabic algabr)...they may use alcohol (Arabic kohl)...they may pay tarrif (Arabic tarifa)...they may rest on a divan or sofa (Arabic dewan and sufa respectively)...they may lay down on a mattress (Arabic matrah) or read a magazine (Arabic Makhzan)". These are vivid reminders of the Islamic empire that was (Armajani, 1970: 14).

The Islamic empire lasted for about a thousand years. At times, it was more centrally and effectively controlled and, at other times, barely nominal and rather ineffective. After the four orthodox Caliphs (Abu-Bakr, Omar, Othman, and Ali), the empire was governed by hereditary dynasties. Each ruled from a different capital within their original sphere of power. First were the Ummayads who, from 660 A.D., ruled from Damascus and initiated the empire's finesse politique. Second were the Abbasids, who ruled from Baghdad from 750 A.D., featuring the popular friendship between Caliph Haroun al-Rasid and Charlemagne, the leader of the West. Third were the Ottomans, who reigned from Constantinople (now Istanbul) from about 1300 A.D. and greatly demonstrated the empire's military prowess. These dynasties were at times so ineffective that they gave rise to smaller dynasties like those in Egypt, Syria, Spain, Sicily and, on an even smaller level, in North Africa. These mini-dynasties intermittently fought the Crusaders from 1096 A.D. (i.e., Richard the Lionhearted versus Salah al-Din al-Ayouby) until the Crusaders were finally expelled in 1291 A.D. The Ottoman Empire continued to decline until, in the 19th century, it became known as the "sick man of Europe." After its defeat in WWI, the Ottoman Empire disintegrated. The remnants of the Ottoman Empire continued in Turkey, Egypt, Syria, and Palestine.

Sources

Armajani, Y. (1970). *Middle East Past and Present*. Englewood Cliffs, NJ: Prentice-Hall.

Bebawy, N. (2003). *Terrorism: a non-Islamic Industry*. Cairo: Alahram Publishers.

Hitti, P. K. (1967). *History of the Arabs: From the Earliest Times to the Present* (9th ed.). New York: St. Martin's Press.

Part II

Islamic Law

4

Overview of Islamic Government and Penal Laws

There is a great deal of skepticism regarding the nature of Islamic government and laws, especially in the area known as Shariah law (criminal and penal laws). In this area, severe punishments are meted out for seemingly insignificant crimes, such as hand amputation for theft and 80 lashes for drinking alcohol. In the eyes of the Western public, and among Western scholars, imposing such severe punishments for such minor offenses is too cruel, and carrying it out so blatantly in public reinforces the perception that Islamic laws are backward and barbaric. The Western observer may legitimately question why, in Islamic justice, a thief should have to lose a hand, while murderers and rapists in Western societies are only punished by prison sentences. Implicit in this reasoning is the broader view that severing a human limb as punishment for a crime is a repulsive thought that shocks the human conscience (Souryal, Alobeid, Potts, 1994).

In Islamic jurisprudence, however, thieves are considered the rapists and murderers of society because they violate its most precious essence—religious communitarianism. Thieves, according to Moslem jurisprudence, atomize society by indiscriminately preying upon property, thus keeping its members in fear for their safety, livelihood, and freedom to worship. Moslem jurists argue that if theft is not so harshly suppressed, it will undermine the spirit of the ummah and eventually destroy the essence of Islam. This view can be better understood in light of the Arab culture that prevailed during early Islam. Most people at the time lived in tents, were concerned for their family privacy, and left their animal stock unguarded. Moslem jurists further argue that crimes of rape and murder in Moslem societies are indeed so rare precisely because of the imposition of such a severe punishment for seemingly less heinous crimes, such as theft. Ironically, this very view, unpopular as it may sound, is consistent with the Western criminological theory of "Broken Windows," one that has been hailed by Western criminologists for its proven effectiveness.

Western observers should also realize that early Islamic governments focused, before any other obligation, on promoting a spiritual community and protecting the Moslems from external or domestic aggression, including social and family disorganization. Given the high rate of illiteracy during the Jahiliyah (ignorance and social decay) era, it was vital for the emerging Moslem state to uphold a draconian Mosaic-type of law known as Shariah (the path to follow), one that is qualitatively different from the Western categories of common law, case law, or civil law. Shariah law is holistic in its approach to guiding all human behaviors and applies to both public and private matters. In this context, Shariah law makes no separation between church and state as many Western laws do. Moslems assume that Shariah laws are directly made by Allah and were dictated to Mohammed in the Quran. As such, Shariah laws are considered theocratic, universally applicable, and just. At least in the category of Huddud (limitations) crimes (one of which is theft), punishment is absolute. It cannot be negotiated, altered, or forgiven. Yet, at the same time, especially in the case of theft, Shariah laws provide stringent sets of checks and balances. Not every thief gets his or her hand amputated, even if the accused confessed to the crime. Strict evidential rules apply concerning the person of the accused, the stolen goods, and the number and condition of witnesses. The purpose of these rules is to maximize the deterrent effect of punishment while, at the same time, minimize bias by judges or prosecutors. If one of these rules is not met, the Qadi (judge) must abstain from imposing the sentence of hand amputation (Souryal, et al: 1994).

Before discussing issues of crime and punishment in Islamic laws which will follow in subsequent chapters, it is appropriate to first review the nature and scope of Islamic government. In this context, we will examine the following topics:

- Characteristics of Islamic Government
- The Pillars of Islamic Worship
- The Sources of Islamic Jurisprudence

- Islamic Law, Theory and Practice
- Religious Minorities in Islamic Law.

Characteristics of Islamic Government

To understand the nature of Islamic government, one must first realize that for any state to survive, it must have three basic elements: (1) sovereignty, (2) territory and population, and (3) organization. Foremost among these elements is sovereignty, without which the other two elements are pointless.

In Western thought, sovereignty has been associated with the concept of state, the culmination of the evolutionary process by which a large number of people—in a fixed territory—form an organization that serves the common good. In Islamic states, this is an alien view; sovereignty belongs to God alone, since He is the creator, organizer, and preserver of the universe. Unlike in democracies or monarchies, the Islamic state, in and of itself, possesses no sovereignty. All the organizations of the state are dependent on what God explicitly permitted or forbade. Should exigencies occur, however, the doctrine of Ijtihad (intellectual industriousness by Islamic scholars) provides the necessary adjustments that need to be made. Islamic jurists believe that, since God is the absolute sovereign, the roles of state, government, and law must be consistent with God's laws (Hassan, 1981: 112).

The second element in Islamic government is that of territory and population. The question arises as to whether the application of Islamic law is based on territorial or personal criteria. If it is the territorial criteria, then all people within the boundaries of a Moslem country must be governed by Islamic law, regardless of whether they are Moslem or non-Moslem. If it is the personal criteria, then Islamic law applies only to Moslems. Moslem scholars have long debated this issue. Most of them support the exclusiveness principle. Thus, if a non-Moslem is in an Islamic country and breaks the rules of that country, for instance, by eating pork or drinking wine, that person will be punished according to Islamic laws. Conversely, if a Moslem visits a non-Moslem country and eats pork or drinks wine, he is still governed by the Islamic laws which prohibit such actions. On the other hand, the famous Moslem scholar, Abu Hanifa, states that Islamic law should be applied within the boundaries of Islamic countries to Moslem people only. It does not apply to the non-Moslems in Islamic countries or to the Moslem in a non-Moslem country. This viewpoint is based on the concept of religious freedom guaranteed by Islamic law to non-Moslems (Sanad, 1991: 20).

The treatment of zimmis, however, may vary depending on the kind of the Islamic state they live in. For instance, in Egypt, while Moslem law forbids drinking alcohol or eating pork, these laws do not apply to Christians or Jews living in the country. Furthermore, Christians and Jews living in Moslem countries can (depending on the toleration of the state at the time) perform their own religious rituals, matrimonies, processions, and festivals. For example, while in Egypt Christmas mass is shown on government-controlled television stations and is partially celebrated by non-Moslems, in Saudi Arabia no churches or synagogues are permitted, and foreigners who are convicted of drinking alcohol are publicly flogged (Bassiouni, 1982:3).

Theoretically, the idea of religious tolerance in Islamic countries was originally practiced by the Prophet Mohammed when he allowed the Jews of Yathrib (later called Medina) to worship freely and the Christians to "ring their church bells" as long as they did not interrupt Moslem prayers (Bebawy, 2003: 143). In a different context, the Prophet showed religious tolerance when he and his Moslem compatriots took Mecca in 628 Hijri. He offered total amnesty to the Christians, and when they needed a place to pray, he—against the will of his compatriots—allowed them to pray in the Mosque (Bebawy, 2003: 81, 106). In practice, however, while Islamic governments are obliged to protect their zimmi populations against external or internal attacks, in orthodox Islamic states non-Moslems may have to pay jizya (personal tax) in return for protection. This requirement can be traced back to the early years of the Islamic state that required such a tax for two reasons: (1) jizya paying was a more humane response than forcing non-Moslems to choose between converting to Islam or fighting for their lives; and (2) jizya paying was a legitimate economic means to provide for the social welfare of the poor and the needy.

The third element of Islamic government is the concept of social and political organization. In theory, the immediate purpose of an Islamic government is to preserve social harmony in accordance with the Quranic verse "the believers are but a single brotherhood" (Quran, Surat XLIX: 10). This verse focuses on the need for fraternity among Moslems, regardless of their nationality, race, color, or language. However, while Islamic social harmony is a worthy theory, its practice has been inconsistent, to say the least. Moslem tribes have been known to fight other Moslem tribes and, at the present time, Moslem countries have invaded other Moslem countries (i.e., Iraq, Kuwait, Iran, and Yemen). From a practical viewpoint, however, expecting social harmony among 23 Islamic countries with different political, social, and economic needs may be too idealistic an expectation. On this point, however, one must be reminded that attempts at practicing social harmony among Christian or Jewish communities have also often failed.

Social harmony in Islamic government is synonymous with the notion of equality. Islam considers this notion both unique and vital. In the Quran, God commanded Mohammed "if thou judgest (concerning the affairs of Moslems and non-Moslems), judge in equity between them (regardless of how hostile their attitude may be toward you), for Allah loves those who judge in equity" (Quran, Surat V: 46). Yet, when the Islamic government speaks of equality, it basically focuses on religious and legal equality since "abstract" equality is physically impossible and socially unattainable (Hassan, 1981: 40). Under religious and legal equality, Islamic governments recognize the equal treatment of all human beings before God and the law. This has been interpreted as providing fairness in all matters of civil rights and equal opportunities. Under these precepts, the Qadis must be both knowledgeable and just. To demonstrate these attributes they must: first, have an intimate knowledge of Shariah law and possess a reputation of piety; second, follow legal evidence in a manner consistent with Shariah laws; third, mete out punishments in a reasonable and merciful manner. Yet if harsh punishments are required, they must be equally applied to the rich and the poor, the powerful and the powerless, the Moslems and the non-Moslems.

Also paramount in Islamic government is the notion of liberty. In pure Islamic thought, Moslems consider themselves freer than non-Moslems because they are not required to obey any other authority except God's. In contrast with Christians, for instance, Islam has no hierarchy of priests, bishops, cardinals, or popes. While this perception of freedom does not absolve the Moslems from obeying their parents, elders, and superiors at work, it clearly requires that compliance must be within the limits prescribed by Shariah law. Furthermore, freedoms of expression and conscience are considered cornerstones of Islamic government. While these freedoms have obviously been denied in many Islamic countries, in pure Islamic philosophy they are considered sacrosanct. Even by today's standards, it is not unusual for an ordinary citizen in one of the more orthodox Islamic states to criticize those who are in power or to approach the ruler's weekly Majlis (open meeting) to petition redress against government officials. In such a case, the petitioner should be politely heard without interruption and, based on the case, should be advised as to the options he may pursue with the assurance that, if unsatisfied, he would be welcomed to return and address the Majlis at a future date (Hassan, 1981: 43).

Another characteristic of the Islamic state is administration by consultation. While this process may not be common in many democratic assemblies and parliaments, in Islam it is expected to be the rule: forthright, religiously inspired, and freely offered. The idea of consultation in Islamic government started with the Quranic verse "O Mohammed consult with them (your companions in the faith). Then when thou hast taken a decision, put thy trust in Allah [since] Allah loves those who put their trust in Him" (Quran, Surat III: 153). Yet, as evident in the practice of consultation, the process may not always lead to good consequences. As mentioned earlier in Chapter Two, when Mohammed fought the battle of Uhud, he followed his companions' advice against his own opinion. Subsequently, that advice later proved to be flawed, and the battle was lost.

Another important characteristic of the Islamic state is its nature as both religious and temporal. Mohammed adopted this dualism after his Hijrah to Yathrib in 622 A.D. He quickly realized that for the Islamic state to survive, it must be involved in both spiritual and temporal matters. He subsequently took charge, leading the believers into battle, sitting in judgment of the accused, and establishing policy pertinent to how Moslems can resolve family, social, and political conflicts. Having said that, it would be misleading to compare the Islamic state with any European state, since it differs qualitatively from all of them (Hassan, 1981: 46). Neither can Islamic states be compared with theocratic institutions in the tradition of the ecclesiastical authorities of Medieval Europe. Islamic states can better be considered "ideological states," since they are based on rules and regulations that are not of the citizens' choosing. Moreover, since the leaders of Islamic states are usually not popularly or representatively elected, any claim by Islamic states to democracy may be questionable. In the final analysis, the ultimate welfare of the subjects of such states will inevitably depend on the degree of enlightenment and compassion of their Islamic rulers.

The Pillars of Islamic Worship

For Islamic states to survive, the citizens of the Ummah (community) are expected to be self-disciplined and religiously well-trained. Without this assumption (at least as a foundation), the integrity of the Islamic state stands a higher risk of being undermined when the ummah is faced with dire odds, especially when these odds are not of the people's making. That is perhaps why most Islamic states emphasize promoting religiosity among their citizens and keeping them reminded that they are living under "the eyes of God." Such a state of affairs, not unlike Christianity and Judaism, legitimately suggests that the Moslems are essentially kept busy carrying out repetitive religious ferud (plural of fard, meaning obligation) and rituals of piety. By the same token, the Moslems are also reminded to avoid sin and, even during their idle time, to keep praying the rosary to purify their souls. From a political perspective, it may be safe to assume that Islamic governments find it necessary to immerse their citizens in a form of sustained religiosity to make them more docile and submissive. Such a condition is considered more conducive to social stability.

To achieve a sustained level of social and political stability, Moslem theologians distinguish between the fundamentals of *iman* (religious belief), *ibada* (acts of worship), and *ihsan* (right doing). All of these maxims are assumed under the subject of *din* (religion). Collectively, they generate a sense of religiosity, which, in turn, can lead to *taqwa* (perpetual piety). In a sense, religiosity is seen as the process of understanding Islam while piety is seen as the application of these fundamentals on a daily basis. To accomplish the goals of religiosity and piety, Islam requires that Moslems perform five ferud. These are known as the pillars of Islam:

1 - Shehada (declaration of Faith): a public declaration that every Moslem must undertake upon being a Moslem. The declaration states "Ishhad alla Ilaha illa Allah, wa anna Mohammeden Rasul Allah" (I witness that there is no God but Allah and that Mohammed is His Messenger). Indeed to convert to Islam, all that one needs is to publicly recite the Shehada.

2 - Salat (Prayer): the obligation to regularly pray to Allah throughout one's life. It unifies all Moslems, including those in remote tribal and social communities. For prayer to be valid, Moslems must set their direction toward the Kaaba in Mecca and perform the ritual in specific acts of physical movements (i.e., kneeling, standing, and sitting) while reciting accompanying Quranic verses. Islam requires five daily prayers, which are to be performed at dawn (fajr), noon (zuhr), afternoon (asr), sunset (maghrib), and night (isha). Islam also provides for practices to be performed if one was sick or unable to pray on time.

3 - Siyam (Fasting): abstention of eating, drinking, smoking, or engaging in sexual relations to develop piety and self-discipline. The Quran stated: "You who believe, fasting is prescribed for you that you may learn self restraint." Siyam is obligatory between dawn and sunset during the month of Ramadan. On the other hand, Moslems who are sick or traveling for some distance are not required to fast and can make up for it later.

4 - Hajj (Pilgrimage): traveling to worship at the Kaaba in the city of Mecca. It is an obligation to be fulfilled at least once in one's lifetime. It is required of all Moslems who are able physically and financially to do so. Making the hajj takes about three hard days and is considered as worthy as the degree of hardship one faces in completing the ritual.

5 - Zakat: Islamic charity offerings to be made by the financially able to help the subsistence of the poor. It symbolizes social solidarity among Moslems throughout the world. In other words, Zakat is the poor's due to be paid by the Islamic treasury. It is imposed on all Moslems who can afford it, and its virtue was mentioned in over thirty verses in the Quran. Zakat can be divided into two categories:

- Zakat al Fitr: this zakat should be paid before the breaking of fast at the end of the month of Ramadan. According to present estimates, the amount of zakat al fitr is about ten Egyptian pounds ($2.00 U.S. in 2004) per person. This amount is to be paid to the Islamic treasury to help the orphans, the poor, and the needy.
- Zakat of wealth: this zakat is required from all Moslem adults who possess some wealth. It is levied on livestock (such as camels, cows, and goats), gold and silver, fruits, and other productions. The amount of this Zakat is a percentage of one's total worth. One's wealth is measured in terms of

what he or she owns including homes, clothing, furniture, weapons, animals, or jewels. On the other hand, any equipment used in earning one's living is not considered subject to this kind of zakat.

Sources of Islamic Jurisprudence

Islamic jurisprudence is based on five important sources. As a Moslem, one must learn these sources and, without any hesitation, accept their validity. Some of these sources are considered more worthy than others, with the Quran as the most worthy source. Moslems, however, are expected to believe in the totality of these sources, since they constitute the religious essence of Islam.

1 - The Quran: the Holy Book for Moslems. Its text is the most holy source of Islamic jurisprudence. It contains the rules that God has laid down and revealed to the Prophet Mohammed for governing human behavior. The Quran governs both the religious and social lives of Moslems. It contains rules for personal hygiene, diet, sexual conduct, inheritance, and matters of child rearing. The Quran presents the body of ordained rules (known as ahkam al-Shariah or limitations of the path). These rules are considered the most pure source of Islam and all other sources must be consistent with these ahkam. Since Quranic rules are usually formulated in general terms, extracting practical, legislative, or judicial regulations out of the Quran is a task designated only to Moslem ulama (plural of alim or scholar) who are religiously trained to carry out such a serious responsibility.

2 - The Sunna (acts of the Prophet): the second highest source of Islamic jurisprudence. It compiles the authentic traditions by the Prophet Mohammed. The Sunna complements the Quran when a Quranic text is hard to understand or interpret. If compared to Christian sources, the Sunna serves a more important role than the Book of Acts, since it is considered far more binding. Sunna consists of the Prophet's acts and sayings as well as his conduct in specific situations. Second only to the Quran, it presents the Islamic precedents that Moslems should follow. While Sunna is not based on any revelation, it is considered divinely inspired. Also, while the Prophet was not considered infallible, his acts and sayings are considered a model for all Moslems.

3 - Ijma' (consensus): the process of reaching agreement among the Moslem ulama regarding a complex matter or event. Ijma' does not require the agreement of all Moslems; it is restricted only to the ulama who are known to be competent in the arts of jurisprudence. Moslem scholars resort to ijma' when a new case or event occurs and Islamic judgment is unclear or hard to reach. The validity of Ijma' judgment depends on its accordance with, and conformity to, the spirit of the Quran and Sunna. The validity of Ijma' as a source of Islamic jurisprudence is derived from the Prophetic saying: "My community shall never unite on error." Nevertheless, judgments based solely on ijma' are, in fact, few.

4 - Ijtihad (intellectual endeavoring): a process of self-exertion or endeavoring to articulate or find a solution to a problem or an issue. In the legal sense, it refers to attempts by jurists to formulate a new rule or law on the basis of evidence found in previous Islamic sources. Since Islam was revealed to Mohammed about fourteen hundred years ago, ijtihad was considered necessary to improve the quality of interpretation, thus enabling Islamic laws to cope with the changing needs and demands. In contemporary terms, ijtihad can be defined as "legal reasoning" or the development of practical solutions compatible with Shariah. Unlike ijma', the process of ijtihad is left to each mujtahid (jurisprudence consultant) in whom strict and precise conditions must be met. Furthermore, neither ijma' nor ijtihad can be considered an independent source of Islamic jurisprudence, since the validity of these two sources depends on their accordance with, and conformity to, the rules set by the Quran and the Sunna.

5 - Qiyas (analogy): the kind of judgment rendered in a new case on the basis of juristic analogy. In other words, it is the use of a previous solution found in the Quran or the Sunna to resolve a new matter. In contemporary legal terms, it is akin to the rule of precedent or *stare decisis*. Qiyas, like ijma and ijtihad, is not an autonomous source of Shariah, since it must depend on the existence of a *prima facie* case. Some Moslem jurists assert that qiyas, given the above-mentioned definition, absorbs and encompasses ijtihad.

In addition to these main sources, Islamic jurisprudence allows three sub-sources: (1) *aurf* (Islamic tradition), (2) *istislah* (reformed ideas), and (3) *istihsan* (preferred ideas) (see Abu-Zahra 1950: 226-32). The first sub-source, like in all other religions, permeates the entire process of Islamic jurisprudence, giving it the cultural flavor of what is being articulated. The other two sub-sources are so intricately similar that they are often treated interchangeably. The difference between a reformed and a preferred idea is ostensibly a choice between "a more advanced theory" and "a more suitable theory." These kinds of arguments have been rarely made, and only by liberal Islamic jurists.

Islamic Law in Theory and Practice

The theory and practice of Islam during the time of Mohammed and the first four Caliphs (Abu Bakr, Omar, Othman, and Ali) were almost identical. That time was known as the era of "true Islam." By the end of that era, however, the Moslem state (almost unexpectedly) found itself in control of a vast empire with different religions, cultures, and languages. Specifically, due to the physical proximity between the Moslems of Arabia and the infidels in non-Arabian lands (all non-Moslems), the new rulers of the Moslem empire had to adapt. To survive, they needed assistance from the infidels in Spain, Russia, and France to run state functions and later to train the Arab armies. As a result, while the theory of Islam remained the same precisely due to the sovereignty of God, Islamic practices in Moslem countries differed.

Because so many countries have adopted Islam as their official religion, the practices they follow may vary, sometimes slightly, and other times radically. For instance, among the 23 countries that currently claim Islam as their official religion, Saudi Arabia and Iran appear to be the most radical. The former claims the puritanical Wahhabi faith, and the latter, the rebellious Shiite faith. On the other end of the continuum, countries like Egypt, Jordan, and Tunisia practice much milder versions of Islam. Precisely, the main difference is whether the country in question applies a pure version of Shariah law (one that includes beheading and hand amputation as penalties for certain crimes) or if, instead, it's policies are commingled with Western ideas and liberal practices. From a political perspective, the former countries are popularly labeled "Islamic states", and the latter "moderate states." Based on the country's level of modernity and Westernization, its practice of Islam may differ from the true theory of Islam. Prominent among these variations are political and social issues. The political issues include individual freedoms, the succession of rulers, the incorporation of democracy, the promotion of economic opportunities, and alignment with the West. The social issues include equal opportunities before the law, the treatment of women, the sale and use of alcohol, the circumcision of girls, and, of course, terrorism. Some of these issues have been chronic and continue to cause considerable instability in the Moslem world.

In interpreting the Quran and Islamic rules, the Islamic community recognizes four schools of thought that exist among the Sunni community. These schools are the Shafi'is, Hanafis, Malikis, and Hanbalis. While these schools agree on the basic tenets of Islam, each school interprets the Quran and Sunna a little differently. Even if the differences are serious, the presence of religious discord does not usually affect the substance of Islamic rules. In addition to these main schools, many Islamic societies recognize lesser-known sub-schools of thought, including the Ismailis in Pakistan, the Sufists in Baghdad, and the Assassins in Syria. This may further explain why differences in the application of Islam occur in Moslem countries.

Finally, there is the impact of colonialization. In the 19th and 20th centuries, many Moslem countries experienced European colonialism, an added factor that may have contributed to the kind of Islam these countries apply. As a result, many Moslem countries have incorporated, at least in part, the kind of religious tolerance they themselves were subjected to. For example, while Egypt and Jordan learned secular constitutionalism and freedom of worship from the British, the Syrians and the North Africans learned the concepts of Liberte,' Equalite,' and Fraternite' from the French. As a result, all of these Islamic states have enacted Western-style laws including more liberal penal codes and rules of criminal procedure. In this context, Napoleon's conquest of Egypt in 1798 may have been one of the most beneficial conquests in history. It introduced the Egyptians to new sciences and arts they were unaware of. And due to the discovery of the Rosetta Stone by the French scientist Champollion, Egyptians learned to unravel hieroglyphics and read their ancient history. Conversely, many argue (rather convincingly) that the reason Saudi Arabia and Iran continue to practice antiquated methods and systems is because they were never colonized. During the pre-oil times, both countries were thought not worth colonizing. Interestingly, Moslem countries that had the misfortune of being colonized by smaller and less progressive foreign powers (e.g., Portugal and Belgium) tended to remain stagnant and rather equivocal in their application of Islamic Shariah. The cases of Indonesia, Malaysia, and central Africa are good examples.

Religious Minorities in Islamic Law

The subjects of an Islamic state are classified under Islamic law into three religious categories: Moslems, Zimmis, and Infidels.

1 - Moslems: These are the people who accepted Islam by declaring the Shehada and recognizing the five pillars of Islam. They are accepted as Moslems regardless of their race, color, gender, place of birth, or their previous religion.

2 - Zimmis: These are people of the Book (mainly Christians and Jews) who live under Islamic suzerainty. They must believe in one of the heavenly revealed scriptures and reside under the protective covenant of the Islamic state.

3 - Infidels: These are non-Moslems who do not believe in one of the heavenly revealed scriptures. They consequently cannot have a protective covenant with the Islamic state.

Some Western writers criticize Islam by claiming that non-Moslem minorities within an Islamic State do not enjoy rights equal to those of the Moslem majority. As mentioned earlier, while this may well be a practical reality in many Moslem countries, it is inconsistent with pure Islamic theory. In some countries, like Saudi Arabia, Kuwait, and in some parts of the United Arab Emirates, non-Moslems cannot own land or businesses unless under the khafala (sponsorship) of a local Moslem. They cannot eat breakfast or lunch in public during the month of Ramadan. Nor can women walk in the streets without a Moslem abaya (a black outer garment). During the 1990 Gulf War, the latter requirement was also applied to female members of the U.S. military. In Egypt, Christians were attacked and killed by extremist Moslems in Alexandria, Minia, and Sohag, especially those who were accused of building or repairing a church, since such an act requires special permission from the country's highest authority (The Coptic Awakening, 2001: 10-14).

Yet, in Islamic jurisprudence there are ample verses that disallow such discriminatory activities and guarantee equality among all citizens, Moslem and non-Moslem. For example, the Quran teaches, "O Mankind! Lo! We have created you from male and female and have made you nations and tribes that ye may know one another... Lo! The noblest of you in the sight of Allah is the best in conduct" (Quran, Surat al Hujurat: 13). There is also the popular Hadith that states: "The people are as equal as the teeth of a comb...an Arab is no better than a non-Arab except in their pursuit of piety." And in another Hadith, the Prophet stated: "The Zimmis enjoy the same rights of Moslems and bear the same obligations" (Sanad, 1991: 24).

As mentioned earlier, many moderate Moslem countries have adapted their constitutions to Western-style democracies and articles of the Human Rights Conventions. Among these, one can clearly note a promising change. For example, Article 40 of the Egyptian Constitution of 1971 states "All citizens are equal before the law. They are equal in their rights and obligations, without distinction on the basis of race, origin, language, religion or creed" (Sanad: 1991: 24). Similarly, article 46 of the same constitution declares "The state guarantees the freedom of creed and the practice of religious worship, while articles 160 and 161 of the Egyptian Criminal Code punish all behaviors that diminish or offend, in any respect, the practices of religious worship or sacred premises" (Sanad, 1991: 24).

By the same token, principle two of the 1962 Constitution of Pakistan declares "All citizens should be equal before the law, be entitled to equal protection of the law, and be treated alike in all respects" (Sanad, 1991: 24). Even if some Moslem states put restrictions on non-Moslems in the field of administration or authority, such situations might arguably be justifiable, based on the need to balance the collective interests of the ummah—the interests of the majority population (Moslems) with those of the minority population (non-Moslems). Moslem scholars argue that such a justification is not unnatural and has been politically expedient in non-Moslem countries such as Ireland, Israel, England, South Africa, and others.

Nevertheless, the issue of requiring Zimmis to pay jizya when they live in Moslem lands has been a thorny issue. Moslem theorists argue that requiring Zimmis to pay the appropriate jizya is not a discriminatory practice for three reasons: (1) these persons enjoy public safety and security under Islamic protection while they are exempt from serving in the military or the public services; (2) these persons are exempt from paying zakat (poor tax) and other taxes otherwise required from all Moslems; and (3) Zimmi females, poor Zimmi men, as well as those Zimmis who voluntarily serve in defense of the Moslem state (by accepting military or public service assignments) are exempt from paying jizya. On these three grounds, Moslem jurists argue that requiring the Zimmis to pay jizya is politically and socially justifiable since, without paying it, the Moslem state would be incapable of protecting not only the Zimmis, but itself.

Sources

Abu-Zahra, M. (1950). *Crime and Punishment in Islamic Jurisprudence: The Punishment*. Cairo.

Ali, A. (1946). *The Holy Quran: Text, Translation and Commentary*: New York, Hafner Publishing Company.

Bebawy, N. (2003). *Terrorism: a non-Islamic Industry*. Cairo: Alahram Publishers.

The Coptic Awakening (2001). The Coptic Association of America, Los Angeles.

Hassan, F. (1981). *The Concept of State and Law in Islam*. Washington, DC: University Press of America.

Hitti, P. K. (1967). *History of the Arabs: From the Earliest Times to the Present* (9th ed.). New York: St. Martin's Press.

Sanad, N. (1991). *The Theory of Crime and Criminal Responsibility in Islamic Law: Shari'a*. Chicago, IL: The University of Illinois at Chicago.

Souryal, S., Alobeid, A., Potts, D (1994). "The Penalty of Hand Amputation for Theft in Islamic Justice." *Journal of Criminal Justice*, vol.22, No.3

5

Crime, Justice, and Punishment in Islamic Jurisprudence

Bassiouni (1982: xviii) states that the Western world has all too often seen the wrong side of Islam. Although he explores several cultural and social reasons, he puts most of the blame, ironically, on two educated groups: (1) Western Orientalists, whose distorted perceptions of Islam failed to grasp the social essence of Islamic justice, and (2) the Moslem Ulema (scholars), who have drastically failed to convince the West of Islam's fair and equitable philosophy. To truly understand and appreciate Islamic justice, it is important that Western scholars remove the mask of positivistic thought, allow for the metaphysical as well as the physical, rely more on transcendentalist philosophy than science, and confront the "cunning of reasoning" which normally manifests itself so compulsively when religious beliefs are judged (Souryal, Al-obeid, Potts, 1994:431). As Malinowski remarks, the Western scientist must be able to "see in the lives of alien people," and before the beliefs of another culture are examined, one must first "wear the mind" of its people (Wilson and Hernstein, 1985:439).

In Islam, justice can have several meanings. One meaning likens it to a sacred trust, a duty imposed on humans to be discharged most sincerely and honestly. This is to identify one's own interests with those of others and to administer the trust as if it is "an act of devotion" (Muslehuddin, 1979: 101). As such, justice requires being morally responsible and merciful and giving each his or her due. Another meaning is based on the notion of mutual respect. As such, a just society is one which offers equal respect for individuals through various social arrangements made in the common interest of all members (Doi, 1984:8;

Muslehuddin, 1979:104-5; Bassiouni, 1982:14). A third meaning characterizes the bond which holds society together and transforms it into a brotherhood in which everyone becomes a keeper of "everyone else and each is held accountable for the welfare of all" (Quran, Surat 10: 13). A fourth meaning identifies justice as "a command from God, and whosoever violates its tenets traces grievous punishment" (Quran, Surat 10: 90). The third and fourth meanings of justice are probably the ones most commonly invoked in Islamic jurisprudence, especially when the topic of theft is discussed. Moreover, Islamic justice is considered to possess a much deeper essence than the formalistic justice enumerated in Roman law or stipulated in the works of the Greek philosophers. Moslems consider issues of justice to be much more penetrative because, as Moslems, they are expected to act as if they are always in the presence of God, to Whom all things, acts, and motives are known (Doi, 1984:5). Both the rich and the poor, the powerful and the weak, are equals under God's protection, as far as their legitimate interests are concerned. However, neither group can be favored at the expense of the other.

There are numerous Quranic injunctions that command justice within the Islamic community. Allah is believed to have dispatched with his Apostles three gifts which characterize the Islamic community: "We sent aforetime our Apostles with clear signals and sent down with them The Book, the Balance, and the Iron, that men may stand forth in Justice" (Quran, Surat 4:4). The Book, the Balance, and the Iron are the elements which effectively hold the Islamic society together. The Book is the body of revelation which commands good and forbids evil; the Balance is the essence of justice which gives each person his or her due; and the Iron is the arm of the law which deters and sanctions evildoers (Doi, 1984:2 3). As mentioned earlier, this third gift of God—the law—is one on which we will focus more closely throughout the remainder of this section.

Islamic law has two primary sources: Shariah, which is a theocratic legal system based on a divine code revealed to the Prophet Mohammed and expressed in the scriptures of the Quran; and Sunna, or acts of the Prophet. The former source is the most essential; the latter will appear only sporadically. In Islamic tradition, God is the only lawgiver, the sovereign who has the right to ordain all commands for the guidance of humankind (Quran, Surat 1-2). Shariah, which literally means "a pathway" but is invariably used to mean "law," represents such commands identifying what is right and wrong, legal and illegal, and proper and improper, in the Moslem's life. Shariah combines within itself the reality of society and the ideal of community: the way society ought to function. The former represents the prowess of the law; the latter represents the benevolence of justice—the supreme end of the law (Muslehuddin, 1979:100). To accomplish this design, Shariah law regulates human conduct by demanding, authorizing, or prohibiting certain behaviors. As such, it provides an all-inclusive scale of religious valuation of human conduct. Behaviors falling under the prescription of Shariah include, without exception, all religious and secular conduct. Accordingly, all aspects of human behavior are classified as obligatory (fard); meritorious or recommended (mandub); indifferent, which means bringing neither reward nor punishment (mubah); reprehensible, which is not punishable but disapproved (makruh); and forbidden (haram).

The main body of Shariah, however, addresses issues of crime and punishment which are commonly known as Huddud Allah, or divine limitations. For all practical purposes, Huddud (plural of Hadd) serve as the constitution, the penal code, and the code of criminal procedure, all in one. Crimes in the Huddud category are offenses against God's community, and, because in Islamic jurisprudence community takes precedence over the individual, it is the interests of the individual that may have to suffer and not vice versa (Doi, 1984: 219). Huddud penalties are decreed by God: they are absolute, universal, non-negotiable, and unpardonable, even under the sentiment of mercy (Quran, Surat 24:2). As such, Huddud cannot be subjected to interpretation by any judge or government official, regardless of power, rank, or status. By the same token, because they represent God's decrees, they are neither subject to rational consideration nor are they to be judged by human reason (Souryal, 1987:433).

As in the Jewish tradition, social goodness and social evil in the Islamic society can be sustained or resisted through a nomos (a set of norms) based on a spiritual commitment to social decency. When the nomos is internalized in the psyche of believers, it produces a collective moral conscience by which society, as a functional organism, can distinguish between right and wrong, abstain from criminal behavior, and adequately resist criminal endeavors. Reprehensible acts, therefore, do not shock the collective conscience of society because they are criminal; they are considered criminal because they shock the collective conscience. When obligatory duties are thus internalized, they are seldom ignored, and it does not become necessary to consciously make them manifest (Souryal, 1987:431).

In contrast to the neatness and precision of Western penal philosophy that legislates morality through an exhaustive enumeration of secular prohibitions, Islamic justice is based on divine law. The Quran states "Be just: that is next to piety and fear of God" (Quran, Surat 5: 9). Moslem jurists further argue that positive laws, despite their "politically correct" provisions, fall short of rendering natural justice (Bassiouni, 1992:239, Muslehuddin, 1979:24-37). In its purest sense, natural justice is *justica virtutis*; it is asocial, apolitical, amoral, and cannot be subjected to the rules of science. As Plato once declared, natural justice is a "perfect circle in the sky," which, if manipulated for any reason, ceases to be perfect. Therefore, justice cannot be legislated, tailored to fit, or replaced by "technological" justice, as is the case in the West. Furthermore, although individual freedoms and amenities should be universally protected, in Islamic justice, they cannot be allowed to take precedence over the benefits of communitarianism—the truism of God's plan for creation. Moslems believe that failure to observe this hierarchical order of justice can exacerbate social disorganization, encourage material hedonism, heighten ethnocentricity, and lead to the high rate of criminality and violence currently experienced in the West. For a spiritual community to be truly spiritual, it must be based on unadulterated natural justice, and because Shariah is considered to be God's natural justice, the entire ummah must be committed to the purposes of justice.

On the other hand, the Western philosophy of compartmentalizing human conduct into religious and secular, sacred and profane, or spiritual and material, is contrary to Islamic doctrine because human judgment always falls short of God's purpose. In Islam, religion and behavior cease to be autonomous categories; they become two sides of the same coin. Each human act must reflect God's will and at the same time be regulated by His guiding command. Human activities receive a transcendent dimension; they become purposeful and sacred, earthly and heavenly, for this day and for the hereafter. Good deeds earn for a person righteousness with God, and bad deeds take away in the same manner (Souryal, 1987:431). That is probably why Shariah law establishes no court jurisdictions; a judge is a judge for every matter, whether it is civil, criminal, or military.

To establish justice in accordance with Islamic doctrine, the head of the Islamic state has a dual judicial responsibility, one positive and the other negative. The positive function relates to the establishment of peace in the realm, the maintenance of accord among the various segments of society, and the protection of the weak from the strong. The negative function involves the punishment of offenders and the restitution of the rights of the injured. Toward that goal, the head of the state must appoint Qadis (judges) who are well versed in Islamic law, are God-fearing, and are of irreproachable character and sterling piety. Qadis, especially in orthodox Islamic countries, are perhaps the closest representation of a medieval inquisitor. In conducting his court (Shariah prohibits female judges), the judge is expected to be upright, sober, and calm. Nothing should distract his mind from the path of rectitude. If he does wrong, he is not only held responsible to the community of believers, but also to God. He is not to feel mercy in the execution of ordained sentences for the prescribed crimes. The Quran states: "Let not pity detain you in the matter of obedience to Allah if you believe in Allah and the Last Day" (Quran, Surat 24:2). Naturally, being a just Qadi under such conditions must be an extremely difficult task. If he is slightly irresponsible or unjust, he will be judged accordingly on the Day of Judgment. On the other hand, if he administers justice strictly by the Shariah and the Sunna, he risks making enemies with highly influential members of society. To illustrate this difficulty a Hadith states: "A just Qadi who administers justice among people is like a person slain without a knife" (Doi, 1984:12).

In the remainder of this chapter, the following topics will be discussed in greater detail:

- The Islamic Theory of Punishment
- Severity in Islamic Punishment: the Case of Hand Amputation
- The Principle of Legality in Islamic Law
- The Principle of Non-retroactivity in Islamic Law
- The Principle of Equality before the Law in Islam
- The Moral Character of Islamic Penal Law

The Islamic Theory of Punishment

The perpetual task of Shariah law is to create and sustain a spiritual bonding committed to the perpetuation of religious beliefs, social order, and proper individual conduct. This task is not only entrusted to elders of the clergy and government officials, but to each and every believer in the commonwealth. The bond that results imposes a dual responsibility on believers: a commitment to do what is good and abstain from what is blameworthy, and a responsibility to directly or indirectly correct the behavior of nonconformists. The principal objective of Islamic jurisprudence, indeed of all justice systems, is determining the proper balance between the interests of a society (a spiritual society being the specific objective of Islamic jurisprudence) and those of the individual. To accomplish that social balance, Western philosophers have searched for answers in the nature of humans, while Islamic jurists claim to find their answers in the nature of God.

Given the Islamic view of Allah as an omniscient God who is stern but benevolent, jealous but compassionate, and militant but merciful, a theory of punishment which is both deterrent and forgiving seems to perfectly fit the Islamic philosophy of justice. Punishment in Islamic justice is designed to be so severe as to deter the most corrupt in the community, but also so magnanimous as to accommodate their re-integration into the society of believers. To manifest this forgiving nature, Shariah urges compassion and mercy by encouraging the forgoing of punishment. This is done either by paying diya (blood money), paying restitution (if one is able to), or forgiving the offender if he comes forward and admits the act before apprehension by the authorities. By maintaining this duality of deterrence and forgiveness, Islamic justice attempts to sustain the chastity of religion and the safety of society without sacrificing the dignity of the individual (Lippman, McConville, and Yerushalmi, 1988: 84).

Based on the Islamic view of God, punishment in Islamic justice is naturally harsh and its application is expedient because the "sword of Shariah" takes priority over social disruption. Furthermore, because punishment has a definite tangible impact, its effectiveness must be maximized by carrying it out in public. Severe punishments are, therefore, justified (if not indeed necessary) not only on the basis of retribution, as most Westerners believe, but more so on the basis of social utility. Examples of Islamic punishment include beheading for murder and robbery, stoning to death for adultery, and eighty lashes for public intoxication. It is important to note, however, that although severe punishments can have a devastating effect on the offender, they are systemic by-products of the "eternal triad" of God, society, and humans. In this relationship, punishment serves a three-tiered obligation: (1) the fulfillment of worship, (2) the purification of society, and (3) the redemption of the individual. If the interests of the individual—the least valuable component in the triad—have to be sacrificed for the wholesomeness and integrity of the encompassing justice system, then it is the natural and rational thing to do. This should, by no means, imply contempt for humans—God's favorite creation—but simply their expendability if the sanctity of God is violated or the integrity of society is threatened. The imposition of capital punishment, for instance, underscores society's deep abhorrence of disorder and its innate affection for spirituality and social conformity. The Prophet proclaimed that beheading, as a punishment for social corruption, is "more effective than forty days of rain" (Souryal, 1987: 433). It is here that the reader should be reminded that rain is very precious to the Arabs because of its rarity. The forty days of rain may also be a reference to the time when God cleansed the Earth during the Great Flood. It is interesting to note that the Prophet's proclamation might have been a precursor to Bentham's "hedonistic calculus," by which he attempted to measure social utility and the prospects of the "greatest felicity" within society. Consistent with Benthamian thought, the calculus of Islamic justice can be summarized as follows:

- The larger interest of society takes precedence over the interest of the individual.
- Although "relieving hardship" and "promoting benefit" are both among the primary objectives of Shariah, the former takes precedence over the latter.
- A bigger loss cannot be inflicted to relieve a smaller loss, nor can a bigger benefit be sacrificed for a smaller one. Conversely, a smaller harm can be inflicted to avoid a bigger harm, and a smaller benefit can be sacrificed for a larger benefit (Doi, 1984: 8-11; Siddiqi, 1995: 8-14).

Severity in Islamic Punishment: The Case of Hand Amputation

Perhaps the most graphic display of the triadic fusion between God, society, and the individual is when hand amputation is applied. It is usually carried out in the center square of town and invariably within sight of the Mosque when worshippers conclude their Friday noon prayer. The condemned person is brought forth, the verdict is read loudly, and the arm is stretched on the surface of a regular table with the body of the condemned person turned backward. In a quick move, a professional executioner (in the presence of at least one male physician and a male nurse) exerts strong pressure, pulling the hand away from the wrist and severing the limb at the joint with a sharp knife. At that moment, the physician intercedes to stop the bleeding and bandage the wrist. The amputation, which is usually watched by a multitude of worshippers, is always carried out with utmost solemnity. Unlike the carnival-like scenes depicted in Western history books, the event represents a welcome solace in which the forces of religion, government, and community climax in a live experience of puritanical justice. The scene and memory of the event serve to reinforce in the conscience of believers the consequences of betraying community standards. Tangible and severe as it may be, believers still find in hand amputation what amounts to an act of mercy, especially to offenders who have a strong tendency to commit thefts. It is further argued that when compared with a long prison sentence, which could lose its effectiveness with subsequent thefts, amputation offers obvious advantages. Besides serving as an act of penance and remission, it allows the offender to resume working within a very short period of time.

Severity (the proportionality issue) in Islamic punishment constitutes the crux of contention by Western observers. Whereas proportionality of punishment is a relative concept which can be raised against virtually any system of justice, in Islamic justice the subject is purely academic for two reasons: (1) it cannot be viewed as a real issue because it is eschewed by divine ordainment; and (2) it is almost never raised because the punishment does not trouble the collective conscience of the spiritual society which practices it (Christie, 1970).

Throughout history, communities have determined severity primarily by indigenous measures: basically traditions, beliefs, and customs that form their sense of theodicy (Hegel's notion of the philosophy of history), as well as the dialectics of their beliefs and experiences. Sovereign societies, even vanquished ones, rarely modify their views on how sacred is sacred or how severe is severe, even in the face of overwhelming exogenous forces. The case of the Jewish people is a perfect example; despite continuous persecution, they hold to their beliefs. Furthermore, when societies do change, they normally follow a slow and arduous process of cultural evolution. If that were not the case, then the U.S. Supreme Court should have ruled against capital punishment long ago because most civilized nations disfavor its use. Obviously, this will take much longer since, by the end of 2004, only 12 states ban capital punishment. The remaining states, on the other hand, cannot be denigrated or ostracized for maintaining their social, legal, or moral standards. In spiritual communities, views on crime and punishment are even more deeply ingrained. What is "just dessert" and what is not can be a dogmatic, if not a fanatical issue, and not without justification. As Durkheim remarked, "There exists a unified system of beliefs and practices relative to sacred things set apart and forbidden" (Berger and Luckman, 1967; Durkheim, 1947; and O'Dea and Aviada, 1983).

Moslem law explains proportionality in terms of Qissas, or equal retaliation. The term, which will be explained later, has its origin in the divine principle of *lex talionis*. Accordingly, Moslems are little bothered by the extent of severity as long as it ensures the equivalence of pain or loss inflicted on the victim. In addition, given the tribal practice of raids and counter-raids over trivial matters in the history of Islam, Qissas came to be a perfectly reasonable alternative to greater retribution against the offender, his family, or his tribe. Furthermore, by carrying out a Qissas sentence, an Islamic community reaches the point of social finality by putting an end to disputes which otherwise would fester and cause greater harm to the parties involved, as well as to the spiritual ummah as a whole.

But how can modern societies judge the severity of a penalty that severs a human body part (i.e., a hand, an eye, a leg, or a tooth) as punishment for crime? Is carrying out such a penalty really barbaric and backward? What universal principles or moral guidelines can support this view? In responding to these questions, the reader should be reminded that in Islamic justice the primary motive behind hand amputation is not to punish the perpetrator vindictively, but to ensure the preservation of a benevolent community. Obviously, a thief with one hand can still commit theft and cause social harm, but at least the spiritual wholesomeness of the community will have been exonerated.

Now let us examine any universal principles or moral guidelines which may bear on the issue of severing a human limb as an act of punishment. History, of course, can be a reliable source because it is replete with events which confirm the presence of such acts in the West. But history can also be a suspect source because: (1) it is descriptive in terms of merely chronicling events without examining the principles or ideals that directed their occurrence; (2) it is unreliable because it is mostly written by those who had the power to direct events rather than by those against whom the events were directed; and (3) even if we were able to verify that severing human limbs had been common for millennia, history cannot justify why it ought to be continued or discontinued. Obviously, more reliable sources must be sought.

If natural law is to be considered a reliable source of judgment, then hand amputation may be as justifiable as pruning a tree, neutering a pet, or performing surgery. These practices are routinely carried out without any hesitation to salvage a weak plant, to redirect the energy of an animal, or to restore a patient to health. Circumcision, as a human example, may have been the longest of such practices which has been religiously commanded, socially accepted, and at times deemed hygienically necessary. Since the beginning of Jewish history, the practice has been perceived as necessary and proper despite the substantial pain involved in its exercise, especially in the earlier times. In applying the natural law view to areas of crime, social control, and punishment, it is not surprising to learn that, in recent rape trials in the United States, judges have imposed chemical or surgical castration as a condition of probation to ensure the proper treatment of compulsive rapists and/or the protection of society.

Moreover, if religious testaments are considered a valid source of judgment, then the practice of hand amputation may not be inconsistent with Judeo-Christian teachings, which state: "if thy right eye offend thee, pluck it out and cast it from thee" (Matthew 5:29) and "if thy right hand offended thee, cut it off... for it is profitable for thee that one of your members should perish, and not that your whole body should be cast in Hell" (Matthew 5:30). References to removing a "sick" body part in these verses represent serious concern for rejuvenating life, in this case human spirituality. Although it is true that many religionists argue that these verses were only meant allegorically, the fact remains that religious allegories contain powerful fields of meaning and establish *de facto* realities, sometimes of quantum social implications. If this were not so, it would be laborious to argue that God, in His grace, would recommend to His chosen people practices which are intrinsically evil or wrong. Moreover, one would be at a loss to justify why it is reasonable to believe that when God refers to severing body parts he means it allegorically, but when he refers to stoning, which was reportedly carried out in the Bible and is obviously much more inhumane than amputation, He does that literally.

In the philosophy of Islamic justice, all human beings are considered salvageable, if not for their intrinsic value then for the benefit of society and the preservation of God's plan. Given this basic premise, it does not seem too contradictory or irrational for the Moslem believer to accept the amputation of a "sick" hand as a method of salvation rather than doing away with the entire person. The amputee, handicapped as he or she may be, will remain alive and Moslem. In the more serious crimes of murder or robbery, for instance, the Moslem believer would naturally not hesitate to condone public execution as the ultimate act of societal purification and redemption.

Based on what has been said, when Islamic penology is compared to its Western counterpart, an interesting analogy can he discerned: physical amputation versus societal amputation. In Islamic philosophy, although the offender suffers enormous physical loss at the initial stage, he (very few offenders are females) is immediately set free and reintegrated into society. He is accepted as a normal person who has paid his debt to the community in full. He, by the grace of God, has become spiritually whole and the entire community acknowledges his reformation. In Western philosophy, by contrast, the offender's freedom is restricted at the initial stage through a prison term, but the offender remains "socially amputated," perhaps for the remainder of his or her life. Western societies have often rejected ex-convicts, relegating them to the role of social outcasts.

Perhaps the final argument against the severing of a human limb as an act of punishment is the repulsiveness of the act itself—it shocks the human conscience. From a psychological viewpoint, the notion of repulsiveness is basically an emotional state which is independent from the utility of the act or the collective conscience which supports its adoption. It can be further argued that if the objection to hand amputation in Western thought is solely based on the issue of disproportionality (that it does not fit the crime of theft), it would be a fairly rational and logical objection, because, if that is true, there ought to be less resentment if hand amputation were to be applied to more serious crimes such as aggravated theft, armed robbery, or terrorism. The notion of repulsiveness, however, seems to be based on much broader sentiments than the single issue of disproportionality of punishment, perhaps involving paradoxical reasoning. It would seem illogical, if not outright contradictory, that some Western-minded penologists (as in the United States) would continue to favor capital punishment and, at the same time, view hand amputation as repulsive. This contradiction can be analogous to one who states, "I can see perfectly in the dark, but I cannot see in dim light." The minor premise obviously negates the major one, and no logician can possibly reconcile the two premises without doing serious harm to human intellect.

One possible reason for this contradiction may be that when offenders are executed, they forever disappear, whereas amputated offenders remain ever visible. Although this may be a relevant reason, it would seem more germane to a condition of guilt (after the act) than to the validity or equity of the punishment itself. Other possible reasons could be: (1) the emotional vacillation in Westernized societies between the clichés of "law and order" and "waging war on crime", and the "appearance of civility" in light of one's concern for effective punishment and for political correctness; (2) the cultural repugnance of having to endure watching more people (perhaps many more people) roaming the downtown streets wearing prostheses; and (3) the sort of "pragmatic reasoning" in the West which seems inclined to interpret God's commandments either literally or allegorically, depending on the social romanticism of the time. In Islamic jurisprudence, the response to crime is serious and straightforward: if deterrence is good, then maximum deterrence is better, especially if society, government, and religion share the same structural foundation—God's ordainment.

The Principle of Legality in Islam

In modern penal law, the principle of legality is the *sine qua non* for protecting each individual from abuses of authority. Some jurists believe this constitutes the basis of penal law. According to the principle of legality, no conduct constitutes an offense unless it is defined as such in a prior law. In other words, the authority for criminalizing a behavior should be left only to the legislative authority. While neither the judicial nor the executive authorities play a direct role in lawmaking, by interpreting the law or putting it in action, these authorities can play an important role.

Over fourteen hundred years ago, Islam adopted the legality principle, the only legitimate means of criminalizing behavior. Islam requires prior notice before incriminating and punishing any behavior. People, both as groups and individuals, must be forewarned of illegal acts and their prescribed punishments. The Quran and the Sunna are replete with evidence that confirms the principle of legality. In Surat al-Isra (V: 15), for example, the Quran states: "And nor shall we be punishing until we had sent them an apostle." In Surat al-Qissas (V: 59), the Quran states, "Nor was your Lord the one to destroy a population until we had sent to it an Apostle who shall divulge upon them our signs." From these Quranic verses one can easily conclude that in Islamic penal law there is no crime without statute and no punishment without a prior notice. These verses may also demonstrate that the principle of legality was not first declared in the Western world as claimed in the 1789 French Declaration of the Rights of Man (Article 8), but might have appeared first in Islamic penal law.

Yet one should ask whether the principle of legality in Islam is applicable to all categories of crimes identified in the Islamic penal law? The answer to this question requires a brief explanation of the nature of these categories. As will be explained later in more detail, the degree of legality in Islamic penal law varies based on the seriousness of the act and the gravity of punishment prescribed for it. Moslem scholars classify crimes into three categories (1) Huddud crimes (crimes against the sovereignty of God), the punishment of which is prescribed by both the Quran and the Sunna; (2) Qissas crimes (crimes against another's bodily integrity), the punishment of which is defined in the Quran and the Sunna but can be modified if the victim or his family choose to forgive the defendant in full or in part; and (3) Tazir crimes, the punishment of which is neither prescribed in the Quran nor the Sunna. The authority for conviction and punishment for Tazir crimes is left to the judge and is determined by balancing community and individual interests, as long as these interests are in compliance with the general rules of the Quran and the Sunna. This being the case, the legality principle in Islam applies completely to the first two categories (Huddud and Qissas crimes). As for Tazir crimes, while some Western scholars hold that this category is excluded from the application of the legality principle, it must be noted that the judge's discretionary power in these cases is not unbridled. He must act legally under the general provisions of the Shariah, in which the principle of legality is foremost.

The Principle of Non-retroactivity in Islam

Associated with the principle of legality in Islam is the principle of non-retroactivity of punishment. This principle is crucial to both justice and legality since, without it, the law can incriminate and punish acts that were permissible at the time of their occurrence. And since Islamic law dictates that people cannot be subjected to punishment without being duly warned beforehand, the principle of non-retroactivity must always be upheld. The significance of this principle is that it protects personal integrity by preventing the abuse of power by public authorities. Shariah is replete with evidence confirming the principle of non-retroactivity. For instance, God prohibited the practice of usury, but he did not punish those who committed such acts before the revelation of his command (Quran, Surat al-Baqarah: 275). He also forbade the marrying of two sisters at the same time, but he did not punish the violators if the marriages occurred during pre-Islamic times (Quran, Surat al-Nisa: 23). Similarly, prohibitions against adultery, drinking alcoholic beverages, and marrying any of one's father's wives were not criminalized if such activities took place before the coming of Islam (Sanad, 1991: 42). There is only one exception to the non-retroactivity principle: when a newly promulgated law includes texts in favor of the accused. In such a case, the new law should be applied retroactively. Moslem scholars assert that Moslem Qadis should adopt the above-mentioned exception, maintaining that if a new law is favorable to the accused, either by providing a lesser penalty than the law in effect at the time the crime was committed, or by legalizing or decriminalizing an illegal act, the new law should be applied.

However, Islam allows certain cases of non-retroactivity if retroactivity would condone conditions that prevailed during pre-Islamic jahiliyah (ignorance and decay) period, that were later prohibited by Islam. There are two main offenses that fall in this category: al-zihar, and al-li'an. Al-zihar was a common offense committed by Arab husbands who, during the jahiliyah period, punished their wives by abstaining from having sexual intercourse with them. The punishment for this offense was a mandatory and permanent divorce. The name zihar (literally meaning the backside of a person) denotes the husband admonishing the wife by calling her as "untouchable as the back of his mother." Under Islamic law, the punishment was less severe. It was reduced to fasting for two months or feeding 60 needy persons. If the husband refused, and the wife took her case to the Qadi, the husband would be required to either make amends, or the wife would divorce him (Sanad, 1991: 42). Al-li'an was the offense of defaming one's wife by accusing her, under oath, of adultery without producing the required four eyewitnesses. In the early days of Islam, this practice was subjected to the same penalty prescribed for defamation (eighty lashes) on the grounds that there was no difference between defaming one's wife or any other woman. Later, a Quranic text legitimized the act of al-li'an (Quran, Surat al-Nur: 6-9). Since the later text was more favorable to the accused, it was applied to all acts committed prior to its revelation (Sanad, 1991: 43).

Exceptions to the Non-retroactivity Principle

Shariah law applies the principle of non-retroactivity to all offenses, regardless of the category they may fall in (e.g., Huddud, Qissas, or Tazir). Nevertheless, some contemporary Moslem scholars argue that there can be exceptions to this principle. Such exceptions may allow new Islamic rulings to be applied retroactively. The supporters of this view offer the following two examples:

1-The Hadd Crime of Defamation: This offense refers to the false accusation of adultery. If proven, the offense is punishable by eighty lashes. Nevertheless, those who support exceptions to the non-retroactivity principle allege that the Prophet Mohammed imposed the Hadd penalty retroactively on the slanderers of his wife, A'isha, when, in reality, the Quranic verses criminalizing and punishing defamation (Quran, Surat al-Nur: 5) preceded the revelation of A'isha's innocence. This case demonstrates that the Prophet felt justified in carrying out the penalty for defamation before the act of defamation was known to be false. The logical excuse for retroactivity in this case might have been the social status of the victim and the danger to Islam if severe punishment was not swiftly applied.

2-The Penalty of Baditry (hiraba): Like defamation, banditry is a Hadd crime which is punishable by beheading, crucifixion, cutting off the wrongdoer's hand and foot on alternate sides, or exile from the land (Quran, Surat al-Ma'idah: 33-34). Those who support exceptions to the non-retroactivity principle argue that the Prophet Mohammed applied the banditry Hadd retroactively to a number of people who were accused of attacking and killing a herdsman and stealing his herd, all before the Quranic revelation of the banditry sentence. The only excuse for retroactivity in this case is that the offense could have also been tried as a Qissas crime (i.e., murder), and the penalty could well have been death.

In the final analysis, it appears that cases of retroactivity of punishment, especially in the early years of Islam, were justified on a case-by-case basis when the social conditions of the ummah were seriously endangered and the integrity of Islam was threatened.

The Principle of Equality before the Law in Islam

As mentioned earlier, there was no principle of equality during Jahiliyah times. There was no expectation of equality between masters and slaves, the leaders of Mecca (the Qurayshites) and the masses of Mecca (non-Qurayshites), the rich and poor, or between men and women. Moslem scholars assert that by the advent of Islam, distinctions based on race, gender, color, language, or creed were all abolished, since Shariah law put great emphasis on the principle of equality before the law. The Quran states: "O Mankind! Lo! We have created you from male and female and have made you nations and tribes that you may know one another, Lo! The noblest of you in the sight of Allah is the best in conduct" (Quran, Surat al-Hujurat: 13). The Prophet Mohammed also stated: "O mankind! You worship the same God, you have the same father. The Arab is not more worthy than the Persian, and the red is not more worthy than the black, except in goodness" (Sanad, 1991: 45).

The principle of equality in Islam was not only held in the Islamic theory of law but was applied in practice by the Prophet and the first caliphs (who were known as al-rashidin, meaning the wise) who succeeded him. For instance, during the Prophet's time, a woman belonging to a powerful tribe was accused of theft. Some of her relatives went to the Prophet requesting him to exempt her from the prescribed punishment. The Prophet firmly rejected their appeal, stating: "If my own daughter, Fatima, committed theft, her kinship ties would not save her the Hadd punishment" (Sanad, 1991: 45).

To institutionalize equality, the Prophet also determined a uniform amount of diya (restitution money) to be paid to the victim (or his family) of Qissas crimes. Mohammed's diya made no distinction between the "blood worth" of men or women, rich or poor, males or females, as well as between criminals or victims. The Prophet also reportedly stated "injustice to a Zimmi (non-Moslem) is worse than that to a Moslem" (Bebawy, 2003: 124). Following the death of Mohammed, the first Caliph, Abu Bakr, followed the Prophet's practice. For example, he stated "O people, the powerful among you is powerless to me until I get the other's right from him, and the powerless among you is powerful to me until I restore him his right." By the same token, the second Caliph, Omar, repeatedly upheld the principles of equality, in particular, the exercise of Islamic penalty. In the tradition of Saint Augustine (354-420 A.D.), two hundred years before him, he was known in the Sira of Islam as "Omar the Just" (Bebawy, 2003: 125).

The Moral Character of Islamic Penal Law

A serious debate has long existed among Western criminologists regarding the role of criminal law in protecting society's moral values and whether the criminal justice system can be legitimately charged with regulating public morality. Moslem scholars argue that such a debate does not exist because the Western-style separation between state and religion does not exist in Islamic tradition. As mentioned earlier, Islam is considered both a theology and a state. It not only regulates the relationship between Moslems and their creator (the religious portion), but also between the people themselves, whether they are governors or governed, or whether they are Moslems or non-Moslems (the secular portion).

This being the case, it can be safely assumed that an integral relationship between religion and morality exists in Islam, and that such a relationship justifies the role of Islamic law as the protector of moral values (Hoffman, 2001). For example, the Quran prohibits certain acts such as drinking alcoholic beverages, committing fornication, dancing, gambling, usury, and false testimony, on the basis of their dangerous moral consequences (al-Awa, 1979 : 47). The Prophet has succinctly expressed his moral authority by saying in Hadith: "I was sent to perfect moral values" (al-Awa, 1979: 48).

To a considerable extent, the morality of Islamic penal law can be perceived in the consensus among Moslem jurists that the community of Islam is required, by divine command, to ordain what is good and prohibit what is wrong. Subsequently, it is the duty of the Islamic community (ummah) to watch over the practice of what is good and decent and prohibit that which is evil and blameworthy. In Saudi Arabia, this practice can be demonstrated by the presence of Mutaweens (lay moralists) who roam the streets watching for immoral activities. If such activities are observed, the Mutawee can stop the person, lecture him or her, and if necessary, arrest the violators and take them before a special judge. The ultimate purpose of this moral system is to achieve the objectives of the Quranic verse "Ye are the best community that hath been raised up for mankind, Ye enjoin right conduct, and forbid indecency" (Quran, Surat al-Imran: 10).

Closely associated with the moral character of Islamic penal law is its religious character. This character necessitates certain consequences, the most important of which are:

- There is an inseparable relationship between the prohibitions prescribed in Islamic penal law and the Moslem's unshaken belief in God. The Quran states "O ye who believe! Observe your duty to Allah, and give up what remaineth from usury, if ye are believers" (Quran, Surat al-Baqarah: 278). It also states: "The adulterer and the adulteress, scourge ye each one of them a hundred lashes, and let not pity for the twain withhold you from obedience of Allah, if ye believe in Allah and the Last Day" (Quran, Surat al-Nur: 2).
- Islamic criminal law provides both an earthly and an eternal punishment for violating God's prohibitions. Theoretically, if the perpetrator of a prohibited act succeeds in escaping from the first punishment, he or she will be subject to the second punishment on the Day of Judgment, unless he or she repents. So, after defining the earthly punishment to be

imposed upon the bandits, the Quran adds "Such will be their degradation in the world, and in the hereafter theirs will be an awful doom" (Quran, Surat al-Ma'idah: 33).

- Regardless of the strictness of the Moslem state and the success of its security forces in deterring and suppressing criminal activity, unless religious restraint is internalized in the Moslem community, law and order will be lacking. Islam requires each and every Moslem to be his or her own moral judge. Belief in Allah and His word is therefore the most dominant factor in preserving a safe and spiritual society.
- The application of Islamic penal law is not an optional task left to the Moslem state to apply or to reject. It is an obligatory function that all Moslem governments must perform. This is perhaps one reason for Osama bin Laden's fury against Moslem governments that do not apply Shariah law.

Sources

Al-Awa, M. S. (1979). *The Basics of Islamic Criminal Law*. Cairo.

Ali, A. (1946). *The Holy Quran: Text, Translation and Commentary*. New York, Hafner Publishing Company.

Bassiouni, M. C. (1982). *The Islamic Criminal Justice System*. New York: Oceana Publications, Inc.

Bebawy, N. (2003). *Terrorism: a non-Islamic Industry*. Cairo: Alahram Publishers.

Berger, P., & Luckman, T. (1967). *The Social Construction of Reality*. New York: Doubleday.

Christie, N. (1970). "Comparative Criminology." *Canadian Journal of Corrections*, 12, 40-60.

Doi, A. R. I. (1984). *Shari'ah: The Islamic law*. London: Delux Press (Ta Ha Publishers).

Durkheim, E. (1947). *The Elementary Forms of Religious Life*. New York: Free Press.

Hoffman, M. (2001). *Islam as an Alternative*. Bavaria: Bavaria Verlag & Handel.

Lippman, M., McConville, S., & Yerushalmi, M. (1988). *Islamic Criminal Justice Procedures*. New York Praeger.

Muslehuddin, M. (1979). *Philosophy of Islamic Law and the Orientalists*. Lashore, Pakistan: Islamic Publications

O'Dea, T., & Aviada, J. (1983). *Sociology of Religion*. Englewood Cliffs, NJ: Prentice Hall.

Sanad, N. (1991). *The Theory of Crime and Criminal Responsibility in Islamic Law*: Shari'a. Chicago, IL: The University of Illinois at Chicago.

Siddiqi, M. (1985). *The Penal Law of Islam*. Lahor, Pakistan: Kazi Publishers.

Souryal, S. (1987). "The Religionization of a Society: The Continuing Application of Shari'ah Law in Saudi Arabia." *Journal of the Scientific Study of Religion*, 26, 429-449.

Souryal, S., Alobied, A. I., & Potts, D. W. (1994). "The Penalty of Hand Amputation for Theft in Islamic Justice." *Journal of Criminal Justice*, Vol. 22, p. 249-265. Material from this article has been used by permission from the Journal of Criminal Justice. The permission was granted on November 12, 2003.

Wilson, J. Q., and Hernstein, R. (1985). *Crime and Human Nature*. New York: Simon and Schuster.

6

The Classification of Crime in Islamic Penal Law

In Western positive law, crime has been defined as "voluntary conduct that violates a public law and for which punishment may be imposed in the name of the State" (Sanad, 1991: 49). In Islamic law, crime is defined as "the commission of a prohibited act or the omission of a duty that is commanded" (Abu-Zahra, 1950: 23). Based on these two definitions, it is evident that the concepts of crime in Western law and in Shariah law do not differ significantly.

However, some major differences exist between the Western application of criminal law and the Islamic. Islamic Shariah, as mentioned earlier, is primarily designed as both a preventive and a moralizing instrument. This can be better understood in light of the following characteristics:

- It seeks to reform the individual and purify his conscience through the use of sublime Islamic ideals and morals.
- It warns would-be violators against committing offenses and admonishes the offender with dreadful punishment in this world and in the hereafter.
- It commands Moslems to assist one another on the path of righteousness by offering counsel, moral support, and exchanging religious teaching.
- It prevents crime by blocking the path to its commission, for example, by prohibiting the use of intoxicants and segregating the sexes.

- It reinforces the moral integrity of Moslems by urging marriage at a young age and requiring the rich to contribute to the needs of the less fortunate in accordance with the concept of Zakat (alms giving).

Categories of Crime in Islamic Penal Law

Offenses in Islamic criminal law are categorized according to a complex criteria which takes into consideration the gravity of the act committed, the manner by which the person is incriminated, the severity of punishment, and the religious and social interests to be served by the process of exacting justice. Based on this criteria, crimes in Shariah law are divided into three categories: Huddud crimes, Qissas crimes, and Tazir crimes.

Huddud Crimes

As mentioned earlier, Huddud (limitations) crimes are the most serious and grave crimes in Islamic penal law. The reason for this is that they are committed against Huddud Allah, or God's rights. Huddud crimes are based on one of the Quran's most stern verses: "These are the limitations of God. Do not transgress them" (Souryal, 1994: 441). This does not mean that Huddud crimes do not address private interests, but that the predominant rights they violate are those designated by God.

The prosecution of Huddud crimes is mandatory, and punishment must be imposed exactly as prescribed in the Quran or the Sunna. However, due to the severity of punishment associated with Huddud crimes, judgment requires a rigorous set of evidentiary rules which far exceeds the strictest rules in any Western code. For the crime of adultery, for instance, the rules of evidence require either confession or the sworn testimony of four pious eyewitnesses who saw the act of carnal conjugation as clearly as they could distinguish a "white thread from a black thread." For the crime of drinking alcohol, either confession or the testimony of two male eyewitnesses is required. The crime of theft requires either confession or the testimony of two eyewitnesses to the commission of the stealthy act (Souryal, 1994: 441). Once guilt has been proven, no human judge, governor, or Imam (ruler) can increase, reduce, probate, or suspend the sentence (Mustafa, 1979: 11-12). Moslem scholars, however, differ slightly regarding the crimes that fall in this category. They agree on four Huddud crimes (adultery, theft, banditry, and defamation) but disagree on three others (transgression, drinking alcohol, and apostasy). The majority of Moslem scholars, however, maintain that the last three crimes fall within the Huddud crime category, since these acts and their punishments are stated in both the Quran or the Sunna.

Adultery (Zena)

In Islamic law, adultery is an act of voluntary sexual intercourse with anyone other than one's spouse, regardless of whether he or she is married. This Islamic concept of adultery is different from that in Western positive laws, which stipulate that one or both partners must be married to someone else, and that the act must take place during the course of this marriage (Mustafa, 1979: 48). Most notably, Islamic law does not differentiate between adultery and the Western offense of fornication.

Adultery is defined as the physical penetration by the male organ into the female organ. Any sexual contact short of penetration cannot be legally considered adultery and the Hadd punishment described above cannot be meted out. That is perhaps why more sexual acts fall into the Tazir category and are punished as prescribed for that category.

Adultery was a widely practiced behavior in pre-Islamic tribal society. Since the Islamic faith pays particular attention to the protection and preservation of a clear and honorable bloodline among the community of believers, committing adultery was strongly condemned because it could cast a doubt on the purity of society. Offspring might not know who their natural parents are, causing family units to disintegrate. If guilt for adultery is proven through the Islamic modes of evidence, and if the adulterer and adulteress are subject to Islamic criminal responsibility, they must be subject to the prescribed sanctions. Adultery carries different penalties, depending on the status of the guilty party. If he or she is a married person (ma'soum), he or she is stoned to death, as defined in the Hadith. On the other hand, if he or she is unmarried, the penalty would be one hundred lashes.

Theft (Sariqa)

Theft takes place when a person carries away movable property from another person's possession without the consent of its owner and with the specific intent of appropriating the stolen goods. The seriousness of a theft often depends upon the value of property that is stolen and by the method used in stealing the property. For the application of the theft Hadd, the majority of Moslem scholars require that the stolen property be kept in a private place (hirz) and that the thief breaks into this private place to get to the property. To them, theft that takes place in public places is not a Hadd, but a Tazir crime.

Moslem jurists also require that the stolen property be of some value (nisab), but they differ on the exact extent of this value. Hanafi says it should not be less than ten dirhams (the equivalent of $3.00 in 2004); while Malik, Shafi'i, and Ibn-Hanbal maintain that it should be the equivalent of a quarter of a dinar, or three dirhams (Al-awa, 1979: 165).

Moslem jurists exclude the application of the theft Hadd if there is a reasonable dispute over the ownership of the stolen money. The Shariah punishment for theft is stated in the Quranic text: "As for the thief, both male and female, cut off their hands; it is the reward for their own deeds, an exemplary punishment from Allah" (Quran, Surat al Ma'idah: 38). Furthermore, for punishment to be effective, the hand amputation must be carried out publicly. This is deemed conducive to safeguarding the property of everyone by deterring the offender from committing new crimes (specific deterrence) and by deterring potential criminals from following suit (general deterrence).

Banditry (Hiraba)

Banditry (highway robbery) is a more serious crime than theft because it is committed by means of force—laying in wait and attacking travelers. The penalty for this crime was made particularly severe in order to eradicate it: "The reward for those who wage war upon Allah, and his Messenger and strive with might and main for mischief through the land is execution, or crucifixion, or cutting off of hands and feet from opposite sides, or exile from the land" (Quran, Surat al-Ma'idah: 33).

There is disagreement, however, among Moslem jurists on whether the punishments stated for banditry can be applied differently according to the degree of the seriousness of the act committed. Malik states that the judge has a greater degree of flexibility in selecting the proper penalty with no restriction upon his discretionary power. But Hanafi, Shafi'i, and Ibn-Hanbal maintain that these penalties are ranked according to the gravity of the act committed, with no discretion left to the judge. According to these scholars:

- If the bandit commits murder, he will be subject to execution by the sword.
- If he steals money, his hands and feet will be cut off from opposite sides.
- If he only threatens the travelers without murdering or stealing, he will be expelled out of the land (this may include imprisonment).
- If he kills and steals property at the same time, he will be crucified.

Defamation (Qadhj)

Defamation is the false accusation of promiscuity against a woman. If someone accuses a woman, whether married or unmarried, of adultery without providing the required four witnesses, he or she is a defamer (slanderer) and must be punished for defamation. The Quran says: "And those who accuse an honorable woman, but bring not four witnesses, scourge them with eighty lashes, and never accept their testimony, they indeed are evildoers (Quran, Surat al-Nur).

Defamation, however, does not occur if a husband accuses his wife of adultery without providing witnesses. As mentioned earlier, he would be committing al-li'an. Malik states that defamation could be committed either by an explicit accusation of promiscuity or an implicit one, whereas Hanafi, Shafi'i, and Ibn-Hanbal hold that the defamation Hadd should not be applied unless the accusation of an honorable woman takes place by the use of direct and clear words (i.e., explicitly).

Transgression (Baghi)

Transgression, or rebellion, is defined by the majority of Moslem scholars as rising against the legitimate imam by the use of force. The transgressors must have reasonable grounds, in their own view, to rebel against the imam. If the rebellion is groundless, they are considered bandits and punished accordingly. The Quran states: "if two parties among the believers fall into quarrel, make ye peace between them, but if one of them transgresses beyond bounds against the other, then fight ye all against him until he complies, then make peace between them with justice, and be fair. For God loves those who are fair" (Quran, Surat al-Hujurat: 9).

Moslem scholars hold that for transgression to occur the following requirements must be met (Mustafa, 1979: 188-190):

- The Imam should not take the initiative and fight the transgressors until he knows their arguments and calls on them to stop the uprising.
- If the transgressors refuse to respond to the Imam's peaceful invitation, he is allowed to fight them until they surrender or are defeated.
- If the suspects were unable to fight or surrendered, they should not be punished by the Hadd (killing) but may be punished according to the Tazir penalty
- If the suspects' claims are found to be just because the Imam has deviated from the correct path, then the Iman is considered the transgressor. Those who revolted against him will not be subject to punishment because Islamic law gives Moslems the right to revolt against an unjust ruler.
- If the transgressors' claims are found to be groundless, then the Moslems should support the Imam in his fight against the transgressors.

Drinking Alcohol (Shorb al-khamr)

Drinking alcohol was a habit widely practiced among Arabs in pre-Islamic times as well as in the early period of Islam. Therefore a sudden and complete prohibition was illogical. The Quran prohibited drinking alcohol at three stages. First, a Quranic text stated: "They ask thee concerning wine and gambling…say to them they are great sins even though they make some men some profit. But the sin is greater than the profit" (Quran, Surat al-Baqarah: 219). At a later time, another text stated: "Ye who believe, approach not prayers with a mind befogged until ye can understand all ye say" (Quran, Surat al-Nisa: 43). Finally, the Quran prohibited drinking alcohol in any form and at any time.

Because Moslems were forbidden from drinking wine while they were doing prayers, and as prayers were required of Moslems five times a day from dawn until night, a new text which forbade and outlawed drinking alcohol at all times was appropriate. God said: "O ye who believe, intoxicants and gambling, idolatry, and divination by arrows, are an abomination and Satan's handiwork. Avoid them so that you may prosper" (Quran, Surat al-Ma'idah: 91). It should be, therefore, clear that this prohibition includes all types of substances that befog the mind and make a person lose his sense and conscience, no matter what these intoxicants are called (e.g.,wine, cocaine, opium, hashish, marijuana, etc.) (Mustafa, 1979:90-98)

The punishment for drinking alcohol was prescribed in a Hadith. The Prophet Mohammed stated: "He who drinks wine, whip him." Although the Hadith determined the type of penalty to be applied, it did not determine the number of lashes that should be inflicted upon the accused. Moslem jurists disagree on this issue. Malik, Hanafi, and a few others maintain that it is eighty lashes. They refer to the practice of Omar (the second caliph). Shafi'i and some other Moslems hold that it is forty lashes, referring to the practice of the Prophet himself.

Apostasy (Ridda)

Apostasy is the turning away from Islam after having adhered to it. It is forbidden by a large number of Quranic texts. For example, the Quran states: "And whoever of you turns from his religion and dies disbelieving, their works have failed in this world and the next. Those are the inhabitants of fire: therein they shall dwell forever" (Quran, Surat al-Baqarah: 217).

All the Quranic texts prohibiting apostasy demonstrate the awful doom in the hereafter awaiting those who commit this crime, but none define an earthly punishment. The Sunna, however, provides such a penalty—death. The Hadith states: "Whoever changes his religion, kill him" (see Ibn-Rusd in Sanad, 1991:56). Moslem scholars maintain that the application of the Hadd of apostasy requires two prerequisites:

(1) The accused must commit an intentional and explicit act, positive or negative, that shows his rejection of the Islamic faith, such as denying the existence of the one God, his messengers, and the hereafter, or denying any of the Islamic tenets (e.g., prayer, zakat, fasting).

(2) The accused is allowed an adequate period of time to repent and return to Islam before the application of the penalty. If he does repent, no penalty will be imposed upon him. Moslem jurists do not agree on

the length of this period for repentance. Some say it is three days; others hold that it should be left to the judge's discretion.

The Effectiveness of Huddud Penalties

After discussing Huddud crimes and the punishments prescribed for them, it may be safe to suggest that these punishments are distinguished by the severe corporal harm they cause to the convicted person. Some Western scholars see this distinction as a social failure and criticize Shariah as inhumane. A fair and logical discussion of the Western view may demonstrate that this view is inaccurate.

In the Moslem mind, Islam is a divinely ordained law revealed by God and directed to all mankind. As an eternal law, Islam regulates all aspects of life in order to achieve a high level of social harmony. The role of the individual in the Moslem society, however, is a crucial one. He is considered the cornerstone of the society and, as such, cannot exist separate from it. The individual enjoys as many privileges as society can afford, and the society offers the individual as many privileges as it receives from the individual.

Corporal punishments in Islamic penal law are also carried out within a short period of time, causing temporary physical pain to the criminal. These punishments deter him from committing any more crime and keep him from being held in prison for a long time, during which he would be unable to either earn a living for himself or his family, or have the opportunity to maintain a healthy relationship with his children.

Beside the fact that prisons impose a heavy financial burden on the public treasury, they may not be the most fertile ground for rehabilitating first-time offenders and restoring them to society. Islamic criminal law, by contrast, requires the application of Huddud penalties to take place in public. Moslem scholars argue that this requirement, unlike a prison term, is more effective in preventing crime by deterring criminality and reshaping the behavior of the youths.

The effectiveness of Huddud penalties in deterring crime in Moslem countries can be inferred by examining the following 5-year tables of crime rates in the categories of murder and theft in a number of Middle Eastern countries in comparison with the rates in the United States. The Middle Eastern countries selected are Saudi Arabia, Oman, the United Arab Emirates, Lebanon, and Algeria. All of these countries are either totally Moslem or mostly Moslem. They also vary in terms of whether they apply Shariah law or non-Shariah laws (i.e., Western law), with Saudi Arabia as the leader in the use of Shariah law and Lebanon as the leader in the use of Western law (basically French law). The tables cover these countries during the period between 1996 and 2000. After an examination of these numbers, the reader can conclude that: (1) the total number of crimes committed in the United States are (for whatever reason or combination of reasons) higher than the number of crimes in all of the other countries combined; (2) the rates of murder per 100,000 in countries known for orthodoxy in applying Shariah law (i.e., Saudi Arabia, Oman, Algeria) are substantially lower than in the countries known for being less orthodox (Lebanon); and (3) the lowest number of thefts per 100,000 in the year 2000 was in Algeria, arguably because the government at the time had moved toward the application of Shariah law. The following tables are gleaned from the International Crime Statistics, Interpol, 2003.

Total Numbers of Offenses for 5 Years (1996 - 2000)

Country	1996	1997	1998	1999	2000
Saudi Arabia	28,992	22,292	25,232	60,722	72,512
Oman	1,483	2,741	6,609	7,580	10,001
United Arab Emirates (UAE)	37,359	34,216	8,790	63,633	63,729
Lebanon	35,918	87,461	108,513	122,507	121,478
Algeria	—	—	42,501	52,108	62,425
United States	—	13,867,143	13,473,619	13,175,070	11,608,070

Table 1

Total Numbers of Offenses by Population and Rate per 100,000 (2000)

Country	Population	Number of Offenses	Crime per 100,000
Saudi Arabia	20,846,884	72,512	347.83
Oman	2,409,780	10,001	415.02
United Arab Emirates (UAE)	2,463,729	63,729	821.32
Lebanon	4,000,000	121,478	3,036.95
Algeria	29,276,766	62,425	213.22
United States	281,421,900	11,608,070	4,124.79

Table 2

Total Numbers of Murders by Population and Rate per 100,000 (2000)

Country	Population	Number of Cases	Crime per 100,000
Saudi Arabia	20,846,884	147	0.71
Oman	2,409,780	22	0.91
United Arab Emirates (UAE)	2,463,729	75	—
Lebanon	4,000,000	177	4.43
Algeria	29,276,766	286	0.98
United States	281,421,900	15,586	5.54

Table 3

Total Numbers of Thefts by Population and Rate per 100,000 (2000)

Country Population	Theft		Aggravated Theft		Robbery		Theft of Motor Car	
	No	Rate	No	Rate	No	Rate	No	Rate
Saudi Arabia 20,846,884	33,669	161.50	1,123	5.39	30	0.14	15,896	76.25
Oman 2,409,780	4,481	185.95	—	—	—	—	517	21.45
United Arab Emirates (UAE) 2,463,729	8,613	—	227	—	13	—	678	—
Lebanon 4,000,000	21,846	546.15	3,269	81.73	380	9.50	1,524	38.10
Algeria 29,276,766	27,600	71.00	4,560	74.20	—	—	2,480	28.20
United States 281,421,900	10,835,316	3,804.58	2,532,688	889.30	422,921	148.50	1,226,457	430.64

Table 4

Qissas Crimes

While Qissas (retaliation) crimes may appear more serious than Huddud crimes because they include murder, they are considered a lower category than Huddud since murder, despite its gravity, is not a crime against God's limitations. Literally, the word Qissas means "the equivalent" as in "equal retaliation," "lex Talionis," or the biblical phrase "an eye for an eye." Qissas is the infliction upon the offender an amount of bodily harm equal to that which the offender inflicted upon the victim. Qissas crimes include: (1) murder and its related areas of manslaughter and criminal negligence, and (2) assault, battery, and similar acts of violence against the person. It is also important to note that the right to return equal harm in these crimes does not belong to the state, but to the victim or the victim's family. This is why murder is not among the Huddud crimes, but theft is. Murder is against an individual, but theft is against God's spiritual community.

Qissas crimes are acts committed against the bodily integrity of another, whether intentionally or unintentionally. These offenses are what the Western penal codes call "crimes against persons." The punishment for Qissas crimes is either retaliation or Diya (blood money). Retaliation penalties are only applicable to intentional crimes committed against the bodily integrity of another. This is consistent with the Quranic text that states:

> *"O ye who believe! Retaliation is prescribed for you in the matter of the murdered; the free man for the free man and the slave for the slave and the female for the female. And for him who is forgiven somewhat by his brother, prosecution according to usage and payment unto him in kindness. This is an alleviation and a mercy from Our Lord. He who transgresseth after this will have a painful doom" (Quran, Surat al-Baqarah: 178).*

In Surat al-Medina, the Quran also states:

> *"And we prescribed for them therein: The life for the life, and the eye for the eye, and the nose for the nose, and the ear for the ear, and the tooth for the tooth, and for wounds retaliation. But who so forgoeth, it shall be expiation for him who so judgeth not by that which Allah hath revealed, such are wrongdoers."*

It should be clear by now that Qissas punishment is only applicable to crimes against bodily integrity and is not applicable to other crimes against a person's property, honor, dignity, reputation, etc. For instance, according to Qissas, if someone sets a fire in another's house, the victim has no right to set the offender's house on fire.

In Shariah law, Qissas is established to satisfy the human tendency to retaliate on the part of a victim or members of his family. By so doing, the parties involved avoid any potential escalation of violence that might cause more serious bodily harm. Diya (blood money), on the other hand, is a legitimate settlement that can be paid by the wrongdoer (or his family) to the victim (or his family) in order to end the dispute. In modern terms, Diya is equivalent to compensation paid to a harmed person. The only difference is that in Islamic penal law, it is a criminal penalty, whereas in Western law, it is a civil one.

In order to establish the principle of equality among people before the law, the Prophet Mohammed determined a standard amount of Diya for all people without any distinction between criminals and victims, rich or poor. The standard Diya during the times of the Prophet was a hundred cattle. Today, it is the equivalent of 27,000 Saudi Rials, or $6,750 in 2004 (Sanad, 1991:62).

In Islamic law, Diya is normally assigned to unintentional crimes against bodily integrity (i.e., involuntary killing, unintentional physical injury or maiming). The use of Diya was mentioned in the Quran: "Never should a believer kill a believer, but [if it happened] by accident, he who does must liberate a believer's neck and diya is due to the deceased's family" (Quran, Surat al-Nisa: 92). Diya can also be applied in cases of intentional bodily harm if the victim or the avenger of the blood waives his right to Qissas. Moreover, Diya would be the only punishment applicable in intentional crimes against bodily integrity when there is uncertainty due to inconclusiveness of evidence against the accused. In such cases, the existence of doubt nullifies the application of the Qissas penalty.

The Western reader should also note that in Islamic jurisprudence, the amount of Diya required for a female is half that for the male. In traditional Moslem countries, this has been justified by the fact that in Islamic Shariah, men form the economic foundation of society. They are the breadwinners of the family, even if the women have their own income and are wealthier than the men (Sanad, 1991: 62). The absence of equivalency between male and female has been rapidly changing in moderate and progressive Islamic countries. In moderate Islamic states, the Diya is the same for males and females.

Limitations on the Application of Qissas

For Qissas penalties to be consistent in Shariah law, the following requirements must be met (Bassiouni, 1982: 208-209):

- The accused must be an adult who is of sound mind and understanding at the time of the act, and the act must have been done intentionally.
- The victim must be a Moslem or a Zimmi (Christian or Jew) or, according to the majority of writers, a musta'min

(a non-Christian or non-Jew who has entered the land of Islam pursuant to a peace treaty).

- Only the male blood relatives (father, grandfather, or son) in a line of ascendancy can claim Qissas in the case of the death of the victim, and only the victim can claim it in the case of injury or maiming.
- A Moslem or a Zimmi cannot be executed or maimed for the killing or maiming of someone who is not a musta'min (i.e., a pagan or an apostate).
- The infliction of Qissas must be in the least painful manner.
- The person who inflicts Qissas must have the knowledge and competence which enable him to inflict it. Otherwise, a professional person (i.e., physician or nurse) is assigned to carry out the sentence on behalf of the victim or his family.
- The retaliator or the professional person cannot inflict a greater degree of harm than that which has been inflicted.
- Qissas should not be applied unless conclusive evidence exists. Doubtful evidence is valid only to sustain Diya.

Tazir Crimes

Tazir crimes are technically the least serious crimes in Islamic penal law. The legality of these crimes and their punishments is based on ijma (consensus) regarding the Moslem state's right to criminalize and punish all inappropriate behaviors that cause any physical, social, political, financial, or moral damages to an individual or the community as a whole. This category can, therefore, include all inappropriate behaviors that cannot be included in the categories of Huddud or Qissas. As a result, an exhaustive list of the acts constituting Tazir crimes cannot be made. This is especially the case since new crimes can be added (or even removed) depending on the discretion of the Islamic ruler or the specific Qadi examining the case. Such a discretionary power is, however, not an absolute one. Moslem scholars hold that this authority must: (1) be exercised within the spirit of the general rules of Islamic Shariah; (2) be consistent with the public interest of the Moslem society; and (3) be made without any deviation or abuse.

The following criminal acts fall into the category of Tazir crimes (Sanad, 1991:64):

- Criminal acts in the category of Huddud crimes that, for some legal reason or technicality, do not exactly fit the requirements of a Hadd crime. Examples include petty theft, attempted adultery, homosexuality, and cases supported by doubtful evidence.
- Acts prohibited by the Islamic Shariah without providing specific earthly punishments. Examples include eating pork, providing false testimony, usury, and tampering with measurements and lengths.
- Acts that might cause damage to public interest, public order, or to an individual's rights. This stipulation enables the Islamic Shariah—as an eternal and universal law—to cope with the new requirements of modern life and to safeguard the Moslem society. Examples include traffic violations, fraud, embezzlement, corruption, economic crimes, or forgery.

Tazir Penalties

As mentioned earlier, the punishments for Tazir crimes are left to the discretionary authority of the ruler or the judge. The judge can use his discretion according to the gravity of the act committed, the personal aspects of the accused person (i.e., previous criminal record, motive, lifestyle, etc.), the damage caused to society, and the totality of the surrounding circumstances. As a general rule, however, the purpose of Tazir punishment is to achieve two goals: (1) deterring would-be criminals, and (2) rehabilitating the criminal and restoring him or her to society as a law-abiding individual. With this in mind, the judge can choose from the following penalties (Sanad, 1991: 64-65).

The Death Penalty

The imposition of death as a Tazir punishment has been questionable; some Moslem jurists agree while others do not. Those who agree require it for serious acts that can seriously harm the public interest (i.e., treason) or for incorrigible criminals who cannot be rehabilitated (i.e., habitual offenders). The jurists who do not agree assert that the death penalty should be limited exclusively to Huddud and Qissas crimes.

Flagellation

This penalty is highly recommended by Moslem scholars for Tazir crimes on the grounds that it is in the interest of both the criminal and the society. Since this penalty can be administered at any time or place, the condemned can attend to his business soon after and serve the interests of his family. In addition, flagellation does not cause financial burden to the public treasury and saves the first-time offender from being corrupted by the habitual criminals in prison. The minimum number of lashes to be imposed is three; the maximum number is not agreed on. Some scholars maintain that it is thirty-nine, whereas others say that it is seventy-five (Sanad, 1991: 65).

Incarceration

Moslem jurists maintain that a judge can legitimately impose a prison sentence only when flagellation is deemed ineffective in rehabilitating and reforming the criminal. Imprisonment could be for a fixed term left to the judge to decide, or for an indeterminate sentence (until the convicted person repents).

Fine

There is no consensus among Moslem scholars regarding this penalty. Some say it should be the sole principal penalty inflicted, yet others maintain it is a supplementary penalty to be applied in addition to the principal one.

A fine can be imposed by confiscating a segment of the criminal's wealth to go to the public treasury. The amount to be confiscated is left to the judge's discretion. In addition to the fine, the judge can "admonish" the accused either in an open court or in private. He can also "preach" to him to induce him or her to do good and to avoid evil deeds. The judge can also rule that the defendant be dismissed from employment if he or she brought about harm to the public interest. The judge may also order the public disclosure of the convicted person's deeds in cases such as perjury and fraud (Sanad, 1991: 64).

Comparison between Huddud, Qissas, and Tazir Crimes

Several procedural differences exist among the categories of crime in the Islamic penal code:

- In Huddud crimes, once guilt is established, the offender cannot be acquitted, nor can his punishment be commuted to a lesser one. This is based on the doctrine that Huddud crimes are offenses against God's rights and their punishments are fixed by the rules of God. Therefore, no one can intercede to reduce the Huddud penalty or suspend its execution, no matter what political or social status this person has. As for Qissas or Tazir crimes, the victim or his family or the state can intercede under certain conditions.
- Huddud crimes are prerogatives of God. They do not require a formal complaint by the victim's family or the state, except in cases of defamation and theft. The Imam or any other Moslem can bring charges against the defendant in court. In Qissas and Tazir crimes, legal action must be initiated by the harmed party or by the state on behalf of society.
- Doubtful evidence, as will be discussed later, nullifies Huddud and Qissas penalties, whereas Diya and Tazir punishments can be applied with the existence of doubtful evidence.
- Unlike Huddud crimes, Qissas crimes are of a restitutionable character. Once a sentence is pronounced, it is the victim's right (or his family's) to demand its execution in full or in part, to accept Diya instead, or to forgive the offender completely.
- While Huddud crimes are considered the most serious category, they do not necessarily require the most severe penalties. For example, while a person accused of drinking alcohol (a Hadd crime) may be punished by 80 lashes, a person accused of murder (a Qissas crime) or of treason (a Tazir crime) can be punished by death.

Sources

Abu-Zahra, M. (1950). *Crime and Punishment in Islamic Jurisprudence: The Punishment*. Cairo.

Al-Awa, M. S. (1979). *The Basis of the Islamic Criminal Law*. Cairo.

Ali, A. (1946). *The Holy Quran: Text, Translation and Commentary*. New York: Hafner Publishing Company.

Bassiouni, M. C. (1982). *The Islamic Criminal Justice System*. New York: Oceana Publications, Inc.

Mustafa, M. A. (1979). *Huddud and Qissas Crimes: Comparative Study between the Shari'a and Positive Law*. Cairo.

Sanad, N. (1991). *The Theory of Crime and Criminal Responsibility in Islamic Law: Shari'a*. Chicago, IL: The University of Illinois at Chicago.

Souryal, S., Alobied, A. I., & Potts, D. W. (1994). "The Penalty of Hand Amputation for Theft in Islamic Justice." *Journal of Criminal Justice*, Vol. 22, p. 249-265.

7

Fundamentals of Islamic Penal Law

In Shariah law, the Islamic theory of responsibility is governed by certain fundamental principles that must be observed in all cases, regardless of the type of crime (i.e., Huddud, Qissas, or Tazir), the criminal history of the accused (i.e., first offender or habitual offender), or the circumstances surrounding the act committed. Before the emergence of Islam, it was possible for a person to be held responsible for an act in which he did not participate in any way. In certain crimes (i.e., political crimes or revenge crimes) one's family name or social ties were reasonable grounds for assigning criminal responsibility. A person could also be held responsible for an act committed by his son, daughter, father, or even by any of his friends. Criminal responsibility was very likely to extend to a person who did not take part in a crime at all. With the advent of Islam, this tradition changed.

The main issues of criminal responsibility in Islamic jurisprudence include:

- The Principle of Individual Responsibility.
- The Presumption of Innocence.
- Nullification of Penalty by Doubt.
- Guarantees for the Accused

The Principle of Individual Responsibility

The Islamic theory of individual responsibility rejected the egotistical Jahiliyah theory. The Islamic theory developed cautiously and gradually due to two reasons: (1) the stubborn jahiliyah culture needed to be dislodged without causing any radical repercussions to the burgeoning religion of Islam, and (2) the length of time the Quran took to be completed. Not until the time of Mohammed's death was the Islamic theory of individual responsibility complete.

The Quran is replete with religious provisions asserting that no person can be held criminally responsible unless he or she is involved in the commission of a prohibited act, either as a principal or as an accomplice. This view is consistent with the Quranic principle, "Each soul earneth on its own account" (Quran, Surat al-An'an: 164); "No burdened soul can bear another's burden" (Quran, Surat Fatir: 18); "Who so doth right, it is for his soul, and who so doth wrong, it is against it" (Quran, Surat Fussilat: 46). The Sunna also confirms this principle. The Prophet Mohammed reportedly stated: "A soul is not held responsible for acts committed by his father or by his brother" (Quran, Surat al-An'an: 164).

Given this information, it is interesting to note that the theory of individual criminal responsibility in Islam preceded the same theory established by positive law in the Western world. According to Sanad, the first reference to a Western theory of individual responsibility appeared after the French Revolution of 1789 (Sanad, 1991:72).

The Presumption of Innocence

An inevitable consequence of the Islamic principle of individual responsibility for crime is the principle of lawfulness or permissibility. According to this principle, all human acts are presumed to be permissible unless a law proves them otherwise. As a corollary to the principle of lawfulness is the assumption that any accused person is presumed to be innocent unless proven guilty in a court of law. Furthermore (perhaps as a higher corollary to the previous ones), no person can be found guilty of wrongdoing unless the evidence against him is beyond any reasonable doubt. If reasonable doubt is shown to exist, the accused person must be acquitted.

The concept of presumption of innocence was laid down in Islamic law long before its acknowledgment in Western positivist thought. Fourteen hundred years ago, the Prophet Mohammed reportedly said in a Hadith: "Avoid condemning the Moslem to Huddud crimes whenever you can, and if you can find a way out for the Moslem, then release him for if the Imam errs it is better that he errs in favor of innocence than in favor of guilt" (Sanad, 1991: 72).

The presumption of innocence in Islamic law has an important consequence: the burden of proof rests with the accuser. Without this principle, the burden of proof would then rest with the accused. In Islamic law, the accuser is charged with the duty of proving the accusation. If that cannot be shown, the charge must be dismissed. One of the most traditional principles in Islamic jurisprudence in this context has been: "al-baina ala min ida' wa al yamin ala min ankar." This can be translated as: "the burden of proof is on the accuser, and if the accused denies the charge, he must accept to take an oath." Subsequently, all criminal justice systems in Moslem countries currently operate on the basis of this principle.

Nullification of Penalty by Doubt

Closely connected to the presumption of innocence and its consequences is the rule that nullifies penalties in the case of doubt. This rule rests on the Hadith: "Prevent punishment in case of doubt. Release the accused if possible, for it is better that the ruler be wrong in forgiving than wrong in punishing" (Abu-Zuhra, 1950: 222). According to this rule, criminal conviction must be founded upon assertion and certainty. If the circumstances surrounding the case cast doubt upon the occurrence of the crime, its attribution to the individual accused, or the evidence established against him, the judge *must* rule in favor of acquitting the accused. The other side of this rule requires that when circumstantial evidence is considered favorable to the accused (exonerating evidence), it should be considered, whereas when circumstantial evidence is considered unfavorable (incriminating evidence), it should be disregarded (Sanad, 1991: 73). Furthermore, to ensure that the accused does not go free because the evidence against him is doubtful, the judge in Huddud crimes has the discretion to impose a Tazir punishment instead, if the public interest necessitates that.

The rule of nullification of penalty by doubt was originally meant to be applied to Huddud crimes because penalties in these crimes are both non-negotiable and unpardonable. The consensus among Moslem scholars today, however, is that the principle applies to both Huddud and Qissas crimes, but not to Tazir crimes. On the other hand, the minority view maintains that Tazir crimes should not be excluded on the grounds that nothing in Shariah law precludes such an exception (al-Awa, 1979: 143). According to the minority view, the rule was established to ensure justice and to guarantee the interests of the accused who would equally need both of these considerations whether he or she is accused of a Hadd, Qissas, or Tazir crime. I support the minority view, especially since some Tazir penalties can be as severe as those prescribed for Huddud or Qissas crimes. As mentioned earlier, a person accused of a Tazir crime can be sentenced to death for treason or transgression against the government. For this reason, and in addition to the above-mentioned grounds, Tazir crimes should be treated in the manner Huddud or Qissas crimes are, if Islamic justice is to be consistent.

Currently, the rule in all Islamic states is that doubt nullifies penalty, regardless of the type of crime committed or the severity of punishment assigned to it. For instance, in Egypt, the Supreme Court has repeatedly upheld that "criminal conviction should not be based on doubt or guess. It should only be founded on assertion and conclusiveness. If there is doubt in the attribution of the act to the accused person or in the sufficiency of the incriminating evidence, the accused must be acquitted" (Sanad, 1991: 74). All Islamic states now follow the Egyptian rule.

Guarantees for the Accused in Islamic Shariah

In Shariah law, justice is founded on the basis that it is better served if a judge acquits a culpable person than if he convicts an innocent one. This rule was clearly stated in the Hadith: "If the imam errs it is better that he errs in favor of innocence than in favor of guilt" (Sanad, 1991: 75).

A criminal proceeding in Islamic law is a contest between a defendant and a government acting on behalf of society. Each seeks to win, the latter by convicting the accused in order to protect society and maintain public order, and the former by proving his innocence and securing his acquittal from the sentencing judge. Since the tools and resources available to the government are infinitely greater than those available to even the wealthiest of defendants, accused persons would be more vulnerable to the power of the government unless some strict guarantees are made in their favor. Without such guarantees, it would be very likely that a defendant might be subject to unlawful measures affecting personal rights, and the chances of an acquittal would be minimal at best. For these reasons, Islamic Shariah contains a set of safeguards to mediate between the government's interest in punishing criminals and the individual's interest in practicing his or her personal rights without any undue intrusion.

Legal guarantees to the accused are furnished by Islamic criminal law throughout the stages of the legal procedure. Since the legal procedure in Islamic law passes through two main stages, (a) the investigation stage, and (b) the trial stage, the guarantees held in each stage will be discussed separately.

Guarantees during the Investigation Stage

Moslem scholars admit that in Islamic criminal law there is no dividing line between the investigation and trial stages. This does not mean that a trial in Islam can take place without prior investigation, but it does mean that investigation is not always regarded as an autonomous phase to be conducted by a competent authority other than the court. Often the official deciding the case is the same person who investigated it and gathered the evidence.

The guarantees recognized by Islam to the accused during this stage are:

- Guarantees against Warrantless Search and Seizure.
- Guarantees against Illegal Arrest or Investigative Detention.
- Guarantees during Interrogation.

Guarantees against Warrantless Search and Seizure

Islam safeguards individual privacy. The Quran is replete with texts ensuring the inviolability of the person and his or her dwelling. The Quran specifically stated "Do not spy." The Prophet in a Hadith stated "A man should not look inside a house unless he receives permission...if a person does, and you pelt him with a stone putting out his eye, no guilt will be on you" (Sanad, 1991: 76). Second Caliph Omar Ibn-al-Khatab was even more persistent in preserving the inviolability of personal dwellings. Abd al-Rahman-ibn-Awf reportedly told a story about Caliph Omar. He said "One night I and Caliph Omar were on guard duty in Medina. We noticed a night light through an open door and heard loud voices." According to Awf, Omar said "This is the residence of Raby'a ibn Umayya and the people inside are drinking." Awf asked Caliph Omar what they should do. The Caliph replied: "I think we have committed a forbidden act. God stated we shall not spy, but we have." Omar and Awf then left the people inside the house alone and walked away (Sanad, 1991: 76).

Traditional Islam seeks to maintain the inviolability of persons and dwellings and does not recognize the modern rule of probable cause. But once a person is accused of a crime (i.e., by acting in plain view or upon a complaint by another), the interest of society in punishing him or her and maintaining peace and order requires engaging in some conduct that might undermine the inviolability rule. In such a case, the state has the right to search the person and his or her dwelling and seize whatever evidence deemed useful to investigate the case and uncover the truth.

The Islamic state's right to search dwellings and to seize evidence is governed, however, by the following guarantees deemed favorable to the accused:

- Searches of persons or dwellings should not be conducted except under a search warrant issued by wali al-mazalim (the minister of complaints, a position equivalent to today's attorney general) and not by anyone else. The precise and strict manner by which wali al-mazalim is chosen in Islam explains the degree of trust the state has in him and his unwavering piety.
- The issuance of a search warrant should not be founded upon mere suspicion. Sufficient evidence against the accused must support such a warrant. The evaluation of the evidence's sufficiency is left to the discretionary power of wali al-mazalim.
- The evidence supporting the search warrant should be the result of lawful and careful examination; otherwise the evidence must be disregarded.
- If a state agent must search an accused woman, he is not allowed under any circumstances to touch the private parts of her body (i.e., sexual or erogenous zones).

Guarantees against Illegal Arrest or Investigative Detention

In Islamic law, arrest is the apprehension of a person in whom there is probable suspicion to believe that he or she has committed a crime. While the duration of detention may vary for different reasons, it normally should not exceed 24 hours. In modern Islamic states, the police can "stop and frisk" an individual when there is reasonable grounds to suspect that the individual is involved in a crime or is wanted by the authorities in connection with a crime. Under these conditions, the police can only detain a suspect briefly. The length of such detainment depends on the circumstances of the investigation, although it must not exceed the time limit imposed for arrest (Sanad, 1991:445).

While Moslem scholars agree regarding the right of state officials to "stop and frisk" suspected individuals, they disagree regarding the authority of the officials who arrest or hold suspects under preventive or investigative detention. Opponents of preventive detention maintain that it constitutes a serious restraint on personal liberties and violates the general rule that no person should be deprived of his or her liberty except for a lawful reason. They base their view on the conduct of the Prophet Mohammed and his successor, Abu-Bakr, neither of whom held any accused individual under precautionary arrest. The proponents of preventive detention, however, hold that such a measure can be necessary for uncovering the truth in an investigation. Furthermore, holding an accused individual under preventive detention can help prevent him or her from influencing the witnesses, altering or demolishing the evidence against him, or fleeing.

As a compromise, jurists on both sides of the argument agree on certain measures that can achieve a balance between the right of the accused to be protected against the use of unreasonable preventive detention and the interests of the government. Most Islamic states enforce the following checks:

- Preventive detention should not be conducted except under a warrant by a wali al-mazalim.
- When the case is referred to a judge, he becomes the only one responsible for determining the propriety of preventive detention and/or release.

- Preventive detention should only be applied to crimes of a special degree of gravity (such as murder, manslaughter, and serious bodily harm).
- Preventive detention should have a time limit. However, Moslem jurists disagree on the maximum period of this limit. Some say that it should be one month, and others maintain it should be less than that. Some jurists hold that this period should be left to the Imam (the ruler) to decide (al-Mawardi, 1880: 81).

Guarantees during Interrogation

Interrogation involves confronting the accused with the evidence established against him and discussing this evidence so that he may either refute it or admit it. Since the purpose of interrogation is gathering and preparing evidence which may result in the conviction of the accused by the trial judge, Moslem jurists provide numerous safeguards to the accused during interrogation:

- Interrogation should be conducted by designated officials known for good reputation and irreproachable character in order to guarantee that it is done fairly and justly. These officials are known as Wali al-Mazalim and the Al-Mohtasib. They are appointed by the Imam to ensure the enforcement of the spiritual provisions of Shariah and to punish the violators accordingly.
- In Huddud and Qissas crimes, interrogators cannot require an oath from the accused when he is confronted by evidence against him. Since an oath is considered highly valued by Moslems (i.e., an awful doom awaits the perjurer in the hereafter), requiring such an oath might result in the accused admitting to false charges against him.
- In Huddud and Qissas crimes, the accused are allowed to remain silent, and their silence is not held against them as an admission of guilt. Moslem jurists hold that guilt in Huddud and Qissas crimes must be proved through specific modalities determined by Islamic Shariah. Since silence by the accused is not one of these modalities, it cannot be held against the accused. Islamic jurists also maintain that "no

saying could be attributed to a silent person" (Abu-Zahra, 1950: 72).

- The accused shall not be subject to any sort of inhumane treatment (i.e., torture, coercion, beating, threats, etc.). The Prophet said "God shall torture, on the day of judgment, those who inflict torture on people in life" (Awad, 1982: 91). The majority of Moslem scholars agree that a confession should be made by the accused of his own free will. If it is the result of inhumane treatment, the confession must be disregarded, even if it were true. On the other hand, a minority of Moslem jurists disagree and allow the admissibility of a confession obtained by deceit. Ibn-Hazm considers such a confession acceptable as long as no physical coercion exists, whereas Malik states that trickery and/or physical coercion violate the rights of the accused, thus invalidating their confession (Sanad, 1991: 80).
- Islamic Shariah protects the accused against his own weakness, error, and indiscretion. It provides that the statement and responses given by the accused should be repeated by him as many times as the number of witnesses required by Shariah. Thus, the accused should have the opportunity to withdraw his confession, even if it has been given freely, at any time prior to the execution of the sentence. In such cases where the confession is withdrawn, punishment should be suspended (Awad, 1982:91).

Guarantees during the Trial Stage

The trial is the most important phase in the criminal action because it is the final step before the declaration of acquittal or guilt by the presiding judge. Hence, Islamic Shariah has provided the accused with guarantees in order to ensure that the sentence rendered by the court is based on the facts.

The Right to a Defense

Islamic Shariah is replete with provisions securing one's right to a defense, not only at the trial stage but also during all prior stages. In Islamic justice, the right to a defense is of great significance because it enables the accused to deny any accusation against him, either by disproving (refuting) the incriminating evidence or by submitting exonerating evidence (i.e., an alibi). The necessity for the right to a defense becomes even clearer in light of the fact that any accusation that is not countered by a valid defense automatically becomes a verdict.

The Prophet Mohammed reportedly instructed Ali, after appointing him governor of Yemen: "O Ali, people will appeal to you for justice. If two adversaries come to you for arbitration, do not rule for the one before you have similarly heard from the other. It is more proper for justice to become evident to you and for you to know who is right." Caliph Omar ibn-al-Khatib reiterated the same speech to some judges: "If an adversary whose eye had been blinded by another comes to you, do not rule until the other party attends, for perhaps the latter had been blinded in both eyes" (Sanad, 1991: 81).

In Islamic law, the right to a defense has been established along with other rights which are intimately associated with it. Without these rights, the defense process would be meaningless. According to Sanad (1991: 81), these associated rights provide the procedural aspects of defense. Sanad (1991: 82) explains:

- The accused must be informed of the charge against him and of the evidence established against him, whether the evidence is incriminating or exonerating. He or she should be made aware of the totality of circumstances surrounding the case.
- The accused should be capable of defending himself. The Hanafi school of jurisprudence asserts that mute offenders shall not be subject to Huddud penalties even if conclusive evidence is furnished against them. Imam Hanafi elaborates by asserting that such an offender lacks the means to express his defense. Imam Hanafi also asserts that sign language is not enough to present a full defense. Given the state of Islam at the time, that view is likely to be accurate.
- The accused has the right to retain an attorney to assist in his defense. Nothing in the Islamic Shariah prevents the accused from being represented by an attorney before the judge. Such a right may well be a practical requirement because confronting the accused with an indictment can alter the clarity of his mind, thus hindering his ability to

defend himself effectively. Moreover, the accused is often unaware of the legal procedures and of the efficient ways to disprove the evidence against him. Hence, he becomes unequal to his adversary (the public prosecutor) in the trial procedure. The presence of an attorney, however, does not eliminate the defendant's right to defend himself. In Islamic justice, he is the primary party to the defense, whereas the attorney is only his agent. By the same token, the right to retain counsel is not limited to the accused only; the accuser has the same right.

- The accused must be given a reasonable opportunity to present his defense and should be permitted to meet and correspond in private with counsel. He should also be allowed to confront and cross-examine the accuser, the witnesses, and any other accused persons.

The Right to Impartial Trial

Islam places a great emphasis on establishing justice and equality among people, particularly those who are on trial. The Quran states: "Judge between them [the people] in accordance with what God has revealed and do not follow their whims" (Quran, Surat al-Ma'idah: 49). The Quran also states: "God commands you to fulfill your obligations towards the people and if you judge between them your judgment should be founded on justice" (Quran, Surat al-Nisa: 58). The Prophet stated: "Avoid injustice because it is a darkness on the day of resurrection." He also stated: "The judges are of three kinds, two of them will go to Hell and one to Heaven. The judge who is aware of the rights [of individuals] and rules in accordance with them will go to Heaven, and the judges who rule by ignorance or deviate [from the right] will go to Hell" (Sanad, 1991: 83).

As if to reinforce the Prophet's edict about the role of judges and their strong commitment to justice, Caliph Omar reportedly sent a message to Abu-Mussa al-Asha'ary upon the latter's appointment as judge. The message emphasized the following rules:

- The right to adjudication is an absolute duty in accordance with the Sunna.

- Investigate any case you suspect (to bring about the right), for a right without execution is futile.
- Equalize between the parties before you in your expressions and in your judgment.
- Your judgment should not be reason for the noble to hope for your favor, nor for the poor to despair from your justice.
- If you render a judgment and after a period of time you find it to be unjust, do not hesitate to revise it, unless it is so old that no one can change it. The revision of judgments is better than preserving injustice.

The Right to Damages for Erroneous Judgment

In the Islamic theory of justice, if a judge renders an erroneous decision unintentionally, the condemned is entitled to compensation from the public treasury. The condemned can also appeal to Wali al-Mazalim. If it is shown that the judge's error was intentional and issued on the basis of an unjust judgment favorable to someone because he is a noble, wealthy, or powerful, the judge should be dismissed and the victim entitled to damages to be collected from the judge's own property (Madkur, 1966:258).

In the next chapters, the reader will be exposed to the concepts of criminal responsibility and systems of proof in Islamic jurisprudence.

Sources

Abu-Zahra, M. (1950). *Crime and Punishment in Islamic Jurisprudence: The Punishment*. Cairo.

Al-Awa, M. S. (1979). *The Basis of the Islamic Criminal Law*. Cairo.

Al-Mawardi, A. (1880). *Al-Ahkam al-Sultaniyah Matba' at Al-Watan*. Cairo.

Ali, A. (1946). *The Holy Quran: Text, Translations and Commentary*. New York: Hafner Publishing Company.

Awad, A. (1982). *The Rights of the Accused under Islamic Criminal Procedure*.

Madkur, M. S. (1966). *Introduction to Islamic Jurisprudence*. Cairo.

Sanad, N. (1991). *The Theory of Crime and Criminal Responsibility in Islamic Law: Shari'a*. Chicago, IL: The University of Illinois at Chicago.

8

Criminal Responsibility in Islamic Criminal Law

The theory of criminal responsibility in Islamic law consists of two elements: criminal conduct and criminal intent. While both of these elements must be present to establish criminal responsibility, there are circumstances under which criminal responsibility may not exist.

Criminal Conduct

Criminal conduct includes all the physical elements of an offense without which there is no basis to believe that a criminal act has been committed. If that were not the case, there would be no criminal responsibility. Criminal conduct may be the result of either the voluntary commission of an act forbidden by law (active crime) or the omission of an act or another obligation required by law (passive crime). Without either of these physical elements, there can be no crime. Dreams and thoughts are not considered forms of conduct because they do not constitute physical acts or omissions.

In addition to the physical elements of criminal conduct, there must be a criminal consequence and a causal relationship that connects this consequence to the act or the omission. Moslem jurists maintain that a causal relationship must exist in order to establish criminal responsibility. In this context, they refer to three Quranic texts: "Each soul earneth on its own account;" "No burdened soul can bear another's burden;" and "He who doth wrong will have the recompense thereof" (Sanad: 1991: 85).

Therefore, a person is held criminally responsible for a criminal offense whenever it is possible to trace that result back to the act or the omission attributed to him or her. For instance, it would be an offense of homicide if someone were to open up a river dam causing people to drown or to start a fire and destroy a building with the intention of causing death. In a controversial case, it was reported that Ibn-Hazm stated: "a man was traveling with his mother [on a donkey] when another man came on a horse galloping at a high speed. The donkey was frightened as a result and jumped. The woman fell off the donkey and was killed. The man appealed to Caliph Omar Ibn-al-Khatab who asked, 'Did he hit the donkey?' The man answered, 'No.' Omar asked, 'Did the horse injure the donkey in any way'? The man answered, 'No.' So Omar said, 'Your mother's time had come, resign yourself to God's will" (Ibn Ahmad, 1927: 9 as cited in Sanad, 1991: 86).

In Islamic jurisprudence, the requirement of a causal relationship between an act or omission and a criminal consequence does not mean that the act or omission need be the only cause that brings about the criminal consequence. A person can be held criminally responsible even if some other contributing factors intervene in causing the criminal consequence. This, however, can only be valid as long as the contributing factors are insufficient in and of themselves to bring about the consequence and do not break the causal relationship between the act or omission and the consequence (Ubayd, 1974, as cited in Sanad, 1994: 86).

Criminal Intent

In Islamic jurisprudence, criminal intent refers to a person's mental determination to violate a criminal law for a wrongful purpose. The purpose of a person's conduct is wrongful when he or she intends to cause harm to the body or property of another person, to the public at large, or to the state. Criminal intent is often referred to in legal terms as an evil state of mind (Jones, 1978: 30). Criminal responsibility, however, can only exist if the person had a criminal intent at the moment he or she engages in criminal conduct. In legal terms, this is referred to as the concurrence between criminal conduct and criminal intent.

In Islamic jurisprudence, criminal intent is either general or specific. Moslem jurists agree that a person has a general criminal intent whenever he or she voluntarily participates in criminal conduct of any kind. This is because the law presumes that a person who is of sound mind is able to realize the natural and probable consequences of his or her behavior and to anticipate when harm to a person or to property is a foreseeable consequence of the illegal behavior. Yet a general criminal intent may not always be sufficient to hold a person criminally responsible for unlawful behavior. Sometimes a specific criminal intent must be proven. Specific criminal intent is required, for example, in crimes of murder, theft, rape, and burglary. Moslem scholars maintain that a specific intent is required for a person to be held criminally responsible in the following crimes (Bassiouni, 1982: 177-178):

- Treason (the intent to harm the Moslem state).
- Rebellion (the intent to overthrow a pious Moslem ruler).
- Bribery (the intent to promise personal gain to induce another to perform a prohibited act or refrain from doing a required act).
- Apostasy (the intent to reject Islam).
- Murder (the intent to bring about death).
- Embezzlement (the intent to obtain unlawful possession).

In Islamic law, there are degrees of criminal intent Usually, the higher the degree of the criminal intent, the greater the criminal responsibility. Degrees of criminal intent are also known as degrees of culpability, or blame. These degrees are generally defined in terms such as *intentionally, knowingly, recklessly,* and *negligently*, with *intentionally* being the highest degree of culpability. One engages in criminal conduct intentionally when the behavior is purposeful; that is when the perpetrator specifically plans to either commit a prohibited act or to abstain from performing a required act. A slightly lower degree of culpability exists when a person knowingly—but not intentionally—engages in an illegal conduct. This ordinarily means that the person understands what he or she is doing without having a specific purpose or a motive. A lesser degree of culpability exists when a person engages in conduct recklessly. Reckless conduct involves a gross deviation from the acceptable standards of behavior, yet it need not involve an intentional or even a knowing state of mind. The lowest degree of culpability exists when a person acts negligently; that is, when he or she fails to exercise the care that a reasonably prudent person would be expected to exercise under identical circumstances.

Moslem jurists hold that, in Huddud or Qissas crimes, no one shall be held criminally responsible unless he or she has intentionally committed the act. For example, if a woman is brought to a man on his wedding night and, mistakenly believing she is his wife, he has sexual intercourse with her, he would not be held responsible for adultery, and, therefore, would not be legally culpable. A mistake, however, is not an excuse as far as the rights of the victims are concerned. A person who makes a mistake can still be liable for his behavior if he accidentally causes damage to another's property (Sanad, 1991: 89).

Reasons for Denying Responsibility

In Islamic jurisprudence, a person who is charged with a crime may raise one or more defenses based on the absence of his or her capacity to be held criminally responsible. Criminal capacity in Islamic law requires the existence of one, or both, of the following elements: (1) consciousness (reason) and (2) willingness.

In Islam, a person cannot be held criminally responsible if he or she was: (1) unable to know the difference between right and wrong, (2) unable to understand the consequences of his actions, (3) unable to understand what conduct is prohibited by criminal laws, and/or (4) able to understand all of the above, but had to commit the prohibited act unwillingly (Sanad, 1991: 89). The reasons for denying criminal responsibility in Islamic law are considered legal excuses without which any person, without exception, must be held responsible for his or her criminal acts or omissions. These excuses include: infancy, insanity, intoxication, coercion, or necessity. Each of these will be discussed here in greater detail.

Infancy

In Islamic jurisprudence, a child lacks both of the elements required for criminal responsibility: consciousness and willingness. As such, no child can be held criminally responsible for an act he or she commits or omits. Moslem scholars, however, maintain that the criminal capacity of a child increases with age. They recognize three stages of age:

Under the age of seven: An infant who is not yet seven years old cannot be considered capable of committing a crime under any condition. It does not matter if the child is more physically mature than other children of the same age. In Islamic law, children under seven years of age are presumed not to have reached the age of reason. They are not regarded as rational human beings who can be held criminally responsible for their behavior. However, such children could be held responsible on civil grounds (i.e., where restitution is required).

Between the age of seven and the onset of puberty: Puberty in Islam is determined either by age (some scholars say it occurs at eleven years old, and some say at twelve; others differentiate between males and females) or by the signs of puberty, or by both. Therefore, a child in this stage is not completely exempt from criminal responsibility. He or she may possess a partial criminal capacity and, as such, can be held partially responsible on criminal grounds. However, such a child cannot be held responsible for Huddud or Qissas crimes. Most Moslem jurists agree that premeditation on the part of a child at this stage can only be regarded as a mistake, and the child could only be held responsible for a Tazir crime. In this case, an indemnity is usually paid by the child's family or clan.

Beyond the onset of puberty: A person of sound mind is held criminally responsible after the onset of puberty.

Insanity

In civilized societies, it is a general legal presumption that no person can be held criminally responsible for an offense while he or she is insane, even if the person recovers his or her sanity after the criminal act of commission or omission. Fourteen hundred years ago, the Prophet Mohammed reportedly made the same observation. In a Hadith, he stated: "The pen is left out [meaning no responsibility can be assigned] in three conditions: The child until he reaches the age of puberty, the insane until he recovers his sanity, and the sleeping person until he wakes up" (Sanad, 1991: 91). In Islamic jurisprudence, therefore, an insane person is incapable of criminal responsibility because insanity deprives the person of reason and, subsequently, the ability to discriminate between good and evil.

Insanity, in Islamic law, is of two types: (1) prolonged, which totally vitiates one's perception, and (2) interrupted (sporadic), which attacks a person intermittently. Criminal responsibility is completely denied in the case of prolonged insanity and during periods of interrupted insanity if the crime is committed during one of these periods. Yet, a person who commits a crime while sane and then becomes insane would be held criminally responsible.

It should also be clear that insanity is significantly different from mental deficiencies such as mental retardation or feeblemindedness. People who are mentally deficient are not necessarily insane. Mental deficiency by itself is not a sufficient excuse to deny criminal responsibility, unless it causes the loss of one's ability to discriminate between good and evil at the time the crime is committed.

Moslem scholars disagree, however, on the effect of insanity that occurs after the commission of crime but before a verdict is pronounced. In the Hanbali and Shafii schools, jurists argue that this should not be grounds for dismissing the case or suspending the trial. By contrast, in the Maliki and Hanafi schools, jurists argue that insanity prior to a verdict is grounds for suspending the trial until the person recovers. Jurists also differ on whether insanity that occurs after the verdict has been pronounced can suspend the execution of this verdict (Sanad, 1991: 91).

Intoxication

A person is considered intoxicated when he or she has consumed enough of an intoxicating substance, such as alcohol, to cause a loss of control over his or her mind. The reader should not mistake this discussion as a commentary on the offense of drinking alcohol, since the latter falls in the category of Huddud crimes with its prescribed punishment of 80 lashes—a penalty which is both non-negotiable and unpardonable. When considering intoxication as a reason for denying criminal responsibility, Moslem scholars differentiate between involuntary intoxication and voluntary intoxication:

(1) Involuntary intoxication nullifies criminal responsibility for any offense because the acts or omissions of an involuntarily intoxicated person are neither the result of his free will nor his sound mind. Intoxication is considered involuntary if it is due to coercion, fraud, mistake, or the ingestion of a prescribed substance for medical reasons.

(2) Voluntary intoxication is the consumption of an intoxicating substance by choice for pleasure. The majority of Moslem jurists agree that all acts or omissions committed in a state of voluntary intoxication are culpable, and the person should be held criminally responsible. They add, however, that the criminal responsibility of the voluntarily intoxicated person should not extend to crimes requir-

ing specific criminal intent. In such cases, they agree not to impose Huddud or Qissas penalties, although they can replace such penalties with Tazir punishments.

Because intoxication can cause people to lose control over their will and their mind, most Moslem scholars agree with contemporary positive laws that prohibit intoxicating substances. They further argue that to maintain public order and to protect a spiritual community, those who violate the rules against drinking alcohol must be punished. Nevertheless, a minority of Moslem scholars, including Ibn al-Qayyim and Ibn Hazm, absolve the acts of drunks whether they have an excuse for being drunk or not and regardless of the substance that caused their intoxication. They argue that no retaliation is due such persons, no indemnities should be imposed on them, nor should they be held liable in any other way (Sanad, 1991: 92).

Coercion or Necessity

Coercion or duress occurs when a person commits an act or an omission under the compelling force of another person. Individuals who act or fail to act under coercion or duress are considered deprived of their free will. In other words, they act or fail to act unwillingly.

Individuals act under coercion when they are physically forced by others. They also act under duress when they are threatened with physical violence if they do not do what others command them to do. Moslem jurists argue that coercion or duress can be an excuse for denying criminal responsibility if the following conditions are met:

- The perpetrator must be able to carry out the physical violence or the threatened harm. For example, no coercion or duress is possible from a young child.
- The victims must believe that their act or omission is necessary to avoid death or serious bodily injury and that such death or injury will result immediately, not in the distant future.
- The threatened harm, though not directed toward one's own body, is directed toward someone else, and the person acts or fails to act in order to avoid the imminent death or serious bodily injury of that person.

Based on these conditions, violations of one's property or legal rights, such as the damaging of one's property or a false accusation, are not legitimate acts of coercion or duress.

Moslem scholars agree that when these conditions are met, no Hudud or Qissas penalties can be imposed on the person so compelled. For example, the Hadd penalty cannot be imposed on a person coerced into stealing or apostasy. Yet, Moslem jurists differ in their judgment of coerced murder. Abu Hanifa and al-Shafi'i hold that a compelled murderer should not be punished by a Qissas penalty, only by a Tazir one. The compeller, in this case, can be punished by a Qissas penalty. Abu Youssef asserts that a Qissas penalty cannot be imposed upon either the compelled murderer or the compeller. Both should be made to pay restitution to the victim or his or her family (Sanad, 1991: 93).

Necessity exists when a person commits an act or an omission because of a compelling physical force of nature. It should be evident that while necessity has the same effect that coercion has on one's free will, they differ in the nature of the compelling force. Islamic jurisprudence maintains that necessity may excuse a person from criminal responsibility under the following mitigating conditions (Sanad, 1991: 93):

- The person is confronted with a choice between two evils with no way out. Necessity does not exist when the defendant has an alternative that is less harmful than the criminal act or omission he or she eventually commits. For instance, if a bull attacks a person and there is a safe way to avoid harm by escaping, but the person kills the bull anyway, the person cannot claim necessity as a defense.
- The person reasonably believes that any harm he or she causes will prevent a greater harm. Harm to human life is considered greater than harm to property. Thus, a person who reasonably believes he or she must damage or destroy property to save one's own or another person's life may be acting out of necessity. For example, Moslem scholars argue that a person who drinks alcohol to ward off choking should not be punished.
- The defendant must not, of his own free will, have been the cause of the compelling force. For instance, if a person intentionally blows up a building and injures someone as he is fleeing the scene, he cannot use necessity as a

defense for the injury or death caused to that person (Rashid, 1968: 263).

In Islamic law, the general rule is that necessity renders prohibited acts permissible. For example, Moslem scholars maintain that if a hungry man in the desert with no food or money meets a companion who has enough food for both of them yet refuses to share voluntarily, the hungry man is entitled to fight for the food. If he kills the companion, no punishment shall be imposed on him, because a person in such a case must fight to survive (Abu Zahra, 1950: 504). Ibn al-Qayyim mentions some interesting instances that can constitute a proper case of necessity. For instance, a person who sees someone's ewe or an edible animal dying and then slaughters it to save it's owner money; someone who hires a boy who later develops a gangrenous sore on his leg and so amputates the leg to prevent the spread of gangrene; and someone who sees a flood rushing toward a house and so tears down a wall to divert the flow of water to save the house (Awad, 1985: 509 512).

Reasons for Permissibility

In Islamic law, permissibility is a doctrine that legally allows a person who commits (or omits) a criminal act, and who may be subject to full criminal responsibility, to go free because the act (or omission) is considered permissible. In Islamic jurisprudence, the reasons for permissibility are:

- Acting in lawful defense.
- Acting with implied consent.
- Acting in the performance of duty.
- Acting in the performance of sports.

Acting in Lawful Defense

According to Islamic Shariah, Moslems are entitled to defend their own life, property, honor, or chastity, as well as those of others. The Prophet reportedly stated: "Those of you who see vice should repel it first with their hands; if unable, then with their tongues; and if unable, then with their hearts, that would be the lowest level of belief." Based on this defense, Moslem scholars maintain that if a person is attacked by another with a murderous intent and that there is no other way to stave off the attack except by killing or maiming the aggressor, no punishment should be imposed on the original victim. This judgment is also applicable to defending anyone else's life (see al-Gahyyz, as cited in Sanad, 1991: 95).

This view is supported by the Hadith: "He who is killed in self-defense is a martyr, he who is killed in the defense of others is a martyr, and he who is killed in the defense of his property is a martyr" (Sanad, 1991: 96). Moslem jurists follow the same rule in cases involving the defense of one's honor or property. Ibn Qudamah asserts that "If someone attacks another wanting his money, his soul, or his woman to sleep with, then any Moslem watching the incident is entitled by Shariah to assist in repelling the aggression" (Ibn Qudamah, 1974: 322).

In support of this open assistance view, it was reported that an excited man entered Caliph Omar's room carrying a bloody sword and was followed by a few men who claimed that he (the first man) had killed his wife along with one of their friends who was visiting her at the time. Omar asked the accused, "What do you say to that?" The accused answered "I hit my wife's thighs with the sword, and if someone was between them, I killed him." Omar confronted the dead man's friends, and they all concurred. Omar released the accused, instructing him "If they repeat it, do it again" (Sanad, 1991: 96).

In Islamic law, lawful defense can decriminalize an act under the following conditions:

- When the act is committed to protect oneself or another from a crime against the person, property, or honor, as described above.
- If the defender only uses the amount of force that is necessary to repel aggression without abuse or excess. If the force used is excessive, the defender can be held criminally culpable. Moslem Qadis evaluate the degree of the force used based on the circumstances surrounding each case.
- If at the crucial moment it is impossible for the defender to rely on protection by the public authorities. It is reported that a man went to the Prophet saying "Messenger of God, a man came to me and wanted my money." The Prophet said, "Remind him of God." The man responded, "If he does not respond?" The Prophet said, "Ask the nearby Moslems to help you." The man responded, "If there are no Moslems

close to me?" The Prophet said, "Rely on the Imam." The man responded, "If the Imam is too far away?" Then the Prophet answered, "Fight until you protect your money and become a martyr in the Hereafter" (Abu Zahra, 1950: 509).

Acting with Implied Consent

When an Islamic law grants certain rights to certain individuals, subject to certain restrictions, then any conduct undertaken by another who is selected by these individuals should be considered lawful as long as it complies with the same restrictions. For instance, Shariah law allows fathers, grandfathers, and guardians the right to discipline their minors on the condition they first use persuasive and peaceful means, and if these means fail, to physically beat the minor as long as the beatings do not leave scars, break bones, maim, or cause death. Consistent with this concept of implied consent, a tutor selected by a parent or a guardian can rightfully beat a minor as long as the restrictions on the severity of beating are not violated. If the tutor, in this case, exceeds the limits of this implied right, he or she would be subject to punishment. However, Islamic jurists disagree on the responsibility of the tutor who exceeds this right, causing the minor to die. Hanafi, for example, argues that the tutor should be held liable and punished by a Tazir penalty. Al-Sahiban argues that the tutor, in this case, should not be held liable since his act was legal (Sanad, 1991: 97).

Acting in the Performance of Duty

According to Shariah law, when a person acts in accordance to duty, no crime can be attributed to him or her even if the elements of the act constituted a crime. For example, a police officer would be justified in using reasonable force to make a lawful arrest or to prevent the escape of a suspect who has been lawfully arrested. Also, a public official who acts pursuant to a lawful court order is justified in using necessary force to execute the court order. Similarly, an executioner who kills a condemned prisoner pursuant to a lawful death sentence is not subject to punishment for murder (Rashid, 1968:386).

Accordingly, Malik states that a physician who treats a patient or circumcises a boy cannot be criminally liable if the patient dies, as long as the doctor is knowledgeable and made no mistakes. However, if the doctor is knowledgeable, yet made a mistake, indemnity is due from him, his family, or his clan. Moreover, if it can be shown that the doctor was not knowledgeable, he should be punished by a Tazir penalty because, in such a case, no legal privilege exists.

Acting in the Performance of Sports

Normally, all positive laws allow playing sports, even those requiring the use of violence (i.e., boxing, wrestling, football, etc.). According to positive laws, if the rules of the game are observed and a player is injured, no criminal responsibility exists on the part of the player causing the injury. However, if the player violates the rules of the game, he or she can be held responsible. The degree of responsibility depends upon whether the defendant commits the act intentionally or unintentionally.

While Shariah law does not directly address these issues, by using Qiyas (analogy), it agrees with these assumptions as long as the privileges assigned to the players are observed in good faith. Islamic jurists refer more often to cases of sports injuries when injury or death is caused intentionally. Al-Qarafi, for instance, asserts that if injury or death results from the accidental use of violence in games such as wrestling or boxing, one-fifth of the indemnity for injury or death is due from the player, his family, or his clan. If the violence is shown to be intentional, then retribution should be due in full and the player should be punished by a Qissas penalty (Al Qarafi, 1961:381).

Sources

Abu-Zahra, M. (1950). *Crime and Punishment in Islamic Jurisprudence: The Punishment*. Cairo.

Al-Gahyyz. *Ankham al Qur'an*, Vol. I. Cairo.

Al-Qarafi, S. (1961). *Al-Dhakhirah Matba'at Kulliyat al-shari'a*. Cairo.

Ali, A. (1946), *The Holy Quran, Text, Translation and Commentary*. New York: Hafner Publishing Company.

Awad, A. (1985). *The Penal Law: General Sector*. Alexandria.

Bassiouni, M. C. (1982). *The Islamic Criminal Justice System*. New York: Oceana Publications, Inc.

Ibn Ahmad. (1927). *Al-Muhalla*. Cairo.

Ibn Qudamah, M. (1974). *Al-Mughni*, Vol. 8. Cairo

Jones, D. A. (1978). *Crime and Criminal Responsibility*. Chicago.

Rashid, A. A. (1968). *The Criminal Law: General Sector*. Cairo.

Sanad, N. (1991). *The Theory of Crime and Criminal Responsibility in Islamic Law: Shari'a*. Chicago, IL: The University of Illinois at Chicago.

Ubayd, R. (1974). "The Link of Causality." *The Criminal Law: Analytic and Comparative Study*. Cairo.

9

The System of Proof in Islamic Law

Rules governing criminal evidence, are not only designed to prove the guilt of a culprit but also to prove the innocence of the wrongfully accused. As was mentioned earlier, justice is better served if a judge acquits a culpable person than if an innocent person is convicted. Understanding the system of proof in Islamic jurisprudence requires discussing two main subjects: (1) the modes of criminal evidence in Shariah law, and (2) the validity of criminal evidence in Shariah law.

Modes of Criminal Evidence in Shariah Law

A relevant question in Shariah law is whether the Islamic Qadi (judge) is bound to observe rules of evidence, and if so, what types of evidence are required in criminal cases. A majority of Moslem scholars (Shafi'i, Hanafi, and Hanbali) adopt a restricted view. They maintain that evidence in criminal cases is restricted basically to testimony and confession. The judge cannot render a criminal conviction on the basis of any other type of evidence, such as personal knowledge or hearsay information. The majority of Islamic jurists, however, allow the use of other methods of proof in non-criminal cases. On the other hand, there is a minority of Islamic jurists, including Ibn Taymia and Ibn Al Qiyyain, who adopt a more liberal view. They hold that nothing in the Quran or in the Sunna restricts criminal evidence to either testimony or confession. To these jurists, different types of evidence can be used without any restriction in both criminal and civil cases (Bassiouni,

1982: 110). In this chapter, we will only discuss issues in testimony and confession.

Eye Witness Testimony

In Islamic jurisprudence, the issues of testimony as evidence in criminal cases are basically those dealing with the number of witnesses and those dealing with the condition of the witnesses.

Number of Eye Witnesses

The majority of Moslem scholars hold that in Huddud and Qissas crimes, Shariah law requires at least two witnesses before the Qadi can render a judgment. In the case of adultery, the law requires at least four witnesses. This may explain why not a single case of adultery has been proven by witnesses in Islamic history (al-Awa, 1979: 290). However, a minority of Islamic jurists, including Ibn Hazm, argues that judgment in Huddud and Qissas cases can be founded on the basis of one witness in addition to an oath by the plaintiff (Sanad, 1991: 100).

Condition of the Eye Witnesses

Moslem jurists maintain that eye witnesses before a Moslem court must meet certain conditions. While in the old days these conditions were determined directly by the Qadi, in modern times Qadis can rely on advice of medical personnel (Sanad, 1991: 100).

Maturity: Witnesses must be of age, as determined by the judge or a medical examination. The majority of jurists agree that the testimony of minors is inadmissible, even if they understood the substance of their testimony. On the other hand, Malik allows the testimony of adolescents against other minors in homicide cases. Hanbal allows the testimony of minors in cases of assault and battery if their testimony was corroborated by someone who had heard it before the trial.

Memory: Witnesses must possess an "adequate" memory to be able to recall their observations. Those who are known to be forgetful are not considered competent witnesses.

Speech: Witnesses must be able to speak clearly. Moslem scholars differ on the testimony of mutes. Malik and ibn-Hanbal accept a mute's testimony if he or she is capable of writing it. Hanafi rejects such testimony under all circumstances.

Reason: Witnesses must be of sound mind. This can be confirmed by the Qadi or by medical examination, if necessary. No testimony is acceptable from insane or mentally retarded persons.

Visual and Aural Perception: In general, the testimony of blind and/or deaf persons is considered inadmissible, although there are differences among jurists on this issue. It is left to the Qadi to interpret the ability of blind and/or deaf people to appropriately testify.

Good Character: All witnesses are assumed to be of good character until proven otherwise. Malik and Shafi'i state that a witness is of good character when he or she avoids grave and venial sins, is trustworthy, and has good relationships with people.

Authenticity: Acceptable testimony must be authentic. The witnesses must have perceived the events they are testifying about with their own senses (i.e., eyes, nose, ears). Hearsay testimony is considered inadmissible because of the element of doubt.

Islam: Jurists agree that adherence to the Islamic faith is a necessary condition for the acceptability of testimony. However, Hanafi would admit the testimony of a non-Moslem against a Moslem.

Gender: Moslem jurists agree that testimony in Huddud and Qissas crimes must be by male witnesses only. Female testimony would be inadmissible. Yet, al-Zahiri is the only Moslem jurist who accepts the testimony of females in Huddud and Qissas crimes. In this case, the testimony of two females would be the equivalent to that of one male. For example, in an adultery case, where four male witnesses are required, al-Zahiri would accept the testimony of three males and two females, two males and four females, one male and six females, or eight females (Ibn Qudamah, 1974: 69-70).

Reasons for Disqualifying Testimony

In Islamic jurisprudence, a witness may meet all of the above mentioned conditions, yet have his or her testimony invalidated by one or more of the following conditions:

Blood and Conjugal Relations: With the exception of Shafi'i, the majority of Moslem jurists (i.e., Hanafi, Maliki, and Hanbali) reject the testimony of family members either for or against another member of the family. They also disqualify the testimony of spouses, either for or against one another.

Enmity: For testimony to be truly helpful in establishing justice, security, and tranquility in the Moslem community, witnesses must be inspired only by these considerations. If a witness is found to hold any hostile feelings toward the defendant or any other party, his or her testimony is disqualified.

Partiality: Like enmity, partiality disqualifies testimony. If a witness is found to be partial for or against the defendant, his or her testimony should be deemed inadmissible. A witness is considered partial when his or her personal interests, whether it is his own interest or someone else's, influence the testimony. In order to avoid partiality, Moslem jurists require witnesses to provide testimony under oath. Moslem jurists, who normally put a great weight on the oath, believe that the oath reminds the witness of the omniscient power of God and warns them of God's wrath if they lie.

Confession (Iqrar) as Evidence

In Islamic jurisprudence, confession is considered a strong and solemn evidence. It is applicable in all categories of crime. Confession is deemed to occur when the accused voluntarily admits to the charge (or charges) facing him or her.

Conditions for the Admissibility of Iqrar

In Islamic jurisprudence, the validity of Iqrar as evidence depends on the existence of the following conditions:

(1) The confessor must be a mature person who is capable of understanding the substance of what he or she is admitting to and its legal consequences. Confession attributed to an insane or mentally retarded person is inadmissible.

(2) Confession should be rendered by the accused of his own free will. If the confession is a result of torture, beating, threat, deception, or any other kind of inhumane treatment, it should be disregarded even if it is true. If the confession is a result of coercion, Moslem jurists state that, in addition to its inadmissibility, the compeller must be punished. This is also applicable in the case of a judge who accepts a confession of a witness without investigating whether or not it was offered by the confessor's free will (Al Awa, 1979: 294).

(3) A confession must assert the commission of the crime clearly, explicitly, and without any doubt. If a person admits that he or she held

hostile feelings toward the victim and previously warned the victim that he or she would take revenge, this cannot be considered a confession because it does not explicitly admit to committing the crime. Doubtful and vague confessions are inadmissible in Islamic Shariah. The requirement for assertion in Islamic confessions leads some Moslem jurists (i.e., Hanafi) to maintain that confessions must be verbal, not written or in sign language. On the other hand, other jurists (i.e., Shaf'i, Hanbali, and Maliki) accept the confession of a mute person as long as the signs he or she uses are intelligible (Sanad, 1991: 103).

(4) The confession must take place in and during the legal hearing. Hanafi maintains that a confession that takes place outside the court is invalid, whereas Malik, Shafi'i, and ibn-Hanbal admit such confession if it is witnessed by two people.

(5) Moslem scholars agree that confession in Huddud, Qissas, or Tazir cases is admissible as long as it is stated once. Repetition by the confessor is not required except in the case of adultery. Hanafi, Hanbali, and Zaydi require the repetition of the confession as many times as the required number of witnesses (i.e., four times). The supporters of this view see the need for making punishment a reformative matter, as well as a retributive action. As such, allowing the defendant to repeat the confession allows him or her to reflect on what he or she is saying, allowing the person the opportunity to withdraw the confession before receiving a stiff, non-negotiable penalty. This might also motivate the accused to repent and return to the correct path. Malik, Shafi'i, and Zahiri, on the other hand, do not require such a repetition, stating instead that only one opportunity to confess is sufficient (Sanad, 1991: 102).

The Judge's Discretion in Admitting Confessions

If a confession meets the conditions for admissibility, the judge may still have to determine its validity to sustain criminal conviction. He has the right to disregard the confession if he realizes that it contradicts other circumstances in the case. For instance, a judge can reject a woman's confession to adultery if it is proven that she is still a virgin. The judge must also determine that the confession implicates only the confessor and no one else, not even his or her accomplices. For example, if a man confesses to committing adultery with a woman, she should not be convicted on the basis of his confession, but only if she also confesses of her own free will.

Withdrawal of Confessions

Since confession must be made voluntarily, it follows that the accused should be allowed to retract his or her confession when necessary. In such a case, while most Moslem scholars agree with this view, they differentiate among Huddud, Qissas, or Tazir crimes in determining the effect of retraction.

Most Moslem jurists argue that in the case of Huddud and Qissas crimes, the withdrawal of confession prevents the judge from rendering conviction, sparing the accused the heavy penalties usually meted out in these cases. They further argue that if withdrawing the confession takes place after the judgment is rendered but before it is enforced, the judgment must be suspended. Moreover, if withdrawing the confession takes place after the enforcement has begun but before it was completed, the judgment must be suspended and its consequences abrogated (Sanad, 1991: 104).

In the case of Tazir crimes, retracting the confession would have no effect. Moslem scholars allow the continuance of the hearing, the examination of evidence, and the enforcement of the penalty, even after the withdrawal of a defendant's confession. This distinction is based on the original doctrine that allows the nullification of Huddud and Qissas penalties whenever doubtful evidence exists. But since no such nullification was allowed in the category of Tazir crime, retracting one's confession in a Tazir crime should have no impact on the judicial process Yet, as has been suggested earlier, the doctrine of nullifying Huddud and Qissas penalties (whenever there is doubt) should be logically extended to Tazir penalties, since the need for justice is the same regardless of the category of crime committed.

Presumptions

In Islamic law, a presumption is an assumption of fact based on another set of facts discovered or otherwise established at a prior stage. A presumption is considered conclusive when the presumed fact is irrefutable. For example, a child under seven years of age is presumed to be incapable of criminal responsibility regardless of his or her physical or mental state. Conclusive presumptions in Islamic law are comparatively few in number.

Moslem jurists disagree on whether a judge can render a criminal conviction on the sole basis of presumptions in Huddud and Qissas crimes. The majority (Shafi'i, Hanafi, Hanbali) maintains that criminal conviction in such cases must be founded exclusively on legal testimony or confession. To them, any presumption in these categories would constitute doubtful evidence and, as such, invalidate conviction.

On the other hand, Malik argues that presumptions can be used in proving Huddud crimes if they are conclusive (irrefutable). He refers to statements by Caliph Omar that the Hadd of adultery should be imposed on a pregnant woman who has no husband and the Hadd of drinking alcohol should be imposed on a person who smells of alcohol, even if there is no testimony or confession. Ibn Taymia and Ibn al Qiyyam share Malik's view. They argue that the judge is not restricted to testimony or confession in rendering a criminal conviction. He can admit any other evidence, including presumption, as long as he is convinced there is sufficient basis for criminal conviction.

The Judge's Use of Personal Knowledge as Evidence

The question that arises here is whether a Moslem judge is allowed to render a criminal conviction on the basis of extrajudicial knowledge. Apart from Zahiri, Moslem scholars prevent the judge from using his personal knowledge as evidence to sustain a criminal conviction because by so doing, he becomes both a judge and a witness at the same time. They also refer to the practice of Caliph Omar when he refused to judge a case in which he was aware of its details, saying "Either I judge or testify." Nevertheless, some Islamic jurists do allow a judge to rule on extrajudicial knowledge, but only in Tazir crimes (al-Awa, 1979: 295).

Conditions for the Validity of Criminal Evidence

In order for evidence (i.e., witnesses or confession) to be considered legally sufficient for criminal conviction, it must meet the following conditions:

(1) Evidence must be conclusive; it must prove the occurrence of the crime and the guilt of the accused clearly and explicitly. Evidence loses its conclusiveness when it relies on other evidence or facts to explain it. The requirement of conclusiveness is a corollary to the presumption of innocence, which is seen as a cornerstone in the structure of the

Islamic criminal system. On the other hand, the certainty of evidence also depends upon its corroboration by other evidence or facts in the case. If a contradiction occurs, then evidence becomes doubtful and, therefore, invalid. As an example of the requirement of conclusiveness of evidence, Caliph Omar Ibn al Khatab imposed the Hadd penalty for defamation on three witnesses who testified against a person accused of adultery when the testimony of the fourth witness clearly failed to corroborate theirs.

(2) Evidence should remain conclusive throughout the criminal procedure until the execution of judgment. It is not enough that the evidence is conclusive in a given stage of the criminal action. For instance, if the defendant confesses during the investigation stage and then retracts his confession before the judge, or confesses during the trial stage but withdraws his confession before rendering judgment, this confession would no longer be conclusive and cannot support a criminal conviction.

(3) The evidence should be presented without delay. However, Moslem jurists disagree on the effect of a delayed presentation of evidence. Hanafi jurists argue that a delayed presentation of evidence casts doubt on its validity, therefore invalidating it and nullifying the penalty. Shafi'i, Maliki, and Hanbali jurists argue that a delay of presenting evidence does not necessarily cast doubt on its validity. Thus, the testimony or confession presented cannot be nullified by delay. In the final analysis, the matter should be left to the Qadi to determine the persuasiveness and admissibility of such evidence (Sanad, 1991: 106).

Sources

Ali, A. (1946). *The Holy Quran: Text, Translation and Commentary*. New York: Hafner.

Al-Awa, M. S. (1979). *The Basics of Islamic Criminal Law*. Cairo.

Bassiouni, M. C. (1982). *The Islamic Criminal Justice System*. New York: Oceana Publications, Inc.

Ibn Qudamah, M. (1974). *Al-Mughni*, Vol. 9. Cairo.

Sanad, N. (1991). *The Theory of Crime and Criminal Responsibility in Islamic Law: Shari'a*. Chicago: The University of Illinois at Chicago.

Part III

Islamic Fundamentalism and the Turn to Violence

10

From the Book to the Kalashnikov: Islam, Fundamentalism, and Terrorism

Not unlike Moses or Jesus, Mohammed neither expected nor wanted to conquer the world. Also, like most Moslem Arabs, when Mohammed died he was buried in an unmarked grave. Mohammed only sought to establish a more sublime religion, one based on submission to God and the endorsement of peace, justice, and piety—doctrines the Moslems believe neither the Byzantines, the Persians, nor the "infidels" really possessed. In the perception of Moslems, Islam is the religion of egalitarianism, civilization, and transcendence. By the same token, they also thought that beyond their borders, no other culture was worth learning from. Yet, as mentioned in detail earlier, the new religion swiftly spread, and the Moslem warriors were modestly surprised by the relative ease with which they marched through countries they never dreamed of seeing (Hitti, 1967: 214). Ironically, these early victories and the responses that ensued may have created a stubborn geopolitical paradox that continues to the present time.

The old world was shaken and confused by the tenacious new faith coming out of Arabia. While the Moslems were disappointed by how little substance the West had to offer, they found themselves faced with an "exotic" religion, one that placed too much emphasis on ritual (i.e., images, statues, titles, symbols, and icons) and too little on piety and communitarianism. To medieval Moslems, Christendom looked like a landscape of temples without a God and a debilitated faith without a message. They also considered the outer lands of Europe to be as backward as the outer lands of dark Africa. These were inhabited by barbarians from whom there was nothing much to learn and very little to trade, except perhaps in slaves (Lewis, 2002:4). The empire of the Franj, as the Moslems called Europe, appeared weakened and gradually declining in size and influence. Conversely, the Moslems may have underestimated the West, especially in the fields of weaponry and warfare, as well as the Westerners' potential to acquire new sciences and industries, which the Moslems ignored simply because such sciences and industries were not mentioned in the Quran.

The first religious clash between the Moslems and the Westerners occurred about five hundred years after the Moslems conquered Spain. The Crusaders (1096-1291 A.D.) marched into the Middle East and attacked the Moslems when they were least ready or willing to fight. The Moslem world at the time offered a spectacle of division and impotence. It was split up among local Arab chieftains: in the north the Seljuk Turks were powerful; in the south the Fatimides of Egypt held sway; and in between there were several schismatic communities, including the Druze, the Maronites, the Ismailites, and the Assassins (Hitti, 1967: 633). The Crusades were mini-wars that were characterized by religious fervor on the part of the Moslems and utter savagery on the part of the Christians. As a result, the memory of the Crusades has left a bitter and lasting taste with the descendants of both sides. It may well have planted the most fertile seeds of hatred toward Westerners by the Moslems, as well as the most irrational sense of contempt toward Moslems by the Westerners.

Nevertheless, the dominance of Islam well beyond the sixteenth century left a lasting mark on the geopolitics of the world (Patai, 1973: 10). What makes the relationship between Islam and the West increasingly untenable is the fact that the message of Islam continues to expand even farther, reducing the "religious share" of Christians and Jews. For instance, from one seventh to one sixth of all mankind are now Moslems. Furthermore, in the huge area extending roughly from the Atlantic coast of Africa to the borders of Western Pakistan and from Central Asia to the Sahara, Islam is the religion of some 95% of the population, as it is in Malaysia and Indonesia. On the peripheries of this solidly Moslem block, there are large contiguous areas in which more than half the population is Moslem. Focusing on the Middle East, it should be safe to state that the region is surrounded by nations that belong to the "House of Islam." The Middle Eastern countries are invariably Moslem and are surrounded by the non-Arab Moslem countries of Turkey, Iran, and Afghanistan (Patai, 1973: 10).

When Moslem history is compared to that of Christendom, it should be safe to note that Islam has not experienced a "religious reformation" in the Lutheran tradition; has largely missed the Scientific Revolution; and has, to a large extent, ignored the "Industrial Revolution." These conditions may have left little for Moslems to bond together except the social solidarity of religion. Subsequently, the Moslem's self-conception of Islam may be substantially different from that of a Christian or a Jew. Moslems unquestionably believe that their religion was directly conveyed to Mohammed by God, a belief that can further reinforce the theonomous and community-oriented nature of Islam. Consistent with this self-conception, Moslems also believe in a divine set of doctrines whose scope comprises all social and human spheres and to which all people in the world should submit. One may also realize that such a "master identity" can more easily flourish in traditional communities where the population is not particularly enlightened and where the capacity to reason is neither indigenously attainable nor is religiously encouraged. Subsequently, in most Islamic countries, no controversial views of Islam are permitted and the advocates of rationalist positions could often find themselves exposed to mental and physical persecution (Senghass, 1998: 37).

It should not be surprising, therefore, that Islam has been the foundation upon which Middle Eastern countries are built. Apart from Lebanon and Israel, which have considerable non-Moslem populations, the constitutions of all Middle Eastern countries state that Islam is the state religion and Shariah is either "the" law of the land or "the dominant legal source." On the other hand, while many Islamic constitutions advocate religious freedom, this is hardly the case outside a few moderate Islamic countries (e.g., Egypt, Lebanon, and Tunisia) where the population is more enlightened, the culture is more Westernized, and the government is more likely a signatory to the International Conventions on Human Rights.

Sources of Islamic Fundamentalism

Fundamentalism is a severe social phenomenon that has been fairly common at all times and in all cultures. It is based on the physical and intellectual assumptions that while most people are relatively healthy and rational, some are neither. The phenomenon can be defined as an "exaggerated concern for or against a belief, an idea, or a practice without a rational reason" (Souryal, 2003: 275). Fundamentalism gives rise to an emotional preoccupation with one's self, religious beliefs, sense of pride, or the group one belongs to. Such a pre-occupation is not only limited to religion, although religion may be one of its main ingredients. Fundamentalist thought may also be desirable and necessary for the evolution of societies. Historically, shades of fundamentalism were certainly associated with some of the great ideas, including philosophy (i.e., Socrates), astronomy (i.e., Galileo), mathematics (i.e., Newton), poverty (i.e., Saint Francis), or non-violence (i.e., Mahatma Gandhi and Martin Luther King, Jr.). As such, fundamentalism may be a neutral sentiment. For instance, fundamentalism in support of liberty promoted the American and the French revolutions; fundamentalism in support of Communism led to the Communist revolution; and fundamentalism in support of totalitarianism created the Nazi Party in Germany and the Holocaust. At a more mundane level, individuals and groups may hold fundamentalist views concerning socio-political issues such as abortion, same-sex marriage, women's rights, or even patriotism.

It is almost inconceivable that any government has not, at some time or another, dealt with issues of social or religious fundamentalism. This includes democratic and non-democratic governments, liberal and conservative governments, as well as rich and poor governments. In Moslem countries, where the practice of democracy is comparatively new and support for Islam is demonstratively potent, governments are at a loss as to how they can legitimately handle issues of social and religious fundamentalism. Ironically, the most devout Moslem fundamentalists seem to be the most devoutly opposed to their own governments. The example of Saudi Arabia is a case in point. In more moderate Moslem countries, fundamentalist groups seem bent on either winning political power through political means (when that is allowed) or overthrowing their governments and replacing them with Islamic Republics. At the heart of the fundamentalist movement in Islamic countries is the seemingly rational slogan "Islam is the Solution." Due to lack of enlightenment, deceptive indoctrination, corrupt government, or a combination of all of these, Islamic fundamentalist groups act as if they are oblivious to the strategic, economic, and geopolitical implications of having to run an efficient government. That may be the reason why some Islamic fundamentalist groups form their own "shadow governments" establishing their own armies, schools, clinics, lending institutions, and self-help institutions. The cases of the PLO, Hamas, and Islamic Jihad are typical examples (Abraham, 1999: 10-13).

While the main causes for the rise of Islamic fundamentalism will be addressed later in greater detail, the most manifest cause is unsurprisingly secularism. In a general sense, secularism means that religion and political authority (i.e., church and state) are qualitatively different and must be kept separate; that dogma and reason are not the same; and that freedom and enlightenment are the most valuable truths. The origins of secularism can be traced to the teachings of Christ as confirmed by the experience of the early Christians. These Christians were taught to distinguish between the realms of God and Caesar. Furthermore, the persecutions endured by the early church members made it clear that a separation between the two was possible (Lewis, 2002: 96). By contrast, secularism never had a chance, or even a need, in Islam. Lewis argues that the main reason for this assertion is because Mohammed was the only prophet who triumphed in his lifetime; Moses was lost with his people for 40 years in the desert and forbidden from entering the Promised Land, while Christ was humiliated and crucified. As a result, Mohammed had to personally build the state, dispense justice, levy taxes, and make war and peace. Therefore, in the early Moslem state there was not a need for a legislative power or an executive branch, since there was only one law for the believers (Allah's law) and one prophet (Mohammed) to rule (Lewis, 2002: 101).

To the Moslem fundamentalists, secularism, especially as exercised in the West, is considered infectiously unholy. Secular practices can only be seen as either violations of God's commandments or inappropriate behavior that offends God's sovereignty. Either way, the influence of secularism can pollute almost all aspects of life, including the cultural (i.e., art, music, and literature), the social (i.e., the mixing of the sexes, the role of women in society, the rearing of children), the sexual (i.e., chastity, homosexuality, prostitution), the political (i.e., the selection of rulers, the making of laws, administering justice), the economic (i.e., the distribution of wealth, the practice of usury, helping the poor and the needy), and, of course, the educational (i.e., teaching religion, family values, and piety). No wonder the vast majority of judges in Saudi Arabia and Iran are clerics and only one Moslem state has formally endorsed secularism as a social norm—The Republic of Turkey.

Moslem fundamentalists also view capitalism as a socially dangerous institution because it invariably serves material pleasures at the price of denigrating religious and social morals. Associated with capitalism, Moslem fundamentalists are equally critical of the doctrines of Human Rights, democratic rule, and Western-style justice systems. Moslem fundamentalists view Human Rights as ostensibly Euro-centric and as such, cannot apply to Moslems because such rights are neither pre-ordained by God, nor are they culturally acceptable. Moslem fundamentalists further argue that the body of Human Rights as it is conceived in New York and formulated in Geneva is corrupted by religious bias. They ask, for instance: if Human Rights are truly human (i.e., universal), why don't they include principles derived from other religions or cultures (e.g., Moslem, Buddhist, or Hindu)? And since they do not, why are people from these religions and cultures expected to comply with them (Abraham, 1999: 10-12)?

Throughout history, however, fundamentalism and terrorism have been intertwined. In general terms, the former concept usually leads to the latter, and the latter is usually the violent expression of the former. Together, they provide calculated responses to geopolitical dynamics which over time can independently act as force multipliers. In a sense akin to the relationship between prejudice and discrimination in social psychology, fundamentalism can be seen as a set of "severe attitudes" based normally on ignorance and stereotyping, while terrorism is the commission of violent acts normally designed to force political change (Souryal, 2003: 241). This analogy, however, should not mean that all fundamentalists are terrorists, nor all terrorists are fundamentalists. In the social experience, there have been fundamentalists who never committed terroristic acts, and terrorists who reacted to violent situations without prior fundamentalism. Examples may include committing terrorist acts simply to avoid arrest by police or because of an emotional predicament.

As mentioned earlier, terrorism cannot be assigned to any given religion. In recent history, terrorism has been committed by Christian groups (e.g., IRA in Ireland, Basque ETA in Spain, Baader-Meinhof in Germany, Direct Action in France); Islamic groups (e.g., Hamas, Islamic Jihad, Black September, Al-Aqsa Brigade) Jewish groups (e.g., Stern, Irgon Zvai Leumi, and possibly Gush Emunim); and Shintoist groups (e.g., the Red Army Brigade in Japan). In The Clash of Civilizations,

Huntington (1996) identifies the root of terrorism as a product of a conflict between civilizations rather than countries. Such conflicts can occur at either the macro level or the micro level. Huntington identifies three kinds of conflict: (1) religious conflicts, (2) nationalistic conflicts, and (3) terroristic conflicts. Huntington explains that religious wars were much more common in Medieval Europe between the time of Martin Luther's Reformation (1517) and the end of the Thirty Year's War (1618-1648). These wars were fought to either support a religion or to replace it with another. The era of religious wars, Huntington states, was later followed by the era of nationalistic wars in which European rulers were mainly motivated by dynastic rights and expansionist goals. The wars of Napoleon and Hitler are typical examples. Huntington adds that after World War II, world conflicts were limited to rivalries between the two superpowers—the United States and the Soviet Union. Neither of them was interested in waging a global war against the other, basically due to the strategic doctrine of mutual deterrence and the fear of starting an apocalyptic nuclear war.

Huntington argues that while the United States now stands as the world's only superpower, and while the theory of conventional wars may have become obsolete, the new conflicts among civilizations will continue, albeit on a small scale, with smaller but equally lethal weapons. These conflicts will entail terroristic attacks in volatile regions where cultural confrontations are severe and where the difference in military might can be technologically equalized. The new arsenal of weapons will most likely include those that can inflict the most damage with the least probability of being detected. In addition to the possibility of using chemical and biological weapons, most terroristic attacks will be committed by cheap weapons and innovative techniques such as suicide bombers and homemade explosive devices. By utilizing such weapons and techniques, countries or groups that do not possess sophisticated fighter planes, missiles, tanks, or armored personnel carriers will, at least to a reasonable measure, have a limited chance of winning against a more technologically advanced country.

The bombings of the Marine's barracks in Beirut in 1983 and of the United States embassies in Nairobi and Dar-Al-Salam in 1998 are cases in point. In the kind of terrorism currently practiced by Moslem groups, and given the unique self-conception of Islam as mentioned earlier, Huntington's classification of wars (i.e., religious, nationalistic, and terroristic) may not be inaccurate. In today's clash of civilizations, and especially after the events of September 11th, Huntington's theory of terroristic conflicts may have been validated. By attacking large numbers of innocent citizens with overwhelming cruelty, terrorist groups may be able to cause mass casualties; by attacking strategic targets such as dams and electricity grids, terrorist groups may be able to cause mass disruption; and by using small size explosives or tactical nuclear devices, they may be able to cause mass destruction. The purpose of all these techniques is to intimidate governments and/or societies and to achieve grand political, religious, or ideological objectives.

At this point, it may be appropriate to illuminate the difficulties in defining the concept of terrorism. There are several reasons for these difficulties. First, the term itself has a pejorative connotation. A person is socially and politically degraded when he or she is labeled as a terrorist. Second, governments tend to stretch state powers and limit civil rights when the fear of terrorism is obvious. It is not infrequent that governments, under the ruse of combating terrorism, act terroristically themselves. Third, innocent people can be held hostage in large numbers as a prelude to expected terror attacks. Business enterprises subsequently diminish, trade dwindles, the economy suffers, and the people experience anxiety. And fourth, the nature of terrorism has changed over time. When the word terrorism was first coined, it was basically used to mean mob activities. It was later used to denote acts of internal subversion, civil disobedience, revolutionary activities, or paramilitary violence (White, 1998; Ezeldin, 1985). Yet, in their zeal to propagate religious faith, religious fundamentalists used the same term to justify what they considered legitimate acts of resistance. Adding to the complexity of reaching an accurate definition is the confusing distinction between the words terror and terrorism. While the former can be as benign as urging legitimate military forces to strike terror in the hearts of the enemy, the latter can be as wicked as inflicting systemic and indiscriminate terror on innocent and unsuspecting citizens (White, 1998: 5).

In Arabic, which is the common language throughout the Middle East, the word terrorism is even more ambivalent. It is derived from the root "rahbah" (immense fear), and the act of terrorism is known as "irhab" (causing immense fear). The Arabic meaning of rahbah, however, is not necessarily as frightening as its English counterpart since the Arabic word could also mean "awe," "respect," or even "piety." For instance, the Quran used the word rahbah to mean piety when it stated "Children of Israel! Call to mind the favor which I bestowed upon you. Fulfill your covenant with me as I fulfill my Covenant with you. And fear none but me" (Quran, Surat Al-Baqara: 40). Aside from these religious interpretations, the common usage of the Arabic word irhab has consistently meant "causing terror by acts of violence such as murder, using explosives, or sabotage" (Ezeldin, 1985:17).

To present a legal definition of terrorism, the following are gleaned from authoritative sources: (1) "premeditated, politically motivated violence perpetrated against noncombatant targets by sub-national groups or clandestine agents, usually intended to influence an audience (State Department: Title 22 of the United States Code Section 2656f); (2) "the unlawful use of force or violence against persons or property to intimidate or coerce a government, the civilian population, or any segment thereof in furtherance of political or social objectives" (FBI); and (3) "the unlawful use or threat of violence against persons or property to further political or social objectives. It is usually intended to intimidate or coerce a government, individuals or groups, or to modify their behavior or politics" (Vice President's Task Force on Terrorism). Furthermore, White (1998: 8) adds: "the use or threatened use of force designed to bring about a political change" and "the illegitimate use of force to achieve a political objective by targeting innocent people."

To more thoroughly investigate the nature of terrorism as committed by Islamic groups, one should first ask: if all Moslems are required to obey the same Quranic commandments, what then distinguishes the benevolent Moslems who are at peace with themselves and the world from the fundamentalist Moslems who are bent on destroying themselves and the world? The answer to this question is both complex and intriguing. Assuming that both groups are acting in good faith, and not unlike in Christianity or Judaism, one must first determine how accurately the commandments are being interpreted. Benevolent Moslems believe that Islam can encompass the entire world by peaceful and evolutionary means, because that is the way it was designed by God. By contrast, most of the fundamentalist groups—in one version or another—interpret God's commandments to mean that Islam is designed to conquer the world by revolutionary means in order to further advance the cause of Islam. This controversy leads us back to the original meaning of the word Islam. There are two scenarios that can explain that meaning: (1) while benevolent Moslems try to peacefully fit Islam into the existing world, fundamentalist Moslems try to force the existing world into Islam; and (2) while benevolent Moslems see peace and submission as a natural process of Islamic worship, fundamentalist Moslems see peace and submission as the "means" to eventually unify the world under the banner of Islam.

Finally, to investigate the geopolitical causes that might have turned benevolent Moslems into fundamentalist Moslems, I will discuss four of the most significant causes. While no one of them is, in and of itself, the prime factor, each cause is certainly a catalyst. When two or more of these causes coincide, the friction they produce can be a force multiplier. Force multipliers reinforce terroristic enterprises by making them more lethal, last longer, and harm more victims. By making terroristic acts gorier and/or more frequent, terrorists believe they can either sap the political resolve of their adversaries or die trying. In either case, they consider themselves deserving of eternal life.

The main causes of fundamentalism/terrorism by Moslem individuals and groups covered in the following chapters are:

- The Crusades: the Ghost behind All Ghosts.
- The Humiliation Due to Military Defeats by Israel.
- The Islamic Revolution: Khomeini's New Export.
- The Fury of Islam: Bin Laden and Beyond.

Sources

Abraham, A. J. (1999). *Khomeini, Islamic Fundamentalism and the Warriors of God: An Islamic Reader*. Bristol: Wyndam Hall Press.

Hitti, P. K. (1967). *History of the Arabs: From the Earliest Times to the Present* (9th Ed.). New York: St. Martin's Press.

Huntington, S. (1996). *The Clash of Civilizations and the Remaking of World Order.* New York.

Lewis, B. (2002). *What Went Wrong? Western Impact and Middle Eastern Response.* New York: Oxford.

Patai, R. (1973). *The Arab Mind.* New York: Charles Scribner's Sons.

Senghass, D. (1998). *The Clash within Civilizations: Coming to Terms with Cultural Conflicts*. New York: Routledge.

Souryal, S. (2003). *Ethics in Criminal Justice: In Search of the Truth*. Cincinnati, Ohio. Andersons.

White, J. R. (1998). *Terrorism: An Introduction* (2nd Edition). Belmont: West/Wadsworth Publishing Company.

11

The Crusades: The Ghost Behind All Ghosts

To Moslems of all ages, the memory of the Crusades is an archetype: a non-erasable sordid memory. The memory is passed down from one generation to another. It still has a distinctively bitter taste even though the conflict ended almost a thousand years ago. To Moslems, the memory symbolizes utter frustration at how savagely, contemptuously, and hypocritically Moslems were treated by the forces of Christendom, a religion they considered an older sister religion. In a historical sense, the role of Crusaders has been perceived as substantially more horrible than that of the Mongols, or the Tartars, who in 1253 sacked Baghdad and threatened to destroy the entire world of Islam. What makes the memory of the Crusades so painful is that the Christians were accepted by Moslems as people of the Book, while the Mongols were not. Viewed from the Moslem fundamentalist perspective, the Crusades were only the medieval chapter in the long saga of humiliation inflicted upon the Moslems by the Westerners.

The Crusades began in 1096 in response to several historical events. First, the emergence of the Teutonic tribes in Europe as a migratory military force. These tribes changed the balance of power in Europe by vanquishing some of the old dynasties in and around Germany and establishing themselves as a mercenary force in search of battle. Second, the unjustified destruction of the Church of the Holy Sepulcher in Jerusalem by Caliph Al-Hakim in 1009. The church had been the object of Christian pilgrimage for many centuries. Third, the reported hardships to which Christian pilgrims were subjected on their way to Jerusalem (Hitti, 1967: 634-635). Fourth, the repeated appeals made to Pope Urban II by Emperor Alexius Comnenus in 1095 regarding the Emperor's possessions in Asia that had been overrun by the Moslem Seljuks. Fifth, the general perception that the feared Moslem warriors had been weakened. In 1050, Castile and Aragon took back Andalusia from the Moslems in Spain, and in 1060 the Normans took back Sicily (Armajani, 1970:126). Hitti also suggests that Pope Urban II might have had a hidden agenda of his own. He probably thought that calling for a Crusadc against the Moslems would help reunite the Greek Church and the Roman Church under his tutelage. In 1095, the Pope finally called upon the Christian soldiers to "enter upon the road to Jerusalem and wrest it from the 'wicked' race that occupied it." According to Hitti, the rallying cry "Deus vult" (God willing) ran throughout Europe and captured the enthusiasm of all able-bodied Christians (Hitti, 1967: 636). By the spring of 1097, about 150,000 men, mostly Norman and Franks, assembled at Constantinople and began their march toward Jerusalem under the banner of the Cross.

It should be noted that while most of the Crusaders were motivated by religious fervor, many of them were not. Hitti reports that many of the European leaders, including Prince Bohemod, were motivated only by the prospect of acquiring new principalities and amassing wealth. Also, while most Crusaders were seen as "romantic, restless, and adventurous," many were indeed criminals who joined in the march as a means of escaping imprisonment or making penance. Many masses were also thought to have followed the Cross rather than endure the depressed economic and social conditions that existed in Europe at the time (Hitti, 1967: 636). It should also be noted that while Western historians list the Crusades by numbers (between seven and nine), Arab historians consider them a continuing stream of barbarous raids without any demarcation between one raid and the next (Hitti, 1967: 636).

In 1097 the Crusaders left Constantinople toward Jerusalem under the leadership of Baldwin the Count of Boulogne. Their route was traditionally simple, cutting across Asia Minor into the Moslem province ruled by Amir Arslan. To reach Jerusalem, however, Baldwin had to first cross the Taurus Mountains, turn sharply southward, attack the Christian Armenians in the eastern region, and capture their capital Al-Roha. Baldwin then had to turn the opposite direction and capture Tarsus, the birthplace of the Apostle Paul (Hitti, 1967: 637). On their way farther southward, the Crusaders captured al-Ramleh, the first Palestinian town. That was followed by battles fought in Maara, Antioch, and Jerusalem, with the last being the most significant and savage.

On June 7, 1099, 40,000 Crusaders stormed the gates of Jerusalem. Hitti (1967) reports that hoping "the walls would fall as those of Jericho had done before," the attackers first marched barefoot around the city, blowing their horns. After a month of siege, the besiegers stormed the city and Godfrey declared himself the King of Jerusalem. The other territories along the northeast border of Jerusalem were also occupied and organized into small Christian kingdoms. Maalouf (1984) reports that in the onslaught of Jerusalem, the Christian forces perpetrated savage and indiscriminate massacres involving people of all ages and both sexes. Clad with "impenetrable armor, they spilled through the city streets, sword in hand, slaughtering men, women, and children, plundering houses and sacking mosques." Maalouf (1984: xiv) offers more repugnant details:

> *"Two days later, when the killing stopped, not a single Moslem was left alive within the city walls. Some had taken advantage of the chaos to slip away escaping through gates battered down by the attackers. Thousands of others lay in pools of blood on the doorsteps of their homes or alongside the mosques. The last survivors were forced to perform the worst tasks: to heave the bodies of their own relatives, to dump them in vacant, unmarked lots and then to set them alight, before being themselves massacred or sold into slavery.*
>
> *"The fate of the Jews of Jerusalem was no less atrocious. During the first hours of battle, some participated in the defense of their quarter, situated on the northern edge of the city. But when that part of the city walls overhanging their homes collapsed and the blonde knights began to pour through the streets, the Jews panicked. Re-enacting the immemorial rite, the entire community gathered in the main synagogue to pray. The Franj barricaded all the exits and stacked all the bundles of wood they could find in a ring around the building. The temple was then put to the torch. Those who managed to escape were massacred in the neighboring alleyways. The rest were burned alive."*

The tide against the Crusaders later changed with the emergence of a new Moslem Sultan, Salah-al-Din, born in 1138 in Takrit (Saddam Hussein's home town). The new Sultan, who was known to have "never refused a request from a man of honor," later welcomed and befriended St. Francis of Assisi (Maalouf, 1984: 197). Salah-al-Din's burning ambition, however, was recapturing Jerusalem and restoring Moslem sovereignty to the Middle East region. His major nemeses were Frederick Barbarossa of Germany, King Richard the Lion-hearted of England, and King Philip Augustus of France. Given the relative complacency of the Crusaders at the time, Salah-al-Din began raiding their small kingdoms and harassing their forces. He typically fought on Fridays, the favorite day for the Moslems because it was their Sabbath. He later won battles in Masyad, Tiberus, and Allepo. In 1187, he fought and won the famous battle of Hittin where he captured Guy de Lusignan, then the current King of Jerusalem, and his assistant Reginald of Chatillon. The Sultan gave them a friendly reception and set them free upon receiving their oath to go back to Europe and not to fight the Moslems again (Hitti, 1967: 647). Salah-al-Din, nevertheless, had to fight them again in the battle of Akka (now Aker), and for reneging on their oath, he made them pay with their lives.

The fall of Akka sealed the fate of Jerusalem and the Christian cause. When Jerusalem finally fell to the Moslems in 1192, Salah-al-Din, in contrast to the Crusaders' savagery, only stipulated a fair ransom since he considered any act of revenge inappropriate. Within the ransom terms, however, he set free all women and children, all those who could not afford to pay, and guaranteed free passage to all Christians who would wish to make the pilgrimage to Jerusalem (Maalouf, 1984: 198). Subsequently, the Frankish cross attached to the Dome of the Rock Mosque was removed; the mosque, which had been turned into a church, became once again a Moslem place of worship after its walls had been sprinkled with rose water (Maalouf, 1984: 199).

An interesting story that demonstrated the magnanimity of Sultan Salah-al-Din was said to occur in November 1183. Salah-al-Din had set up catapults around the citadel of Karak and was bombarding it with huge chunks of rock when the defenders sent word that a princely wedding was being celebrated inside. Although the bride was non-other than the step-daughter of Salah-al-Din's main nemesis, the infamous Prince Reynald, the sultan asked the besieged in which pavilion the newlyweds would reside and ordered his men to spare that sector (Maalouf, 1984: 187).

The Crusades, which spanned almost 200 years, were the first phase in the clash of civilizations between the European Christians and the Moslem Arabs. In a historical sense, they were seen as a replay of the Trojan and Persian wars of antiquity and, in a modern sense, in the same way the Vietnamese people saw the Americans in the 1960s. In the Moslem perception, however, the Crusades were even more humiliating than any other world conflict because they symbolized the triumph of one religion over another. Subsequently, the Moslems believe the Crusades were precursors to latent acts of aggression against them, specifically colonialism and Zionism. It should come as no surprise, therefore, that whenever Osama bin Laden speaks to his followers he invokes the memory of the Crusades and when Saddam Hussein spoke to his people, he invoked the dangers of Zionism.

While the Moslem resentment of the Crusades can be justified, at least to a point, many modern Arab thinkers question the motive behind this resentment and put the blame squarely on the stagnation of the Moslem mind. Edward Atiyah, for example, argues that the deteriorating state of the Moslems today has been self-inflicted. He adds that "the mind of Islam seemed to stand still" and that the Moslem intellect had for centuries been bound with fetters that it is only now beginning to shake off (Patai, 1973: 294-250). Atiyah further states that when Napoleon set foot on Egyptian soil, the Arabs "were still living in the Middle Ages...socially and intellectually, their life had been ossified...they had gradually lost their ability to think their way into fresh fields of endeavor and discovery" (Patai, 1973: 250). Najla Izzeddin also comments on the current state of thinking in Moslem societies by stating "the keen intellectual curiosity and adventurous spirit which characterized the preceding period, the passionate and untiring search for knowledge, and the joy of adventure were all smothered under a hard crust of dogma and fundamentalism, [as a result] free thought was banished [and] traditionalism reigned in its place" (Patai, 1973: 250). Fayez Sayegh states that traditional Islam "has shrunk into hollowed catchwords, and religious fellowships have denigrated into fossilized groupings generating blind fanaticism" (Patai, 1973: 250). The Tunisian Abdallah al-Qasimi states that ignorance based on religious doctrine has tied the Moslem mind with knots upon knots causing "cultural immobility" which cannot be overcome except to the extent to which foreign (i.e., Western) influence and training are accepted and encouraged (Patai, 1973: 252). In many respects, these comments are sad, yet valid. In the final analysis, it may be fair to state that while Islam as a religion can enrich the soul, the Moslem tradition of embracing the past and dimming the lights of liberty and enlightenment may have caused their detachment from the cultural progress around them. If that is the case, one may be able, in a retrospective sense, to explain the 19th century colonization of Moslem countries in terms of the failure of these countries to defend their cultural integrities.

Sources

Armajani, Y. (1970). *Middle East Past and Present*. Englewood Cliffs, NJ: Prentice-Hall.

Hitti, P. K. (1967). *History of the Arabs: From the Earliest Times to the Present* (9th Ed.). New York: St. Martin's Press.

Maalouf, A. (1984). *The Crusades Through Arab Eyes*. New York: Schocken Books.

Patai, R. (1973). *The Arab Mind*. New York: Charles Scribner's Sons.

12

The Humiliation Due to Military Defeats by Israel

When the Moslem populations recall their national tragedies, they cite three in particular: the Crusades (1096-1291), the Mongol invasion (1258), and the wars with Israel. They consider the first and the third religious-based calamities, while the second as a foolish expansionist war. And since Islam is the master identity of Moslems and their predominant "reason for living," the first and third tragedies count very heavily on their minds, while the second is willfully ignored.

The Moslems specifically refer to wars with Israel as Nakbas. The word Nakba is Arabic, meaning "a major setback." By definition, Nakbas are temporary defeats—ones that are caused by extraordinary circumstances beyond one's capacity to resist. By the same token, Nakbas must be later avenged if society is to restore its normalcy. In the Moslem mind, especially the Arab mind, Nakbas are predestined events designed by God to test the community's belief in God and its submission to His commandments. In this narrow sense, most Moslems, Christians, and Jews might agree. Yet, to reverse a Nakba, society must be cleansed by fire to restore its honor.

The Jewish connection to Palestine first began with the Jewish people's Exodus from Egypt during the rule of Pharaoh Merneptah (not Rameses II as is commonly thought) and their subsequent wandering for forty years in Sinai (Bucallie, 1979: 231). Their attachment to Jerusalem has since been immemorial. In Jerusalem, they dwelled under the rule of King David and built their first temple under King Solomon. When they were later forced into slavery in Babylon (587 B.C.) they always dreamt of returning to Jerusalem. After their return (some chose to stay behind and eventually became modern-day Iraqis) they rebuilt the Temple which was later destroyed by the Romans in A.D. 70 (Shipler, 1986: 10).

Palestine was later invaded by the Moslems in 634 A.D. when Amr ibn-al-As marched through it on his way to capture Damascus. Amr triumphed over Serguis, the weak Patrician of Palestine whose headquarters were in Qaysariyah (Hitti, 1967: 148). Forced to comply with Moslem rule, the Jews began several aliyas (migrations) to Europe in search of a better life. They settled mainly in Spain, Russia, Poland, Germany, the Netherlands, and Britain. While they were not equally welcomed in these countries, many of them assimilated into European cultures, religions, and traditions. With the exception of Spain, perhaps, they stayed in these countries until the creation of the State of Israel in 1948. In 1492, the Jews were expelled from Spain and took refuge in North Africa where they prospered, assimilating into the Moslem culture. Nevertheless the Jewish yearning to return to Jerusalem never waned. The North African Jews were among the first groups that returned to Israel after 1948 and constituted what is now known as Sephardi Jews.

After the Moslems took Palestine, they renamed Jerusalem "Al-Quds" (the Sacred City) since the Prophet Abraham—who the Moslems claim as one of their prophets—was buried in the city at the central site where Al-Aqsa Mosque was later built. Ironically, the name of the Mosque has now been adopted by a radical Moslem terrorist brigade. The Arab rule in Palestine lasted for over 1300 years throughout the Ummayad, Abbasid, and the Ottoman dynasties. At the end of WWI, the Allies defeated the Ottoman Empire and occupied all of its previous possessions. Britain occupied Palestine, and France occupied Syria, Lebanon, and most of North Africa. Scattered all over Europe, the Jews, especially those who were influenced by Theodore Hertzl's Zionist movement, continued to press the Allies for a national homeland. European leaders, especially the British Prime Minister Lloyd George, were amenable to oblige, especially because Jewish troops fought gallantly on the side of the Allies in WWI. Earlier in 1902, the British government had proposed Jewish settlement in British East Africa, a proposition that was outright rejected in 1905 by the Seventh Zionist Congress (Wasserstein, 2003: 179-183).

In the meantime, the Arabs in Palestine were also demanding their independence. To appease them, and since they had also fought on the

British side under the legendary Lawrence of Arabia, Britain promised to keep Palestine as an Arab state. This disappointed the Jewish leaders who insisted on Palestine as their lawful ancestral homeland. As both sides kept pressing their demands, the British government responded by issuing the Balfour Declaration (1917) in support of establishing a Jewish state in Palestine. Subsequently, in 1920 anti-Zionist riots broke out in Jerusalem and Haifa. To further press their own demands, the Arabs in 1922 elected Hajji Amin Al-Hussaini (a radical Moslem scholar) as Grand Mufti of Jerusalem and President of the Supreme Moslem Council. This prompted more civil unrest, causing the League of Nations to authorize Britain to rule Palestine under a special mandate issued in 1922 (Wasserstein, 2003: 182-185).

As time progressed, violence and diplomacy marked the continuing Arab-Jewish conflict, with Britain acting as an arbitrator and peace-maker. In 1937, a Royal Commission report proposed the partition of Palestine and, in the meantime, restricting Jewish immigration to 75,000 over five years. In 1946, arguably in response to the Jewish perception of British partiality in favor of the Arabs, a number of Zionist extremists blew up the King David Hotel in Jerusalem where the headquarters of the British forces was located. Ninety British officers were killed in the attack. As a consequence, perhaps, Britain announced in 1947 its intention to hand back its mandate in Palestine to the United Nations (Wasserstein, 2003: 184).

In November 1947, the United Nations voted to partition Palestine into an Arab state and a Jewish state. The Jews accepted the partition but the Arabs rejected it. On May 14th, 1948, the Jewish leaders declared the State of Israel, receiving an almost immediate recognition from both the United States and the Soviet Union. As a result, a combined Arab force from Egypt, Syria, Jordan, and Iraq invaded Palestine, starting the first Arab-Israeli war. Wasserstein chronicles that by the end of the war Israel was able to: (1) win decisive victories over the invading Arab States; (2) cause approximately 700,000 Palestinians to be displaced from their homeland; (3) allow the Principality of Transjordan to annex the entire West Bank territory, recognizing Prince Hussain as the King of Jordan; and (4) begin a large-scale Jewish immigration from Europe and Middle East countries to resettle in Israel under the Israeli "Right of Return" law (Wasserstein, 2003: 184).

In the perception of most Moslems, in particular Moslem Arabs, not only were the Palestinians cheated out of their land and their sovereign right to live freely, the entire Moslem Ummah was betrayed and humiliated. Furthermore, the Moslems could not escape watching as Christian countries (i.e., Britain, France, the United States, and, to a degree, the Soviet Union, which at the time wanted to establish Israel as a communist nation) actively supporting the Jewish state and indirectly failing to protect the Arabs and their lands. In the Moslem mind, these images continue to trigger bitter memories of the Crusaders.

The Moslem arguments at the time will be summarized here regardless of their rationality or irrationality:

- The British government gave what it didn't own to those who didn't deserve, without legal or moral justification. Here again one might see the religious clash between the Jewish belief "We are God's chosen people" and the Moslem's refrain "We are the descendants of Abraham too."
- While the Israelis allowed the "Right of Return" to Jews living anywhere in the world (indeed this right extended to the yet unborn Jews), the Arabs were denied the same right and were consequently forced to disperse and live in other Arab lands.
- Regardless of how the Arab-Israeli conflict is labeled, it is ostensibly seen as another Crusade connived by an unholy alliance among the nations of European Christendom. While the objectives were the same, the strategies were reversed. While the original Crusaders first came charging and then claimed their right to the land, the Jewish warriors first came legally, then they militarily forced their right to the land.
- The defeat of the Arab armies in 1948 was not a function of Israeli military superiority, but the failure of the Arab leaders themselves. For instance, King Abdullah of Jordan was seen as a traitor bought by the Israelis; King Farouk of Egypt as a corrupt weapons dealer; and King Faisal of Iraq as a British "coolie" who received his instructions from London.
- While the state of Israel claims to be the model of democracy in the Middle East and a supporter of Human Rights, it wantonly arrests Palestinians, jails them without charges,

> and razes their homes. Also, while both Israelis and Palestinians have engaged in acts of terrorism in the past, the Palestinians argue they do so only as a means of resisting Israeli occupation.

Closely associated with the political dimension of the Arab-Israeli conflict, Moslems across the region, especially Moslem Arabs, had another equally compelling reason to be ashamed—the poor performance of their armies against Israeli forces during the conflicts that followed 1948. Lewis (2002: 154) articulates the extent of this shame:

> *"With rare exceptions, where hostile stereotypes of the Jew existed in the Islamic tradition, they tended to be contemptuous and dismissive rather than suspicious and obsessive. This made the events of 1948—the failure of five Arab states and armies to prevent half a million Jews from establishing a state in the debris of the British Mandate for Palestine—all the more of a shock. It was bad enough to be defeated by the great imperial powers of the West, yet to suffer the same fate at the hands of a gang of Jews was an intolerable humiliation."*

Collectively, there were four Arab-Israeli wars that occurred about ten years apart. They were the 1948 War, better known in Israel as the War of Independence; the 1956 War, better known as the Suez War; the 1967 War, better known as the Six Day War; and the 1973 War, better known as the Yom Kippur War. While the first three wars ended in humiliating Arab defeats, the last war was not considered a victory for the Israelis. During these wars, the Israeli Air force annihilated the combined Arab air forces on the ground twice; defeated Egypt three times, Syria three times, and Jordan twice. While other Arab armies (i.e., Iraq and Saudi Arabia) offered token forces, these forces did not participate in the war efforts and had no impact whatsoever on the outcome of the wars.

Excerpts from the 1967 War battlefield chronicles demonstrate the failure of the Arab military machine and the almost total absence of military preparedness at the time. These excerpts include (Oren, 2003):

> *"An estimated 20 percent of Egypt's tanks, a quarter of its artillery pieces and a third of its planes were unfit for action when the war began. Less than half of its troops reached their*

designated positions. Of these many were now being ordered to undertake a mission they had never studied, into territory totally unfamiliar to them. There were no provisions for communication, no directives for the artillery or for the administration of the captured areas, no multi-staged plan" (Field Marshal Fawzi, Commander General of the Egyptian forces in Sinai when the 1967 war began).

"Amer (the Supreme Commander of the Egyptian forces and Nasser's closest confidant) was too fixed in his plans for the coming fight and absorbed in the effort to expand his power yet further. Throughout the first days in June, he assiduously altered the army's structure in Sinai, dividing the peninsula into an Eastern and Western Command, a Canal Command, a Forward and a Field Command. Orders from Supreme Headquarters had to pass through the hands of no less than six senior officers before reaching the field. These positions were filled with Amer's cronies, military bureaucrats with little if any combat experience and responsible directly to him. Observing these changes, the Israelis were thrilled... 'He created five new layers of command and with people who'd never fought.' 'We'd be halfway to Suez before they'd even get an order approved" (Israeli General Gavish).

"General Murtagi (the Egyptian Commander of all infantry forces) meanwhile made a note to meet with Amer the next morning to discuss the still-critical shortages of supplies and officers. The General had just issued his own orders to Egypt's fighters (the infantry) exhorting them to 're-conquer the stolen land with...the strength of your arms and your united faith' and reminding them that 'the eyes of the whole world are on you in your glorious war against Israeli aggression.' [Yet] Murtagi himself was on vacation in Ismailiya that evening, while Amer (the Supreme Commander of the Egyptian armed forces) attended an all-night party in Cairo...Nasser's where-abouts were unknown...Sidqi Mahmuud (Commander of the Egyptian Air Force) was at his daughter's wedding...the commander of the Sinai front wasn't in place and the army's commander wasn't

in place neither were their subordinates. It was the first war of its kind where all the commanders were far from their commands" (Maj.General Abd-al-Hamid al-Dudhridi, Chief of the Egyptian Air Force in Sinai).

"The military's fault lines were not merely financial. Senior positions were meted out on the basis of family or political ties, not merit, while subalterns were purposefully chosen for their incompetence, so as not to threaten their commanders. There was little loyalty among officers and even less between them and the common soldier. 'I always felt sorry for the abandoned Egyptians in Sinai when large numbers of their officers took off for long weekends in Cairo" (Gen. Rikhyr, UNEF).

"On both sides of the road were dug-in tanks, anti-tank guns, mortar pits and machine-gun nests all linked by trenches and surrounded with mines. The longest distance between any two positions was 50 meters. [Yet] the Egyptians were so surprised [by the Israeli column] that they did not shoot. The Israeli commander thought the Egyptians had fled and so told his men to hold their fire. Only when the column reached the midway point was it revealed that the Egyptians had not fled" (IDF internal Report).

"Watching that sight [of the retreating Egyptian army], Col. Arvraham Adan, second in command and a veteran of the two previous campaigns in Sinai, was stupefied. 'You ride past burnt-out vehicles and suddenly you see this immense army, too numerous to count, spread out of a vast area as far as your eyes can see...it was not a pleasant feeling, seeing that gigantic enemy and realizing that you're only a single battalion of tanks." (Col. Arraham, an IDF tank commander).

And,

"We sacrifice lives unnecessarily, achieving nothing other than to attract more massive retaliatory humiliation. [But] we are against people who think. [The Jews] survived 2,000 years of pogroms and keep coming back by thinking...We cannot fight

them through brawn alone. We must use our brains also...there is a feeling of hopelessness among the Moslem countries and their people. They feel they can do nothing right. Our own reaction is to become more and more angry (Mahathir Mohammed, Prime Minister of Malaysia, Http//www. nytimes. com, 11-9-2003).

Without a doubt, the most humiliating (and insulting) episode in the Arab- Israeli wars was the 1967 Six Day War. There are four reasons for this assertion: (1) The Israeli victory was so stunning that the State of Israel expanded its territory by an estimated 5 fold; (2) the Israeli forces proved to be so superior that they were able to defeat the forces of three Arab countries simultaneously; (3) the Israeli forces succeeded in capturing East Jerusalem (therefore uniting the Holy city under Jewish control for the first time in about 2000 years), conquered the entire West Bank, and captured the entire Sinai peninsula from the Egyptians and the Golan Heights from the Syrians; (4) the Israeli forces were able to achieve all of their objectives in only six days.

In the Arab mind, the Israeli military victories reflected a two-fold image: (1) the inherent superiority of the Israeli forces who demonstrated advanced military, moral, and spiritual worth under some of the hardest conditions; and (2) the inherently weak performance of the Arab soldiers, who despite their huge numerical superiority, surrendered in mass and were pitifully abandoned in the desert by their inept officers. These two images, which were constantly flashed on the TV screens over the years, brought a sense of deep spiritual shaming to Moslem populations. Although the 1967 Arab Israeli war was avenged—at least to a small measure—by Sadat's 1973 Yom Kippur War, the Arab shame has been turned against the Arab regimes themselves. This, in itself, may have planted the seeds of discontent among the "young Moslems" who dedicated themselves to the cause of Allah in pursuit of redemption under the slogan of *Allahu Akbar* (God is Great). Hence, one can see the beginning of the turn to violence precisely as a means of regaining religious and national pride.

Palestinian Humiliation and Suicide Bombings

The humiliations suffered by Moslems consist of more than just military nakbas. More significant than the military humiliations are the humiliations aimed at the very spirit of the people. The situation in Palestine is a perfect example of this. Because every Moslem is a part of the same ummah, the national and spiritual humiliations of the Palestinians are felt by Moslems everywhere. It is from this shared spiritual humiliation that the seeds of terrorism are sown.

Jessica Stern (2003: 36), a U.S. expert on terrorism, describes the state of humiliation shared by the Palestinians living in the Gaza Strip. It is a space of only 147 square miles in area, roughly twice the size of Washington D.C. This land is shared by 1.2 million Palestinians, three-quarters of which are refugees. Half of the refugees are living in camps. To further complicate matters, 42 percent of the land is retained by Israel under the Oslo accords, most of which is reserved for 6,000 settlers. As Stern notes, most of the land that is actually owned by the Palestinians is littered with garbage and junked cars.

The city of Gaza is even worse. Not only are the sidewalks uneven and strewn with garbage, but attendant with this is the various smells of sewage, sweat, spices, and rotting meat that all mingle together. These conditions give the city the look and feel of other third-world cities throughout the world. There is one critical distinction, one key element that is missing. The lively spirit of consumerism and entrepreneurship that is found in every other third-world city is noticeably absent. Instead, there are the feelings of depression, utter humiliation, and despair that permeate the atmosphere and infect all those who breathe the air (Stern, 2003: 36-37).

Stern (2003: 37-38) points out that since the occupation began, the Israeli Civil Administration has become involved in every aspect of the economic lives of the Palestinians. Respected Israeli reporters Ze'ev Schiff and Ehud Ya'ari explain:

"Each requirement for a permit, grant, or dispensation entailed an exhausting wrestle with a crabbed bureaucracy of mostly indifferent but sometimes hostile clerks and officials—a veritable juggernaut of four hundred Jewish mandarins managing thousands of Arab minions bereft of all authority."

One Palestinian student told Stern of her first experience with this humiliation, at the age of nine. She was traveling with her parents and two siblings when they came to a border crossing. A trip that should have only taken 3 hours lasted more than twenty. All this while she experienced the long lines, toilets filled beyond capacity with excrement, strip searches, arbitrary interrogations, and imprisonment. All of this inestimable waiting was for a simple stamp to be placed by the unwelcoming and belligerent occupiers in their travelling documents—a stamp that some were denied even after all of this waiting.

Stern emphasizes that it is this spiritual humiliation, these conditions of poverty and hopelessness, which increases support for Hamas; a fact not lost on the leaders of this organization (Stern, 2003: 38). "Hardship always brings people back to God" points out one Hamas leader. It makes death seem appealing, especially when they believe that paradise awaits the person after death. "Every good Muslim understands that it's better to die fighting than to live without hope" says an elderly resident of Jenin while explaining the unending supply of volunteers for martyrdom. Stern points out that with these ideas in mind, it is important to note that the economic situation in Gaza has worsened significantly since the Second Intifada began in late September 2000. Unemployment has risen by 11 percent to 40 percent overall. A third of the Palestinian population is estimated by the U.N. to live on less than $2.10 a day; two-thirds are living below the poverty level. The population is experiencing an annual growth rate of 3.1 percent, with half of the population being under the age of 15 years.

According to Stern, these facts have made the job of recruiting suicide bombers so easy that it proceeds in a rather routine fashion for Hamas leaders (Stern, 2003: 48). For example, if the head of Hamas's military wing is planning an operation, he plans all aspects of the operation except one: who will carry out the attacks. This is easily solved with a phone call to the Hamas leader in the target area. That person calls the head of the local student union (or someone else familiar with the students), who will select two volunteers. These volunteers, who are usually troubled youths, are sent to meet with the Hamas leader 48 hours before the operation begins (Stern, 2003: 48).

The profile of the typical suicide bomber prior to the attacks of September 11th, 2001, is as follows (Stern, 2003: 50):

- Young, often a teenager.

- He is mentally immature.
- There is pressure on him to work.
- He has no options, and there is no social safety net to help him.
- He cannot get a job with the Palestinian Authority or with Arafat's army because of lack of connections, or "vitamin W" as it is called (W for wasta, which is the Arabic term for political, social, and personal connections).
- He has no girlfriend or fiancée.
- Marriage is not an option because it's expensive and he can't even take care of his own family.
- He has no means for enjoying life in any way.
- Life has no meaning but pain.
- He feels he has lost everything.
- The only way out is to find refuge in God.
- He goes to the local mosque, five times a day for prayer, even the 4 A.M. prayers that even the average devout Moslems do not normally attend.

While he is there, he is noticed by local Hamas members, who ask about and quickly learn of his situation. These Hamas members begin to recruit this person by telling him about the afterlife in paradise that awaits him if he dies in the jihad. Not only will he receive rewards in the afterlife, but he can make a difference in this existence as well. His family name will be held in the highest respect, and he will be remembered as a shaheed. His family will be given $5,000 and a variety of other supplies and sundries, and they will also be treated as heroes for his actions. The only requirement is that the recruit cannot tell anyone. Once he agrees, he is taken away from his home 48 hours prior to the attack. It is during this time that he fills out his will and writes his last letters. This is done to ensure that it is difficult for him to turn back; he doesn't even have a chance to reconsider in all likelihood. The situation has become such that women are now volunteering to become suicide bombers. There are now so many volunteers, both male and female, that Hamas no longer needs to actively recruit (Stern, 2003: 50-52).

At this point, Stern emphasizes that the confusing fact for many people with at least a passing familiarity with Islam is that suicide (intihar) is strictly forbidden, with many descriptions of the punishments that are reserved for suicides. If suicide is forbidden by Islam, then why are there so many suicide bombers? Stern answers the question by explaining that terrorist leaders portray the suicide bombings not as suicides but as acts of martyrdom (istishhad). This changes the situation entirely: instead of an eternity of torment for being a suicide, the person gains an eternity in paradise. The weakness of this logical argument is that although soldiers are trained to risk their lives for their country, they are also trained how to avoid death. Soldiers therefore go into combat knowing that they might die, but hoping that they won't. Suicide bombers, on the other hand, are trained specifically to die. How do suicide bombers come to view their deaths as more valuable than their lives? The answer lies in an analysis of suicides in general (Stern, 2003: 52-53).

Stern adds that suicides spread through social contagion; usually after one suicide occurs, a number of peers usually follow suit in short order. Suicide is more commonly found among youths who are depressed or exposed to intense social stress. The only difference between ordinary suicides and suicide bombings is that the latter seek to take other lives along with theirs (Stern, 2003: 52-53).

Initially, terrorist leaders had to expend effort to get volunteers for suicide bombings, to train them to value death more than life. But through social contagion, a cult of "suicide-murder" has emerged and taken hold of the youth in that area. "Martyrdom Operations," as the suicide bombings are called, are part of the popular culture: children play a game called shuhada which includes a mock funeral for a suicide bomber; teenage rock groups sing songs of praise for martyrs; and many young Palestinians list suicide bombers as their heroes (Stern, 2003: 52-53).

The humiliation of Moslems seems to continue up to the date of this publication—this time, it was the Americans. In a scandal described as "radioactive" because of the evidence that continues to worsen the longer the investigations continue, the Moslem world is horrified by reports that Iraqi prisoners detained in the Abu Ghraib prison by American forces were subjected to various humiliations and tortures (Hunt, May 10th 2004; McGeary, May 17th 2004). This prison was made infamous by Saddam Hussein as a place of torture and execution.

Now it appears that American Military Police, possibly under the direction of Military Intelligence officers, were continuing the tortures and degradations. Photographs and videos of Iraqi prisoners have surfaced through the efforts of a soldier, Specialist Joseph Darby, who believed that these actions were unethical and violated the international prescriptions of the Geneva Conventions (McGeary, May 17th 2004). These images showed soldiers involved in humiliating the Iraqi prisoners. Some of the prisoners, many of whom had not been charged yet, were forced to perform sexual acts, including nudity (especially in front of female soldiers), masturbation, and simulated sex acts. Some female detainees were reported to have been forced to expose their breasts. Also, some of the prisoners were chained to bars in their cells, put on leashes, had hoods placed on their heads, were hooked up to wires and were told that they would be electrically shocked if they moved or did not comply with demands (in at least one instance, the wires were not actually attached to any electrical source). Reports also indicated that a few prisoners died as a result of these actions. All such acts of torture and humiliation were reportedly designed to "soften them [the prisoners] up" or "fear [the prisoners] up" for interrogation by the military intelligence personnel (McGeary, May 17th 2004; Serrano and Miller, May 9th 2004).

The Moslems, especially in the Middle East, were horrified and interpreted the scandal as a continuing example of humiliation by the West. Despite public apologies and expressions of disgust by President Bush and his administration and promises to investigate and prosecute the guilty, the Moslem world continued to be outraged (Gibbs, May 17th, 2004; Hunt, May 10th 2004; McGeary, May 17th 2004). Senator Carl Levin, a ranking member of the Armed Services Committee, stated "Our troops are less secure and our nation is less secure because these depraved and despicable actions will fuel the hatred and the fury of those who oppose us" (McGeary, May 17th, 2004). In fact, it appears that this has already begun. Moslem terrorists captured and beheaded Nick Berg, an American civilian who was in Iraq helping to rebuild the telecommunications network. The beheading was recorded, and the video was made public on an al-Qaeda linked website on May 11th 2004. The beheading was claimed to avenge the actions against the Iraqis in Abu Ghraib by American forces (Reid, May 12th 2004).

Sources

Bucaille, M. (1979). *The Bible, The Quran and Science*. Indianapolis: American Trust

Gibbs, Nancy. (May 17th, 2004). "Their Humiliation, and Ours." *Time Magazine*. Page 88.

Hitti, P. K. (1967). *History of the Arabs: From the Earliest Times to the Present* (9th Ed.). New York: St. Martin's Press.

Hunt, Terrence. (May 10th, 2004). "Prison Scandal is 'Radioactive.'" Associated Press. *The Sunday Journal*, Albuquerque

Lewis, B. (2002). *What Went Wrong? Western Impact and Middle Eastern Response.* New York: Oxford.

McGeary, Johanna. (May 17th, 2004). "The Scandal's Growing Stain." *Time Magazine*. Pages 26-34.

Oren, Midrad B. (2003) *Six Days of War*. New York: Ballantine Books.

Reid, Robert H. (May 12th, 2004). "American's Beheading Shown on Videotape." Associated Press. *Houston Chronicle* pages 1A, 13A.

Serrano, Richard A. and Miller, Greg. (May 9th, 2004). "Some Answers Emerge from Abu Ghraib." Associated Press. *Houston Chronicle* pages 1A, 22A.

Shipler, D. K. (1986). *Arab and Jew: Wounded Spirits in a Promised Land.* New York: Penguin Books.

Stern, J. (2003). *Terror in the Name of God: Why Religious Militants Kill.* New York: Harper Collins.

Wasserstein, B. (2003). *Israelis and Palestinians: Why Do They Fight? Can They Stop?* New Haven: Yale University Press.

13

The Islamic Revolution: Khomeini's New Export

The 1979 Iranian Revolution was a turning point in the history of Islam and its relations with the Christian "infidels." From a Moslem perspective, there are several reasons for this. The Iranian Revolution succeeded in establishing the first Islamic Republic in modern history; it confronted the West by taking hostage American diplomats, professors, government agents, and media reporters; and it caused the political demise of an American president. Irrational as it may be, most Moslems, and especially Arab Moslems, took a hidden sense of pride in these activities. In a sense, the Iranian revolution was a powerful force multiplier. Against all odds, it was able, at least to an extent, to restore Moslem pride and pave the way for Islamic rebirth everywhere.

On January 16, 1979, the Shah of Iran had to leave his country for the last time. On February 1, 1979, the Ayatollah Khomeini returned to Iran to establish his Islamic Republic, replacing one of the most dictatorial of monarchies. He did not return as president or prime minister. In the tradition of the Prophet Mohammed when he returned to Mecca, the Ayatollah returned as the country's spiritual leader. At the Tehran airport, he was received by an estimated 3,000,000 Moslem revolutionaries. From the airport, the Ayatollah traveled to Tehran's national cemetery where many of his compatriots who had been killed in the disturbances against the Shah were buried. After paying his respects, he made a brief speech in which he declared the current government and the current constitution invalid and demanded the immediate resignation of Bakhtiar, the last prime minister appointed by the Shahinshah (the king of kings). The prime minister obliged on February 11th, and the Islamic Republic began operation under a new prime minister appointed by the Ayatollah and assisted by an army of self-appointed Islamic guards. One of the first acts the new government undertook was to abolish state taxes and, consistent with Quranic teaching, replace it with Islamic Zakat. In the process of making these radical changes, riots and counter-riots continued to shake the country and hundreds of citizens and soldiers were killed (Hoveyda, 2003: 2).

The word Ayatollah is not a proper name. It is a religious title meaning the verse of Allah, one of the highest titles any Shiite cleric can achieve. The Ayatollah's proper name was Rohallah (the soul of Allah). The word Khomeini simply meant from Komein, a small rural town in Esfahan in northern Iran. The Ayatollah was born in 1901 to a modest family of clerics who originally migrated to Komein from India. Shortly after Rohallah was born, his father died. The father's death may have been related to a fight between him and the feudal landowner over the unfairness of having to pay an unjustifiably high rent. The father left behind a destitute mother who could not afford to keep the young child. As a result, Rohallah had to live with his aunt and uncle, a well-off man (the Ayatollah's biographers point out the parallel between the Ayatollah and the Prophet Mohammed, who was also raised by his uncle). In his uncle's house, the child was always reminded of his father's death and the son's obligation to avenge that death. Here perhaps were the initial seeds of Rohallah's revolutionary destiny—avenging the humiliating conditions of the Iranian Shiites, especially when they lived under a repressive ruler who, while claiming Islam, lived in imperial luxury secured by Western infidels.

At the time Rohallah was born, Iran was in a state of great chaos and turbulence. The Russians controlled the northern regions, and the British the southern regions. In between, tribal chieftains (khans in the Indian tradition) held power in their own domains. In 1905, a group of young intellectuals, aristocrats, and high-ranking clerics seized power in Tehran and declared a Constitutional government in the Western tradition. As a result, the traditional clerics, under the leadership of Hojat-ol-Allah Nouri (Hojat-ol-Allah is a title of a middle-rank cleric), revolted against the creation of a Western government in the cradle of the Shiite faith. Nouri, who was a famous mullah, decried the Western-style government declaring "Islam is in danger…what we need is not a parliament or a constitution but an Islamic government" (Hoveyda,

2003: 3). The Shah's regime eventually hanged Nouri in public, and his compatriots, fearing the same fate, escaped into the countryside where they opened inconspicuous Quranic schools. Rohallah was a pupil at the school in Khomein.

Rohallah grew up with his aunt and uncle. His aunt, a devout Shiite, drilled into her nephew's mind the values of having an Islamic government. She also taught him that to establish an Islamic government, the Shiite nation must pursue an all-out struggle against its adversaries. Here perhaps was the first time the young Rohallah heard about an Islamic government. Rohallah was 15 when his aunt and uncle died. Having graduated from the Quranic "madrassa," he moved to the city of Qom where many great Shiite teachers resided and taught. Determined to climb up to the top of the clerical hierarchy, he studied theology under Sheikh Abdul-Kariem Haeri, who had a great reputation as a modest and renowned scholar. At the time, many Shiites from the Caucasus flocked to Qom after escaping the Bolshevik revolution. They spoke in horror of the savage persecution of Moslems at the hands of the Communists, insinuating that they were acting on behalf of God's enemies. These stories profoundly impressed the young cleric, who had internalized his aunt's advice to fight back at all adversaries. As a result, in one of his first published papers, the Ayatollah expressed his pity for Persia (the older name of Iran) and his fears that the Jews might be harboring enmity to the Moslem nations everywhere (Hoveyda, 2003: 7-8).

At age 37, Khomeini made the pilgrimage to Mecca. On his way back to Qom, he was introduced to a Mr. Safavi, a charismatic young fanatic who advocated an armed revolution against the adversaries of Islam. Safavi was connected to the Egyptian Moslem Brotherhood and was later to start a local chapter of the same organization known as Fedyin-e-Islam (Martyrs of Islam). At age 40, Khomeini was an accomplished Shiite and a stern cleric. In 1971, he publicly criticized the Shah for celebrating the 2,500th anniversary of the Iranian monarchy, a Western-style extravaganza that offended the Shiite clerics, as well as most Iranian intellectuals and members of the middle-class (Hoveyda, 2003: 14-16).

Yet the Ayatollah was soon to meet the Shah for the first time. He was asked to head a delegation to meet the Shah on behalf of the Shiite community in Qom that needed financial assistance to repair the famous Fatima Mosque. The meeting was cordial and short, yet the Shah was disinterested in the group's leader, who took it as a slight and a sign of personal disdain. Hoveyda explains that the Ayatollah at the time was not a major figure, and that the Shah, as well as other top-ranking politicians, had not heard of him before (Hoveyda, 2003: 19). The Ayatollah, apparently hurt by the Shah's slight and disappointed in his inability to gain national recognition, spent weeks in solitary meditation in the Shiite tradition. He adopted the slogan "Islam is in Danger" and accused the Shah of anti-Islamic behavior, comparing him to the Ummayad functionaries who assassinated the Prophet's grandson Hussain (Hoveyda, 2003: 21-23). As a result, the Shah imprisoned the Ayatollah and later exiled him to Iraq which, at the time, had strained relations with Iran. While the Shah appeared to have silenced the "black revolutionary" (the Ayatollahs wore black turbans), Khomeini did not admit defeat. Responding to the political events in Iraq, Khomeini later moved to Paris where he contemplated his successful return to Iran and leadership of an absolutist medieval theocracy.

One of the Ayatollah's first acts of governing was proclaiming two major policy changes, one internal and one external. The internal was an Islamization program, and the external was an ideological exportation program. Within weeks of the revolution, Shariah law was applied across the Iranian society; marriage legislation was amended to conform with the Quranic prescriptions; women were pressured to adopt the chador (full length black veil); a ban was placed on the imports of frozen meat, luxury goods and alcoholic beverages; and music was banned on Iranian radio under the ruse that music made the brain "inactive and frivolous." Included in this policy was the closing down of all cinema houses (Wright, 1989: 28).

The ideological exportation program began in 1982 and was designed to spread the Islamic revolution throughout the world. In March, the program was formerly launched from the Tehran Hilton, where the Ayatollah met with some 380 mullahs with various religious and revolutionary credentials. He delivered his first seminar on the inevitability of exporting the Islamic revolution to all Moslem countries and, eventually, to the world. In particular, he emphasized armed resistance to all forces that oppose Islam (Wright, 1985: 26-27). At the Seminar, and in the tradition of the Prophet Mohammed, the Ayatollah professed the superiority of Islam over all other religions, rejected the separation between faith and society, and attributed the success of his revolution to the providence of Islam. The Ayatollah reportedly stated (Hoveyda, 2003: 31):

"True faith is the greatest guarantee of spiritual health and moral perseverance and the most powerful mainstay of every human being in facing life problems, great or small, and at the same time the surest moral guardian of every society.

Our people enjoy the blessing of living under the banner of the most progressive and elevated religious principles, namely those of the sacred faith of Islam. This faith, whose sublime teachings and principles embrace the most perfect material and spiritual advancement of mankind, can be the highest guide to individuals and to society at every stage of social evolution. The pride and the secret of the complete success of our revolution lie in this very fact that the principles of this revolution are throughout inspired by the spirit and essence of the exalted teachings of Islam."

Middle East intelligence agencies did not pay attention to this seminar, or if they did, they did not take it seriously. After all, what could the Iranians do in the midst of a revolution? Yet, while the seminar passed with little notice, the envoys of the Ayatollah were in direct contact with the leaders of the large Shiite community in Southern Lebanon. They met with Yasir Arafat of the PLO and his top aides, who agreed to train foreign revolutionaries in their guerrilla training camps (Hoveyda, 2003: 27). These contacts turned out to have drastic consequences for Moslem nations everywhere and for the savagery of world terrorism.

In the same month of the seminar, the Iranian President Ali Khamenei made a public plea to Moslems in Iran and the surrounding countries. His call pressed upon every able-bodied Moslem to come to Iran to join in the revolution and to assist in liberating the Moslem faith that was smothered by Western ideas and institutions. The call made a dramatic impression, and several thousand Gulf State youths literally "dropped their books" and joined the call. Other students came from Turkey, Libya, Pakistan, North Korea, Yemen, and Palestine. Most of them were idealistic middle-class rebels who wanted radical change in the name of Islam. The largest group came from Iraq, because of the large Shiite community in that country, which was also the most persecuted by the Iraqi regime. The Saudi National Airline offered the revolutionaries a 75% discount on their airfare. The young volunteers wanted to participate in a religious way. Subsequently, they were diverted to "liberation camps" run by Iranian Revolutionary Guards for training and fighting.

The new commandos were trained with automatic rifles, American M-16s, and Soviet AK-47s. Not unlike the Crusaders of 1098, they also underwent religious indoctrination. The main difference between the Crusaders of 1098 and the Iranian commandos of 1982 was the intensity of their readiness to die. The Iranians were Hussainites, followers of Iman Hussain, the martyred grandson of the Prophet and the founder of the Shiite faith (680 Hijri). In the tradition of their assassinated leader, they were willing to give their last measure to avenge Islam through martyrdom. Their slogan was "it is more honorable to die for belief than to live with injustice" (Wright, 1985: 37). The most willing among these fighters were rewarded with red bandanas painted with Quranic scriptures. These became the trainers of the organizations later known as Islamic Amal (Moslem hope) and Hizbollah (the Party of God). Specifically, they were the masters and commanders of today's suicide bombing (Wright, 1985: 37).

Once trained, the foreign volunteers were dispatched back to their original countries where they formed local cells. Wright suggests these cells were so secretive that when an American professor and a French businessman were taken hostage in Lebanon by Shiite extremists, Western intelligence services could not identify who their captors were. Wright adds that the Iranian participation in Middle East terrorism was indeed revolutionary; it was both genuine and dangerous. The Iranian Mullahs demanded more than what religious leaders expected in other faiths. They demanded and received shehada (a declaration of faith, in this case conscious martyrdom). They quoted the Quranic verses "wars come to provide martyrs and that God may prove those who believe" and "Paradise is only attained when God knows who will really strive to endure" (Wright, 1985: 35). Wright describes the new Islamic zeal with a story of a young Iranian fighter who was wounded in battle with the Iraqis. Upon being captured by an Iraqi officer, this young soldier kept sobbing. When the officer told him not to worry because his wounds were not serious, the young Iranian replied "That is not why I am crying…I am crying because I didn't die…God does not want me" (Wright, 1985: 35).

To emphasize her point, Wright quotes a Western official who characterized the Iranian danger saying "these are not the odd men out, whatever hardship comes out of Iran, it remains a source of pride to the

Shiites" (Wright, 1985: 37). In a sense, and as history later demonstrates, the Iranian version of Islam was able to achieve what most Moslems were unable to achieve since the Crusades. These achievements were: (1) it united the Moslem world in resisting the increasing power of the infidels who, as mentioned earlier, had smothered the Moslem faith by secular ideas and secular institutions; (2) it ostensibly revitalized Islamic resistance to the West through Islamic martyrdom, a practice never before used since the Moslem Assassins practiced it against the Crusaders. Even more, the practice was also adopted by female suicide bombers, many of them professionals; and (3) it not only increased the number of acts of Islamic resistance, it intensified their effectiveness. In the perception of most Moslems, if these arguments are accurate, then the Ayatollah's vision is true and Islam is back on the rise.

To universalize the Ayatollah's vision, Iran exported Islamic armed resistance. Such acts of resistance were based on the Iranian experience itself. For resistance to be credible and effective, it was thought, its roots should grow from within and not be imported from without. Lebanon was selected as the natural location for the first Iran-supported armed resistance satellite for three reasons: (1) it was a front state in the war with Israel; (2) it had American and French forces located on its land; and (3) it had a considerably large Shiite community that suffered severely under Lebanon's Christian rulers. Through its Lebanese satellite, Iran-supported armed resistance would be closer to the center of action and capable of attacking the foreign forces without implicating the Iranian government. Hence, there was the need to create a Lebanese Hizbollah (the party of God) in the image of its Iranian example. In the Iranian perception, the winds of the Islamic revolution would be able to create revolutionary currents that could throw out the American and French forces and, hopefully, the Israelis as well (Wright, 1985: 83). By 1983, the Bekkaa valley area in Lebanon looked more like Tehran; women wore black chadors, liquor was pulled off the shelves in grocery stores, pictures of the Ayatollah were in full display, and the area was constantly patrolled by Revolutionary Guards.

Hizbollah is not a political party in the Western sense. It lacks any official structure or membership list. Indeed, it is first and foremost a loose confederation of militant groups and clerical leaders. Yet, to attract serious revolutionaries who are willing to die, Hizballah had to also be committed to social reform. It built schools, hospitals, mosques, and institutions that can reward the families of the fallen. In the Bekkaa valley, for instance, there was the "Khomeini Hospital" and the "Hotel Khayyam" (Wright, 1985: 81). Yet, Hizballah was certainly committed to armed resistance. Musawi, one of its original leaders, called it "the people's march" while another leader, Sheikh Ibrahim, defined its ultimate objective as liberating Palestine and Jerusalem (Wright, 1985: 82). At a 2002 estimate, Hizballah had 500-700 active terrorist cells internationally, as well as 4,000-7,000 militia members in paramilitary units operating in Southern Lebanon. The mammoth organization of Hizballah is governed by a 17 member Supreme Council that decides all administrative, legislative, judicial, political, and military matters, and reports directly to Iran. The organization is also almost totally funded by the Iranian government in the estimated amount of $600 million a year (Hill, 2002: 669).

According to Hill (2003), Hizballah committed over 350 acts of terrorism between 1983 and 2002. These included bombings, kidnappings, executions, hijackings, and guerrilla attacks. These activities were conducted rather indiscriminately around the world, destroying thousands of innocent lives. The worst of these acts, perhaps, was the simultaneous bombings of the Marine barracks and the French peacekeepers' barracks in Beirut on the Sunday morning of October 23, 1983. The bombing killed 241 Marines and 56 French peacekeepers. Wright describes the explosions as possibly the largest non-nuclear explosion since WWII and the single most effective terrorist attack in Middle East history. Within hours of the double blasts, an anonymous spokesman telephoned Agency France Presse in Beirut in classical Arabic stating "We are the soldiers of God" (Wright, 1985: 70). As sad and atrocious as the attacks were, one cannot escape the historical analogy between these attacks and those committed by the Crusades of 1098-1291 when the latter also claimed they were "the soldiers of God." The main force multiplier that arguably made the difference between what the Moslems were unable to do then—but were able to do now—was the Islamic Revolution in Iran that demonstratively reminded the Moslems of Mohammed's first Islamic Revolution.

Finally, while many Moslem countries may have resented the establishment of an Islamic Republic in Iran (including hundreds of thousands of Iranian dissidents in Iran), given the exaggerated self-conception of the Moslems, the theonomous identity of Islam, and the long history of Moslem military Nakbas, the news out of Tehran signaled the first Islamic triumph in a thousand years. In the "bones" of many a Moslem, this triumph symbolized Islam's return to glory, the end of Moslem humiliation, and the first real step toward Islamic recovery. In the final analysis, it was thought that as Nasser of Egypt had begun (but failed) in establishing Pan Arabism in the 1960s, the Ayatollah succeeded in establishing Pan Islamism. By the same token, as the original Moslem Brothers tried (but failed) in establishing Hakimiat Allah (God's government) in the 1950s, the Republican Guards of Tehran succeeded.

Sources

Hill, S. D. (2002). *Extremist Groups: An International Compilation of Terrorist Organizations, Violent Political Groups, and Issue-Oriented Militant Movements* (2nd Ed.). Huntsville: Sam Houston State University.

Hoveyda, F. (2003). *The Shah and the Ayatollah: Iranian Mythology and Islamic Revolution*. Westport: Praeger Publishers.

Wright, M. (editor). (1989). *Iran: The Khomeini Revolution*. Chicago: St. James Press.

Wright, R. (1985). *Sacred Rage: The Wrath of Militant Islam*. New York: Linden Press.

14

The Fury of Islam: Bin Laden and Beyond

Al Qaeda is a common Arabic word that means the "base" or the "rule." Recently, however, the word has been given a highly charged political profile that arouses demonstrative consternation around the world. This political profile of al Qaeda was the brainchild of a hermit-like Saudi Arabian engineer, 47 years old, who reportedly lives in the mountain caves of Afghanistan. His name is Osama bin Laden. In light of the disastrous terrorist attacks recently committed by al-Qaeda terrorist groups, bin Laden—who has been charged with multiple counts of killing Americans, Tanzanians, Kenyans, Saudi Arabians, Pakistanis, and others—is arguably the most infamous terrorist and fugitive the world has known. Yet to millions of "fundamentalist" Moslems, he is considered a "sheik," a man of God and a defender of Islam. To fundamentalist Moslems, and despite his criminal and fugitive status, bin Laden possibly symbolizes the first successful counter-Crusader since Saladin in 1192 liberated Jerusalem and expelled the Christians from the Middle East. Unsurprisingly, the liberation of the two holy cities of Mecca and Medina in Saudi Arabia has been bin Laden's primary objective and al-Qaeda's true battle cry. Fighting against Christians and Jews seemed to be an afterthought. Chase Freeman, the former U.S. ambassador to Saudi Arabia noted "al Qaeda is directed first and foremost at the overthrow of the Saudi Monarchy. You can be damn sure that any al-Qaeda operative is on the Saudi list and that any senior operative is high on that list" (Baer, 2003: 202).

Notwithstanding bin-Laden's true motives, because he is widely considered the CEO of transnational terrorism and the prime suspect of atrocious terroristic attacks around the world, it is only prudent to focus on his history, ideology, and his role in sustaining world-wide terrorism. This focus can hopefully accomplish the following: (1) explain the causes of Islam's final fury; (2) curb the madness of terrorism that the world has been experiencing; and (3) help turn the Islamic faith to its religious "base." Most of the citations in this section are taken from Internet sources and will be accredited as such.

Bin Laden: the Moslem Puritan

Bin Laden was born in 1957 Osama bin Mohammed bin Awad bin Laden, the 17th of 52 children sired by Mohammed bin Laden, one of Saudi Arabia's wealthiest construction magnates. His father (a Wahhabi Moslem) came to the kingdom of Saudi Arabia around 1930 from Hadramout (a province of South Yemen at the time.) He started his life as a porter in the Saudi Arabian Port of Jedda and ended his life as the owner of the biggest construction company in the Kingdom—the Binladen Brothers Group with annual sales of over 255 billion SR (Saudi Rial)—the equivalent of $70 billion (http://www.pbs.org/wgbh/ pages/ frontline/ shows/ binladen/). Bin Laden's father is said to have first attracted the attention of King Abdul Aziz when he performed construction work on the royal palace. As a result, he was awarded much more prestigious contracts, including the renovation of the Holy places in Mecca and Medina as well as the Al-Aqsa mosque in Jerusalem. This enabled the bin Ladens to establish an industrial and financial empire which now extends far beyond religious construction projects. Osama's father was a devout Moslem, a humble and frugal man. He insisted on keeping all his children around him. He had a tough discipline and raised all the children with a strict religious and social code. He maintained a daily religious program and required his children to follow. He dealt with his children as grown men and demanded that they show confidence at a young age (http://www.pbs.org/wgbh/pages/frontline/shows/binladen/).

In the meantime, bin Laden's father was successful in establishing a personal relationship of confidence and friendship with King Abdul Aziz, the founder of the Saudi dynasty. As a result, his relationship with the Saudi royal family was so strong that after a palace conflict between King Saud (the second king of Saudi Arabia) and his younger brother Faisal (who eventually succeeded his older brother), the Saudi treasury was found empty and bin Laden paid the civil servants' wages for the entire Kingdom for six months. This close relationship between the bin Laden clan and the Royal family continued, although it is known to have undergone some serious crises. The most significant of these crises was the 1979 Mecca affair when armed fundamentalist Moslems led by the charismatic Guhaiman militarily occupied the Mosque of Mecca. It was later shown that the attackers smuggled their weapons into Mecca by using some of bin Laden's trucks in use at the time. One of bin Laden's sons was also arrested in the affair but was later released without causing much damage to the continuing friendship between the bin Ladens and the Saudi Royal family. Ironically, when the Saudi forces decided to attack and reoccupy the Grand Mosque, the sole parties in possession of the Mosque's maps were the bin Ladens who, even more ironically, solicited assistance from the French Special Forces to assist in reclaiming the Mosque (http://www.pbs.org/wgbh/pages/frontline/shows/ binladen/).

Osama was exposed very early to the Wahhabi religious and social discipline his father had instilled in all his children. His father died when Osama was 13. Faithful to the Wahhabi tradition, he was married at the age of 17 (a practice encouraged by Moslems who seek to protect themselves from moral corruption) to a Syrian relative (Osama's mother was Syrian). Osama attended school (i.e., primary, secondary and college) in Jedda, perhaps the most cosmopolitan city in the Kingdom. At secondary school and university he adopted the main principles of many educated Moslems at the time—Moslem Brotherhood. The elders of the Brotherhood had moved to Saudi Arabia in the 1950s after being persecuted by Nasser, Egypt's strong man, who himself had survived an assassination attack by members of the Brotherhood in 1954. In 1981, Osama received a degree in Public Administration from King Abdul-Aziz University in Jedda. Upon graduation he traveled the Moslem world; Syria, Sudan, and Pakistan. Contrary to false media reports, he did not visit any European or Christian countries, a fact that might explain his ethnocentric mind. Having inherited an immense amount of wealth, and being the private man he was raised to be, Osama's social contacts followed in his fathers' Wahhabi tradition. He hosted senior Islamic scholars and leaders of Moslem movements. Among these were two influential Moslem scholars who infinitely impressed young Osama and left a perpetual mark on his way of thinking: Professor Abdullah Azzam, and the Moslem Brotherhood doctrinarian writer and teacher, Sayyed Quttb (http://www.pbs.org/wgbh/pages/frontline/shows/binladen/).

Osama's first encounter with organized violence was as early as 1981 during the first two weeks of the Soviet invasion of Afghanistan. As a young puritan Moslem who was endowed with an "unshakable confidence in Allah" and great wealth, he traveled to Pakistan to explore what the new generation of Moslem devotees could, and should, do to confront thc "atheist" Soviets who irreverently invaded the Moslem land of Afghanistan. In Peshawar, he was introduced to members of the old Islam; a widely disorganized battalion of Moslem fighters who also happened to have the tacit approval of the United States government. Baer comments that in 1980 Zbigniew Brzezinski, President Carter's national security advisor, solicited Saudi financial assistance for the Afghan resistance movement against the Soviet occupation. He also promised to match the Saudi contributions (Baer, 2003: 100). Among the leaders Osama met in Peshawar were Khadafy Janjalani (who later became the leader of the Abu Sayyaf terrorist group in the Philippines), and Rabbani, an infamous Afghani warlord.

Perhaps because of his university education in Public Administration, Osama thought he could transform the ragged and disorganized Moslem battalion into a modern army of "mujahedeen" (plural of mujahid meaning a jihadi or a religious warrior). He naturally thought the Mujahedeen needed adequate financial support, more efficient organization, and modern training. Osama endeavored to provide all these with a fervent zeal. He returned to the Kingdom and began organizing what he thought was to be the first counter-Crusade army since the times of Saladin. In the kingdom, and with the blessings of the Saudi government, he turned up the Wahhabi fervor and succeeded in collecting huge amounts of money and material as donations to the Moslem Mujahedeen in Afghanistan.

At the time, the Saudi Royal family was indifferent (to say the least) to Osama's grand Moslem plan. The elders of the Al-Saud clan thought Osama's follies would ameliorate the popular pressures put on them to "do something" in defense of Islam. Failure to "do something," Baer explains, could bring to power a militant Islamic government, one that is more hostile to the clan than Iran's Ayatollah. At the time, the Saudi rulers also had to watch for the continuing problems they had with the Saudi Shiites in the Eastern provinces of the Kingdom (the closest to the Saudi border with Iran). The Shiites, Baer suggests "were ripe for a revolution." Baer estimates that with the rise of Osama's campaign "95 percent of all educated Saudis between the ages of twenty-five and forty-one supported Bin Laden" (Baer, 2003: 202). Osama later returned to Pakistan with a number of Pakistanis and Afghani experts who had worked in his father's enterprises for years. These were to be the new managers, developers, and, in a sense, the young "Napoleons" who would lead the army of Allah under Osama's supreme command.

In 1982, Osama entered Afghanistan for the first time. He put his mujahedeen army to the test. He reportedly participated in several battles against the Russian "infidels," but not on a regular basis. His presence was so encouraging that it attracted more Saudi volunteers and jihadis from other Moslem countries. Their numbers, however, were small. To provide for an adequate flow of highly motivated volunteers, Osama established "Bait-al-Ansar" (guesthouse of the supporters, in the tradition of the Medina residents who supported the Prophet Mohammed upon his Hijra in 622). The guesthouse served primarily as a command center, a think-tank, and a charity bank. Administratively, it was used as a depository for record keeping, documentation of personnel, and public relations. The commander of the guesthouse was Professor Abdullah Azzam, Osama's former teacher and mentor. Azzam, a Jordanian Palestinian, had been recruited into the Moslem Brotherhood as a student at Cairo's Al-Azhar University. Soon after, he became the Amir al-Jihad (Head of Jihad). After Nasser's purge of the Brotherhood, Azzam fled to Saudi Arabia, the only country that would take him. He was offered a teaching position at the university in Jedda where Osama was his student.

Bin Laden: Athanasius Contra Mundum

In 1986, Osama bin Laden established his training camps inside Afghanistan. He wanted to create his own front and to organize battalions under his command. At the time, his "counter-crusade" efforts were supported by the American government as well as the Saudi and the Pakistani governments (http:// news.bbc.uk/1/hi/world/ south_asia). Osama's first battle against the Soviets was in Jaji in the Afghani province of Baktia. During the period of 1984-1989 he reportedly fought more than five major battles and hundreds of small operations and skirmishes. According to Islamic sources, he also participated as a guerilla commander in the fierce battle of Jalalabad that may have directly led the Soviets to finally withdraw from Afghanistan (http://www.pbs.org/wgbh/ pages/ frontline/ shows/ binladen/).

Surprised by the apparently abrupt withdrawal of the Soviets, Osama realized that his Moslem Jihad was incomplete. Al-Qaeda was firmly in place, the Mujahedeen were battle-tested, the American-made Stinger missiles were proven lethal, and the supply of religious and financial support was generously in abundance. Bin Laden had to find a new "front" to continuc Jihad. Such a thought was historically consistent with the tradition of the Prophet who had fought seven consecutive wars. In a sense, after the Russians left, bin Laden had to designate his new "infidels."

Osama returned to the Saudi Kingdom in search of new enlightenment. Not unlike the Prophet's tradition of defending Islam by warning against attacks by opposing tribes, Osama warned the Saudis against possible invasion by Saddam Hussein of Iraq. At the time, the Saudi regime was on good terms with Saddam, and Osama was not totally disenchanted with the Saudi regime. In 1991, Saddam occupied Kuwait and was militarily within one day's march of the Saudi Kingdom's northern oil fields, where, incidentally, the majority of Shiite Saudis lived. Osama, not yet clear on who his next "infidels" were—but fully cognizant of the new-found prowess of his Grand Moslem army back in Afghanistan—wrote to the Saudi King explaining in detail his plan to protect the country of his birth should the Iraqi forces advance on Riyadh. He suggested bringing his victorious army of mujahedeens to defend Mecca and Medina, the two most holy cities in the Moslem world. He probably envisioned his role to be as prominent as that of the Prophet himself.

The Saudi response to Osama was disappointing. At first it was one of "we are in consultation," followed by a more shocking response: "the Americans are coming." According to personal interviews, Osama "felt depressed and decided to change his maneuvers" (http:// www.pbs.org/wgbh/pages/frontline/ shows/ binladen/). He obtained a fatwa (a religious statement) from a senior Moslem cleric that urged training and preparing for the religious duty—a statement he interpreted to mean training under his command in Afghanistan. Consequently, an estimated 4,000 Saudis went to Afghanistan in response to the fatwa. This may have irritated members of the Saudi regime who, threatened by Osama's behavior, limited his movement in the Kingdom to the vicinity of Jedda, under what appeared as a case of house arrest. The regime later began harassing Osama; they summoned him for questioning twice and dispatched the Saudi National Guard to search his farm outside Jedda. As a result, Osama grew impatient and concerned about three main issues: (1) how nonchalant the Saudi government was about accepting American forces to defend the Moslem Kingdom; (2) how indifferent the Saudi government was in response to his offer of assistance to fight Saddam; and, (3) how complacent the Royal family was in allowing the "infidels" to exploit its natural resources, dictate their policies, and support the most corrupt among their leaders. Specifically, Osama was insulted by the humiliating treatment he received from the Saudi Royal family whom, he thought, his father and brothers had faithfully served for over fifty years.

Disenchanted with the way he was treated in his home country, in 1991 Osama sought refuge in Sudan where he was received as a brother and a distinguished guest. While in Sudan, two major sets of events happened that infinitely changed Osama's mind, turning him against the United States: (1) after the Gulf war was won, the Kingdom allowed American forces to set what appeared to be permanent bases in Saudi Arabia, land of the most holy places in Islam—Mecca and Medina; and (2) relatively minor anti-American incidents in Somalia prompted President Clinton to abruptly withdraw all American forces from Somalia. The abruptness factor may have weighed much heavier on Osama's mind than on anyone else's. Abrupt withdrawal, Osama must have concluded, was a universal reaction by all superpowers—the Soviets from Afghanistan, and the Americans from Somalia. Consequently, it would have been natural and logical for Osama to (mistakenly) believe that Allah was on his side, and that his Mujahedeen could, in due course, defeat any combination of superior forces. Here again one can note two interesting revelations: (1) Osama's simple and mystical mind leading him to believe in divine intervention that will eventually win over any military or technological advantages; and (2) Osama's scape-goating logic by which he was able to convince himself and his like-minded companions that Islam's real enemy at this stage of the clash between civilizations was the United States and its allies. He must have also thought that if the United States were to be defeated, even symbolically, Islam would have won, and the world would be Islamized in accordance with the Prophet's prophecy.

Some of Osama's own words may support the previous revelation regarding his simple and mystical mind. In a 1998 interview with

John Miller, Osama stated: (http://www.pbs.org/wgbh/pages/frontline/shows/ binladen/).

> *"Allah has granted the Moslem people and the Afghani Mujahedeen, and those with him, the opportunity to fight the Russians and the Soviet Union...They were defeated by Allah and were wiped out...the flag of the Soviet Union was folded once and for all on the 25th of December just 10 years later. It was thrown in the waste basket...Gone was the Soviet Union forever...we are certain that we shall—with the grace of God—prevail over the Americans...there is lesson here [to be learned].*

Regarding his recognition of an Islamic prophecy, Osama responded to John Miller stating:

> *"Our call is the call of Islam that was revealed to Mohammed. It is a call to all mankind. We have been entrusted to follow in the footsteps of the Messenger and to communicate the message to all nations...It is an invitation we extend to all nations of the world to embrace Islam...We are entrusted to spread this message and to extend that call to all the people."*

Encouraged by the Somalia events, Osama and his companions decided to reinvent al-Qaeda. The direction they took was to adopt a more militant position, one that is akin to Athanasius Contra Mundum (Athanasius against the world); a reference to Bishop Athanasius of Alexandria who, during the Conference of Constantinople in 381, set out to destroy each and every proposal submitted to reunite the Christian Church. Subsequently, in 1992, al-Qaeda's Majlis al shura (consultation council) decided to first target the interests of the United States and Israel (both internally and externally), and secondly, to target the interests of any other country that supports these two countries or threatens Moslem interests anywhere in the world. Toward achieving these objectives, al-Qaeda leaders also decided to: (1) put aside al-Qaeda's differences with all Shiite Moslems and their affiliated terrorist group Hizballah, and to cooperate with other Moslem terrorist groups against the common enemy—the United States and its allies and; (2) target the United States forces stationed on the Saudi peninsula as well as in the Horn of Africa (http://www.pbs.org/wgbh/pages/frontline/ shows/ binladen/).

On the ideological level, al-Qaeda also decided to broaden its definition of legitimate targets. The broader definition was consistent with the doctrines of an archconservative thirteen-century cleric whom all al-Qaeda members were assumed to have studied—Ibn Taymiah. Born in 1263 in Herraan near Urfa in modern Turkey, Ibn Taymiah became one of the most controversial and confrontational thinkers of Islam. Having always been against Islamic orthodox theology, he earned the title of "Patron Saint" of the militant branch of the Brotherhood. According to Ibn Taymiah's teachings, since Christians supported the Crusaders, they deserved death (Baer, 2003: 116). The same judgement he also applied to the Jews. He subsequently glorified the duty of Moslems to die for the cause. Ibn Taymiah was quoted stating "death of the [Moslem] martyrs for the unification of all the people in the cause of God and His word is the happiest, best, easiest, and the most virtuous death" (Baer, 2003: 116). Adopting Ibn Taymiah's views on Islamic martyrdom might have caused the increasing number of suicide bombings by Hizballah members, and more recently by Jammaat Islamiah in Indonesia and Iraq. The same views might also have inspired the never-before practiced suicide bombing by female operatives.

Being the most dangerous transnational terrorist group in the world, al-Qaeda has already been charged with the following activities: (1) the 2002 bombing of a hotel in Mombassa, Kenya; a nightclub in Bali, Indonesia; a U.S. military facility in Kuwait; and a synagogue in Tunisia; (2) the 2001 crashing of four US commercial jets, two into the World Trade Center in New York, one into the Pentagon in Washington, D.C. and the fourth into a field in Shanksville, Pennsylvania; (3) the 2000 attack on the USS Cole in the port of Eden, Yemen; (4) the 1998 bombing of the US Embassies in Nairobi, Kenya and Dar-el-Salam, Tanzania. Al-Qaeda also claimed to have shot down US helicopters in Somalia in 1993, and to have conducted three bombings that targeted US troops in Aden and Yemen (http://www.pbs.org/wgbh/ pages/ frontline/ shows/ binladen/).

Sources

Baer, R. (2003). *Sleeping With the Devil: How Washington Sold Our Soul for Saudi Arabia.* Santa Barbara: Crown Publishers.

BBC News. (September 18, 2001). *Who is Osama Bin Laden?* Retrieved online at http://news.bbc.co.uk/1/hi/world/south_asia/155236.stm on February 16th, 2004.

Frontline: PBS. (September 2001). *Hunting Bin Laden*. Retrieved online at http://www.pbs.org/wgbh/pages/frontline/shows/binladen/ on February 16th, 2004.

15

Beyond Bin Laden: The Future of the Islamic State

The Egyptian writer Nabil Bebawy (2003) presents a twenty-three point thesis in his book *Terrorism: A non-Islamic Industry*. He argues that "despite all the words, sounds, and tragedies of terrorism by Moslem groups, the Islamic faith never in the past nor in the present condoned terrorism or violence, and that all terroristic activities committed in the name of Islam are anti-Islamic and must be considered both criminal and heretical" (Bebawy, 2003: 139-178). The following are a few of Bebawy's more relevant points:

- The vast majority of young Moslems who traveled to fight in Afghanistan or Iraq were poor, illiterate, unemployed, and members of the down-trodden class. They did not travel to fight for the "noble cause" of Islam; they were contracted in groups and were "pushed out" of their native countries by local security personnel who considered them too tough to handle. As a result, other than religious zeal, they were often ineffective fighters.
- Most of the young Moslems who fought for the cause of Islam were indoctrinated into believing they were fighting to topple their own "unholy" governments. They were promised that, after the end of the fighting, they would go back and live in a far better society. Those who would die for the cause of Allah, however, were assured they would wake up in paradise the moment they die.
- Most of the young Moslems who fought for the cause of Islam came from autocratic Moslem countries where

beliefs in enlightenment, freedom, reasoning, democracy, or the rule of law are either unknown or prohibited (e.g., there were much fewer Mujahedeen who came from Tunisia, Jordan, Turkey, or Lebanon).

- Modern acts of terrorism are costly and require sophisticated technology which most terrorists do not possess. For such acts to succeed, the terrorist enterprise has to be well-funded and financed to provide for training and the waging of war. For that to occur, rich Arab states are more than willing to contribute huge financial resources.
- Most of the young Moslems who traveled to fight for the cause of Islam were accompanied by their clerics (e.g., political commissars). These clerics were paid handsomely to inspire the new recruits, to interpret the will of Allah, and to prevent the old recruits from weakening or leaving the battlefront.
- Invariably, the young Moslems who traveled to fight for the cause of Islam did not understand whom they were fighting for or against or for what reasons. They had minimal knowledge of who the Americans, the Russians, the Polish, the Spanish, or, for that matter, any other foreign forces, were. They were subsequently bent to kill indiscriminately.
- The vast majority of young Moslems who traveled to fight for the Moslem cause had not been trained in the rules of war. Therefore, they could not understand that someone in the war zone might be innocent (i.e., men, women, or children). They simply trusted in Hakimiat Allah (God's will, regardless of the consequence).
- It was common for the Moslems who traveled to fight for the cause of Islam to disagree over the ends and means of what they were supposed to do. Subsequently, it was not uncommon, for example, for an Arab Afghan contingent to fight against a Pakistani or Uzbekistani contingent. Such conflicts were usually resolved in accordance to local traditions and to the amount of money paid by the major warlords.

Based on Bebawy's thesis that Islam neither condones nor tolerates terrorism, one would be left with the assumption that terrorism by

Moslem groups must, in effect, be a consequence of the failed Moslem state itself. It would be enormously irrational to believe that so many Moslems who are so fervently dedicated to the righteousness of their faith would—suddenly and without any reason—rise to destroy so many innocent people. And if this is an accurate perspective, it would certainly warrant more contemplation and serious thinking.

With this perspective in mind, and being cognizant of the ideological complexity of the issues involved, I will posit a hypothesis of what the New Islamic State could be in the future and present some propositions that can make this vision a reality.

Preamble for the Future

The New Islamic State will have a new enlightened "Qaeda" (a global social contract), one that allows peacefulness for all, egalitarianism by all, and enlightenment and self-determination to all. The New Islamic State will be secular and democratic. It will fully utilize the Islamic principles of justice, fidelity, fraternity, compassion, mercy, and forgiveness, all connected by the bonds of decency, civility, and mutual respect.

The New Islamic State will adopt an ideology that denounces unjustified violence, abhors bloodshed, and manifests the best in the Quran and the other Holy Books. It will replace the jahiliyah *of terrorism and repression, both externally and internally, with the gentleness of Quranic chant, pious sentiments, communitarianism, and intellectual rejuvenation. It will observe, even rejoice in, the practices of freedom, individualism, reasoning, rule of law, due process, equality, and human rights.*

In a sense, the New Islamic State will bring forth the religious reformation that all the other great faiths found unavoidable. Yet the New Islamic State will not be reborn in an American form, an English form, a Japanese form, or any other form. It will reinvent itself in its own rich and holy heritage, one that, in its purest form, can rival and exceed the benevolence achieved by any of the other great religions.

I here offer three central propositions that can lead to achieving this New Islamic State: (1) social innovation, (2) democracy, and (3) responsible government. For social innovation to be possible, democracy is inevitable, and for democracy to prevail, responsible government is essential. These three propositions must either work together or fail separately. Unlike in *gemeinschaft* (medieval) times, modern Islamic rulers do not have the luxury of choosing among them. Furthermore, these three propositions must be accepted in good faith and executed faithfully.

Social Innovation

The concept of social innovation is as old as humanity. It emerged when communities found it necessary to have more social space to expand and enjoy living. In German, it is *lebensraum* (i.e., a living space), and in Arabic, it is *infitah* (i.e., a source of ventilation). The concept, which has been generally associated with the idea of liberalism, has been the trademark of progressing nations, be they Greeks, Romans, Chinese, or Islamic. Social innovation works well when religious and cultural restrictions are prudently relaxed, and it "suffocates" when the same restrictions are dogmatically intensified. Although all religions have, at one time or another, struggled with the concept, the process of innovation has been stubbornly slow due to the difficulty of identifying the farther reaches of innovation. Understandably, if the limits of social innovation go too far, they may delude religious doctrine and, subsequently, the authority of the clergy. If they fail to go far enough, their pursuit will most likely be seen as a government ploy—a fake attempt to deceive the masses.

Like all other cultures, Islam faced the challenge of social innovation at subsequent stages. First, it had to break with jahiliyah traditions without destroying the native bedouin culture. During the time of the Prophet Mohammed, it had to adapt to Jewish and Christian traditions (Zimmi traditions) without undermining the emerging Islamic doctrines. During the time of the Rashidin Caliphs, it had to adapt to Greek, Roman, and Persian cultures without adulterating the fundamental characteristics of Islamic rule. In the 18th century, it had to adapt to the British and French imperial hegemony. In post-colonial times, Islamic culture—under a more hegemonic West—had to accept a "new world order" and an increasingly pluralistic world. In modern times, Islam has been grudgingly experiencing the values of Human Rights—values which Islamic scholars have basically ignored for being Eurocentric and Christian-based. While some of the early adaptation processes Islam faced were milder than what it is now confronted with, given the phenomenal rise in American military prowess, modern technology, Western economics, and the subsequent global political realignments, Islam has recently been at a doctrinarian impasse regarding the need for, and the utility of, social innovation. Because of this impasse, the roots of Islamic frustration may have finally given way to the final fury against the entire West and what it has always stood for.

Today, Islamic cultures face serious and complicated issues. These include secularization, capitalism, social mobility, women's rights, the treatment of Zimmis, economic productivity, and the risks posed by new technologies of a global dimension. Faced with these challenges, the obstinacy of traditional Islam has come into a clash with the increasing plurality of freedom, wealth, lifestyles, values, and social obligations. Accordingly, for Islamic social innovation to succeed, the past history and the predictable future must be harmoniously bridged. Furthermore, to measure the success of social innovation, social researchers must use indices such as the levels of openness, tolerance, secularization, and the degree to which the grip of religious determinism is relaxed.

Faced with this inescapable need to change, Islam could respond in one of two ways: defense or innovation. If the Islamic culture chooses the former (i.e., ignoring the need for a peaceful and gradual change), the obstinacy of traditional Islam will either snap or further intensify. For example, the case of the Amir of Qatar who found it necessary to forcefully replace his father is a case of the former, while the continuing failure of the Saudi culture to allow women equal rights (i.e., serving on governmental boards, as members of the judiciary, as religious clerics, let alone allowing them to drive automobiles) is a case of the latter. On the other hand, if the Islamic culture chooses peaceful and gradual innovation, society as a whole will be at the "take-off" stage; on its way to achieving social equality, virility, industriousness, and prosperity. The examples of Turkey, Tunisia, and Oman are cases in point.

Two examples of the need for social innovation by Islamic states can be cited here. Both of these examples have been deeply embedded in Islamic tradition and religious dogma. Yet, given the global nature of the world today and the need to demonstrate genuine Islamic tolerance, both examples require a much more reasonable and tolerant mindset.

First is the restriction on non-Moslems to live, visit, or enter the city of Mecca when, in the objective reality of social innovation, removing such a restriction may well be most beneficial to Islam. The reasons behind this assertion are: (1) one of the most effective ways to attract non-Moslems to Islam is by inviting them to witness the true meaning of Islam as best demonstrated in Mecca itself; and (2) the present restriction has not in any effective measure prevented the enemies of Islam or the criminally-minded from entering the city or religiously corrupting the Kabba, as demonstrated by Moslem extremists in 1979. From a cultural perspective, forbidding non-Moslems to visit Mecca is the moral equivalent of preventing non-Christians from entering the Vatican, or non-Jews from entering Jerusalem. Moreover, the logic of forbidding peaceful individuals from visiting the most holy city of Islam based only on their religion can, in itself, engender a powerful motive to doubt the truth of Islam and its sublime message.

The second example of the need for social innovation is the socially unfair practice of punishing Moslems who convert to another religion by death, or for that matter, any punishment at all. Understandably, a milder punishment for such an act could have been justifiable when Islam was in its infancy and needed more able-bodied persons to defend it. Yet, given today's world population, such a need is no longer valid, and punishing "free-willed people" for joining another faith, especially when the Quran explicitly states "compel not mankind to believe against their will" (Quran, Surat 99: 99) may demonstrate an attitude of intolerance.

From a practical perspective, a major obstacle to social innovation in Islamic states may have been the absence of fixed rules of succession within the Islamic state. This obstacle may have seriously undermined the stability of Islam and its long-term plans to pursue social innovation. The principle of primogeniture that has been uniformly applied in European and Asian societies (regardless of its merit) has largely been ignored in Islam, at least during the last 200 years. Except in a few Moslem states, all male members of the extended ruling family are considered acceptable candidates for "rulership"—be they brothers, nephews, cousins, or uncles, as well as sons and grandsons. Furthermore, while, in theory, the Islamic ruler is selected by acclamation, this mode of selection has not been institutionalized. Hence, given the relatively long periods required for implementing social transformation, it would be rather doubtful that a Moslem ruler would courageously embark on any transformational endeavor, not knowing who his successor would be, or if his wishes would be honored after his death. The fact that President Assad of Syria manipulated the constitutional system for electing presidents (allowing his son to follow him as president without activating the electoral process), and the fact that the terminally ill King Fahd of Saudi Arabia continues to be artificially kept alive may lend credibility to the seriousness of this obstacle.

In contrast to South East Asian countries, transformation processes in Moslem states have often ended in crises. In Egypt, for example, the assassination of the progressive President Anwar al-Sadat by Islamic Jihad terrorists in 1981 has been a cause célèbre in the annals of failure of Islam. The numerous acts of murder and robbery routinely committed by Moslem terrorists against wealthy Egyptian Copts in the 1980s and 1990's threatened the country with a serious national upheaval. In Algeria, the cancellation of the parliamentary elections in 1987, when the fundamentalist candidates won the election "fair and square," created a chronic crisis in the politics of the entire North African rim. Such "counterfeit" transformation processes (as they have been called) failed to allow a broad-based upward social mobility to the extent expected in a democracy. On the contrary, such processes can cause more drastic results when the expected transformation fails to touch upon the innermost human aspirations of the masses (e.g., freedom of religion, equality before the law, and the distribution of wealth) and when the expectation of upward mobility—with the exception of a small circle of family members and political cronies—seems to be blocked completely. Recently, the banning of approximately one third of the parliament members in Iran from running for re-election in 2004—when there was no legal or reasonable justification—may well face the Islamic Republic of Iran with one of its fiercest challenges.

Counterfeit transformation processes are neither unique to Islamic states nor can they be simply dismissed as acts of ignorance. Nevertheless, they seem to occur more frequently in Islamic states where the socio-political culture seems to make it easier to deny the "rule of law" for an entire class of people (e.g., Shiites, Druze, Kurds, non-Moslems, women, foreigners) under the ruse of a religious difference. To encourage "true" social innovation in the Islamic state—without causing social snaps or cultural intensification to occur—it may be necessary that the Moslem states "build a mental and emotional bridge between the historical legacy of Islam and the impending requirement of modernity" (Senghass, 1998: 38). Senghass explains that while most Islamic states are, by definition, dogmatic, historically they were able to secularize and modernize. The 1923 Turkish reformation by Kamel Ataturk may have been the most famous example. Yet the relatively more liberal and prosperous United Arab Emirates is another case in point. On a smaller scale, the footprints of genuine social innovation can also be seen in Oman, Bahrain, Qatar, Kuwait, Tunisia, and Lebanon. On a micro level, perhaps, President Mubaruk's recent edict allowing the Coptic Christmas Mass to be shown on government-controlled television was a welcome move toward implementing social innovation in Egypt. Finally, while transformational processes are usually gradual and creeping, in light of the global transformational phenomenon, it would be politically and economically irrational for the Islamic state not to consider institutionalizing.

Democracy

It has been said that un-free people cannot think, and if they do, they cannot reason. This view may explain why the vast majority of slaves in the United States were unable to free themselves. They submissively endured oppression until President Lincoln granted them freedom. Having said that, it is a mystery to discern why in the early period of Islam there were considerably more world-renowned Moslem philosophers (e.g., al-Farabi, Avicenna, Avernos, Ibn Khaldun, al-Tahtawi, and al-Afghani) than in the last two hundred years, when the world Moslem population may have since multiplied by a hundred fold. The virtual absence of democracy in Islamic states in the last two hundred years may be the key to understanding this mystery.

Most Moslem theologians prior to the 19th century (some would say even now) neither understood democracy nor cared to discover it. Although it is true that Islamic theology urges Moslems to honor fraternity, equality, liberty, and justice (Hassan, 1981: 40-43), the Islamic state was (and perhaps still is) unable to translate these benevolent principles into a socio-political agenda. Islamic states have traditionally been theocratic, and Moslems were most obliged to obey without questioning. Furthermore, while the Quran suggested "consultation among the believers" (Quran, Surat XLII: 40), this suggestion lacked specificity and was too hard to adequately interpret or enforce. As a result, after the death of the Prophet and the four Rashidin Caliphs—and notwithstanding the Quranic consultation obligation—virtually all matters of governance were left to the wisdom and temperament of the Moslem leader. In more cases than not, these leaders ruled autocratically and with total impunity. Recent examples of autocratic Moslem rulers may include Saddam Hussain of Iraq, Nasser of Egypt, Gadhafi of Libya, Assad of Syria, Soharto of Indonesia, and, in a more masked manner, the kings of Saudi Arabia and Mahathir Mohammed, the Prime Minister of Malaysia.

Historically, the Moslem dynasties that came to power after the four Rashideen Caliphs (e.g., Ummayads, Abbassides, Fatimides, Seljuks, and Ottomans) were all tribal in origin. Indeed, original Islam emerged from a tribal society to the extent that tribal influences were naturally imbedded in the Islamic concept of government. Ibn Khaldun, the renowned Moslem sociologist, argued that Bedouin tribesmen "provided for their own defense and did not entrust it to, or relied upon, others for it" (Hurewitz; 1969: 16). Ibn Khaldun explains that with the advent of urbanization, the Moslem rulers "lifted society to heights of glory by yielding leisure and tranquility [and] then thrusted it downward to the level of waste and squandering when the dynasty was seized by senility and chronic diseases causing its eventual destruction"(Hurewitz, 1969:16). While Ibn Khaldun was most likely accurate in his characterization, in recent Islamic history, most rulers appear to be more inept statesmen, if for no other reason than failing to capture and learn the moral of Ibn Khaldun's thesis.

While this book is not meant to be a commentary on political science, in the objective reality of the Islamic state, and given the impetus of social change, most Islamic states seem to suffer from a legitimacy crisis: the failure of the masses to recognize their rulers as their rightful representatives or as honest agents of change. Subsequently, a *prima facia* case can be made that as long as there are no constitutional mechanisms (social contractual agreements) to hold the rulers accountable to the will of the ruled, even the most benevolent Quranic obligations of liberty, fraternity, equality, and justice will be left to the whims of the state. Accordingly, the Islamic state (legitimately or not) will enforce its political will by condoning what it deems is in its interest and condemning what it deems not. The history of Islamic rule seems to have been replete with such political indiscretions. Needless to say, the final terroristic fury fueled by Osama bin Laden and his fundamentalist cadres demonstrates, to a substantial measure, a violent response to the legitimacy crisis they perceived in Saudi Arabia—the land of the most Holy Moslem shrines.

What makes the neglect of democracy in Islamic states more politically and socially damaging (than in non-Islamic states) is the fact that the masses in the Islamic state have historically been so harshly ruled; they have no other recourse to voice their will than by reacting as unimpressed spectators. Under such conditions, Islamic rulers found it convenient to restrict individual freedoms, suppress women and minorities, detain political prisoners, forbid traveling abroad, shut down newspapers, or unlawfully grab property that belongs to others—all with virtually no risk to their legitimacy as rulers. As an added insurance, most Islamic rulers typically keep a well-armed (yet highly pampered) military, the commanders of which are usually chosen from among the ruler's close family relatives. This allows the "aggressive" ruler to act autocratically; he may dismiss the parliament, manipulate the judiciary, misuse the police, impose unreasonable policies, and violate his own policies at will. In a composite sense, it can be fairly safe to state that the failures of democracy in the Islamic state is not necessarily because the rulers are more powerful or deviant than elsewhere, but because the "masses," deprived of democratic protection, are left "politically naked."

Having said that, it should be more apparent that the challenge of creating and strengthening democracy in the Islamic state is one of the most important (and most difficult) tasks the Islamic rulers now face. To achieve that, they must first recognize the unquestionable principle of "popular sovereignty" and willingly institutionalize a viable system of checks and balances to safeguard such sovereignty. Subsequently, it should be safe to assume that without a secular-type constitution that can, on the one hand, represent the wills and desires of the populace and, on the other hand, restrict the powers of government, the legitimacy of the Islamic state will always remain in question. Yet the fact remains that in most Moslem states a viable and empowering constitution does not exist, and, if it does, no solid popular support can be marshaled in its defense. One may then begin to understand why unreasonable rulers can, so easily, evade constitutional accountability under the ruse of some theological or political excuse. In more extremist Islamic republics, the rulers simply invoke "Hakimiat Allah" (the sacred power of God) as an all-encompassing excuse. The government of the Talibans of Afghanistan or the Mullahs of Iran is an example of this.

Finally, while monarchies, republics, and even dictatorships can claim democratic rule (e.g., Hitler came to power by the democratic electoral process, and he even appointed a Minister of Justice!), mature democracies evolve "maturely." Regulated by an enshrined constitution and supported by the true "consent of the governed," they can grow politically consistent, ideologically rational, and pluralistically responsible. Yet, for democracy to organically mature in the Islamic state, the state must "faithfully and persistently" support the democratic tenets of individualism, equality, rule of law, and due process, and it must enforce these principles without bias, deception, or prejudice. Furthermore, for democracy to flourish, the Islamic masses must be empowered to demand political reform, to demonstrate against injustice, and to be always assured that doing so will only be perceived as strengthening the state by reinvigorating democracy.

Responsible Government

Historically, all governments have at one time or another been accused of corruption. This is consistent with the universal belief that human beings, especially in the governance of one another, are neither "saints nor apes." In a sense, they are all fallible; no one is too good to be blameworthy or too bad to be unsalvageable. Yet, for the state to survive and prosper, the mechanism of government must observe certain rules and principles that are conducive to survival and progress and avoid practices that can cause society to falter and collapse.

Moreover, in the course of governance there have been governments that are more civil than others. Governments known for their civility make their societies safer, calmer, stronger, and more prosperous, while governments short on civility make their societies more vulnerable, erratic, weak, and hapless. In this context, a civil government can be characterized as one that is faithfully capable of: (1) executing all laws of the land; (2) administering society in an open, honest, fair, and reasonable manner; (3) accepting accountability for its mistakes; (4) acting always in good faith, and; (5) holding the trust of its citizens or their representatives.

At this point, the curious reader may be interested to know that the United Nations annually conducts a "responsible government" evaluation of its member states using a well-designed civility scale (e.g., the frequency of acts of political corruption, economic embezzlements, social scandals, crime rates, etc.). It should come as no surprise that, according to these evaluations, the Scandinavian countries consistently rank at the top of the list, with Finland as the country with the most responsible system of government, and most of the Moslem States rank at the bottom (Corruption, The Economist, August, 2002:78).

In pure Islamic doctrine, issues of responsible government have been paramount. Second only to ensuring monotheism, the most central purpose of the Islamic state has been promoting a civil society. Hassan chronicles that, before Islam, the pagan Arabs were substantially lacking in civility. Hassan states:

> *"[they] were possessed of [a] group feeling and overbearing pride...they were least willing to subordinate themselves to each other...they were rude, ambitious, and eager to be leaders... Bani Ishmael [in particular] were predominated by elements opposed to social harmony...they were by habit and nature misconceived in understanding and unable to fully grasp the benefits of social order" (Hassan, 1981: 21-25).*

Hassan suggests, however, that much of these uncivil qualities were promptly corrected upon the advent of Islam. The Islamic tradition, he adds, had a restraining influence upon the pagan qualities of arrogance, corruption, betrayal, and jealousy. For example, the Quran, in the story of Shuaib, emphasizes the need for Moslems to treat each other in a civil manner. Like Socrates, Shuaib, a pre-Islamic prophet, devoted his life to teaching the people to tell the truth, to be faithful, to honor each other, and to shun acts of social and economic corruption. Specifically, he implored merchants and traders to not overcharge their customers and to ensure the measures and weights they use are fair and well-calibrated. If in doubt, Shuaib recommended, the seller must add a free extra unit of measure (Bahgat, 1993: 156).

As evidence, Hassan explains that with the advent of Islam the government of Mecca was greatly improved. The residents of the city were united in an Ummah (community), and since tribal loyalty was the cornerstone of social life, one's identification with a tribe was expanded beyond blood-kinship. It included identification by adoption, allegiance, or acclamation. Furthermore, Mecca became better administered. All governmental posts were held accountable to a board of elected tribal leaders. The city established an assembly (senate) which framed rules of behavior and enforced them equally on all citizens . Even in military matters, a social contract was framed by which the commanding general of the fighting army was given one-fourth of the war booty, and the rest was to be distributed equitably among the soldiers (Hassan, 1981: 23).

Based on Hassan's commentary, it appears that the influence of Islam was effective in establishing an impressive level of civility during the time of the Prophet and his Rashideen Caliphs. This level of civility was even more apparent when the Moslems later occupied Persia, Egypt, North Africa, and Spain (Armajani, 1970, Hitti, 1967; Lewis, 2002). Yet, while the civility of the Islamic state may have been successful in introducing fair and egalitarian systems in the conquered lands, such civility may have been considerably diminished when the Islamic state—as Ibn Khaldoun predicted—later became wealthy and prosperous. And if Ibn Khaldoun's commentary was accurate, then the future of some modern Islamic states may hang in the balance, since they are virtually "drowned in sudden wealth" generated by the high prices of seemingly unending oil reserves.

Baer (2003) paints a dismal picture of the extent of social and economic corruption in Islamic states in general, and in the Kingdom of Saudi Arabia in particular. He provides an alarming socio-economic profile of government recklessness in Saudi Arabia. The following are only examples:

> *Saudis with money don't have to take no for an answer. In the early 1970s, when the petrodollars started flooding in, enterprising Lebanese began smuggling hookers into the kingdom for the princes. Since the women were posing as Middle East Airlines flight attendants and were driven directly to the royal palaces, the muttawee (religious police) couldn't do anything about it. Since no one in the royal family knows how to balance the checkbook, the Lebanese became fabulously rich (Baer, 2003: 26).*

> *King Fahd's administrator for the palace near Antibes, France, once made a formal proposal to the French government that is still talked about today. The King wanted to move the Paris-Nice railroad track away from the palace. It didn't matter that the existing line didn't run all that near the palace, or that moving it would cost millions. Fahd, the administrator explained, would be annoyed to hear even the distant sound of passing trains while strolling in his garden (Baer, 2003: 27).*

King Hassan of Morocco allowed dozens of Saudi princes to build secluded estates in Morocco, many in the rugged mountains of Tangiers, the area called the RIF. The area was wild and lawless—a perfect place to hold an orgy or go on a drinking binge, away from the prying eyes of the Wahhabis back home and the Western press in Europe's old watering holes. In return for Morocco's delicate diplomacy, the governments of Saudi Arabia and the Gulf states dumped loads of money into the country (Morocco). It's impossible to calculate precisely how much, but there are tantalizing hints: the Saudi Defense minister secretly bought Societe' Annonyme Marocaine de LiIndustrie du Raffinage (SAMIR) Morocco's oil refinery, for $420 million. The transaction was handled through a cascade of nominees, shelf companies, and middlemen to keep the minister's name out of the press (Baer, 2003: 28).

Baer also provides a profile of administrative corruption in Saudi Arabia. He states:

Right through September 11, 2001, Saudis were not even required to appear at the US Embassy in Riyadh or the consulate in Jeddah for a visa interview. Under a Saudi system called Visa Express, a Saudi had only to send his passport, an application, and a fee to a travel agent to get a visa. The Saudi travel agent, in other words, stood in for the American government. A short wait, and any Saudi who had the money for a flight was on his way to New York—to disappear like a diamond in an inkwell or to run his airplane into a skyscraper (Baer, 2003: 32).

Even after the 1998 attacks on the U.S. embassies in Kenya and Tanzania, organized by bin Laden from Afghanistan, Saudi Arabia continued to aid his host, the Taliban. In July 2002 the Petroleum Intelligence Weekly reported that the government of Saudi Arabia was sending as many as 150,000 barrels of oil a day to Afghanistan and Pakistan in off-the-books foreign aid. This tactic of sending free oil in lieu of cash was, apparently, an established Saudi government practice (Baer, 2003: 33-34).

Princess Haifa (wife of the Saudi Ambassador to the United States) allegedly contributed $130,000 to a Saudi national who aided two of the September 11 hijackers. When added to another contribution by an anonymous Saudi in the amount of $550,000, the total contribution would exceed the $550,000 the FBI estimated as the total cost of the 9/11 attacks. Baer points out that through an unbroken string of pretences, intrigues and deceptive acts, the Saudi State managed to support and finance the Wahhabi movement that, to a large measure, fueled hatred and violence throughout the Moslem world. Baer adds that the same corruption (by the Saudi government) is believed to take place in the other rich oil states, including Kuwait, the United Arab Emirates, Libya, Bahrain, and Qatar. Through similarly corrupt practices, these Moslem states were also able to support and finance the Talibans of Afghanistan and their Pakistani surrogates. As a result, through similarly irresponsible government deals, it was possible for the obscure Moslem Brotherhood organization to thrive and dominate the entire Moslem world and for its favorite son, Osama bin Laden, to preside over the most extensive terrorist organization in history (Baer, 2003: 69).

Sources

Armajani, Y. (1970). *Middle East Past and Present*. Englewood Cliffs, NJ: Prentice-Hall.

Bahgat, A. (1993). *Anbia' Al-Allah (The Prophets of God)*. Cairo: Dar Al-Shoroq.

Bebawy, N. (2003). *Terrorism: a non-Islamic Industry*. Cairo: Alahram Publishers.

Baer, R. (2003). *Sleeping With the Devil: How Washington Sold Our Soul for Saudi Arabia*. Santa Barbara: Crown Publishers.

"Corruption," *The Economist*, August, 2002, p.78.

Hurewitz, J.C. (1969). *Middle East Politics: The Military Dimension*. New York: Praeger Publishers.

Friedman, T. (February 21, 2004). "Arabs Wondering how they ever tolerated Hussein" *The Dallas Morning News*.

Gibran, K. (1979). *A Third Treasury of Kahihlil Gibran*.New York, N.Y. Castle Books.

Hassan, F. (1981). *The Concept of State and Law in Islam*. Washington, DC: University Press of America.

Hitti, P. K. (1967). *History of the Arabs: From the Earliest Times to the Present* (9th Ed.). New York: St. Martin's Press.

"Saudis Ban Barbie Dolls" *Japan Today News*. (2004). . Retrieved online at www.japantoday.com/gidx/news272237.html on February 16th, 2004.

Lewis, B. (2002). *What Went Wrong? Western Impact and Middle Eastern Response*. New York: Oxford.

Epilogue

Is there any hope for the New Islamic State? Will social innovation, democracy, and responsible government succeed? The answer to these two questions is definitely yes. This judgment is based on the unfailing theory of history. Since the inception of Islam, or for that matter any other faith, there have been religious ebbs and tides, socio-political alignments and de-alignments, as well as military Nakbas and redemptions. Since the days of Mohammed, the Islamic state has survived numerous crises, including the Prophet's forced Hijrah to Medina, the apostasy movement that followed Mohammed's death, the assassination of three of the four Rashidin Caliphs (i.e., Omar, Othman, and Ali), the split between Sunni and Shiite Moslems, the estrangement (if not the military conflicts) between the Moslem Caliphs (e.g., Ummayads, Abbassides, and Ottomans) and their wallis (local rulers) overseas (e.g., Spain, Egypt, Syria, Iraq, Morocco), the devastating Crusaders, the imperial Colonials, the Israelis, and, of course, the calamitous terrorism.

Yet each of these crises was followed by an intellectual awakening, a renaissance, so to speak, one that was led by neo-romanticist thinkers who rejected the rigidity of the Islamic state. Famous among these thinkers are Mohammed Ali, Gamal El-din al-Afghani, Mohammed Abdu, Mohammed Farid, Mustafa Kamel, Kamal Attaturk, and, Taha Hussain. Yet, in the trans-cultural history of the Arabs, no one expressed this neo-romanticist sentiment better than Kahlil Gibran (1883-1931).

Gibran, an American-Lebanese poet who, in the early 1920s, was outraged by the disastrous occupation of his homeland by the reactionary Ottoman forces, implored his countrymen to rise and reverse the Nakba.

In an inspiring yet scathing poem, Gibran addressed his countrymen saying (Gibran, 1979:24-25):

> *What do you seek of me my countrymen?*
> *Do you wish that I falsely promise to build for you great palaces out of words, and temples roofed with dreams?*
> *Or would you rather I destroy the work of liars and cowards and demolish the work of hypocrites and tyrants?*
>
> *I sang for you but you did not dance;*
> *I lamented but you did not cry.*
> *Do you wish that I sing and lament at the same time?*
>
> *Your souls are hungry and the bread of knowledge is more plentiful than the stones of the valleys, but you do not eat.*
>
> *The sea has its ebb and tide, the moon its crescent and fullness, and the year has its seasons of summer and winter, but justice never changes, never falters, never perishes.*
>
> *Why, then, do you attempt to distort the truth?*

Recently, two Moslem neo-romanticist thinkers (neither of whom is of Gibran's caliber) addressed the status of the Moslem world (Friedman, 2004). They were Osama al-Ghazali Harb, an Egyptian journalist, and Abd-al-Hamid al-Ansari, a Qatarian academic. Harb stated:

> *What we, [as Moslems], should be humiliated about are the prevailing political and social conditions in the Arab world especially in Iraq which allowed someone such as Saddam Hussein to assume the presidency. We should feel humiliated that he was single-handedly able to initiate a number of catastrophic policies that transformed Iraq, a relatively rich [country] in natural, human, and financial resources, into the poorest, most debt-ridden country in the Arab world, not to mention the hundreds of thousands [he] killed and displaced.*
>
> *We should feel humiliated that some of our intellectuals, supposedly representatives of our national consciences and the defenders of their liberty and dignity, not only dealt with Sad-*

dam Hussein but also supported him. The Arabs should have been the ones to bring down Saddam Hussein in defense of their own dignity and their true interests.

Ansari stated:

Let us describe the situation of the Arabs, especially those of Iraq, had America listened to the European counsel that said: Democracy isn't suited to the Moslems; their culture is contrary to it...See now how many [Moslem] countries are turning to democracy. Even Afghanistan has a constitution [and] in Iraq, they are drafting a new constitution and handing over the regime and Libya has also changed.

In the tradition of Gibran who implored his countrymen's children, I too, as an academician, implore the children of my former classmates, friends, and neighbors in the Islamic world, be they Moslems, Christians, or Jews. Here also, I use Gibran's undying words (Gibran, 1979: 31):

The soul is a sacred blue-burning flame, illuminating the face of the gods. [Our] children are the lamps that cannot be snuffed by the winds and the salt which remains unspoiled through the ages. [You] are the ones who must be moving toward perfection, beauty and the truth.

I say this because, if for no other reason, it is, and forever will be, the will of the Creator, without whom no religion would have existed, let alone made any sense.

Sources

Friedman, T. (February 21, 2004). "Arabs Wondering how they ever tolerated Hussein" *The Dallas Morning News.*

Gibran, K. (1979). *A Third Treasury of Kahihlil Gibran*. New York, N.Y. Castle Books.

Glossary

(All terms are Arabic unless noted otherwise)

Abaya: a black outer garment worn by some Moslem women.

Abdullah: literally "the slave of God," one of the most common Moslem names.

Adha: the day of atonement.

Ahkam al-Shariah: limitations of the path, the body of ordained rules from the Quran.

Ahl-il-Kitab: non-Moslem people who believe in a holy scripture, i.e., Jews and Christians.

Al-Alameen: all people universally.

Al-Ansar: the local residents of Yathrib who offered refuge to, and supported, Mohammed and his Muhajirin.

"Al-baina ala men ida' wa al yamin ala men ankar": literally, "the burden of proof is on the accuser and the burden of denial is by taking an oath."

Al-barid: postal service.

Algabr: a branch of mathematics which meant "the study of fractions."

Aliyas: (Hebrew) migrations.

Allah: Islamic name for God.

Allahu Akbar: God is Great, the most common religious phrase pronounced by Moslems whenever there is great fear or celebration.

Al-li'an: the offense of accusing one's wife of adultery without producing the required evidence.

Al-Medina al-Munawara: "the enlightened city," the name given by Mohammed to the old city of Yathrib.

Al-Mohtasib: designated officials known for good reputation and irreproachable character, often used to conduct interrogations.

Al-Muhajirun: the emigrants who came with Mohammed from Mecca to Yathrib.

Al Qaeda: a common Arabic word that means the "base" or the "rule; more commonly known now as the name of Osama bin Laden's terrorist group.

Al-rashidin: the most wise, a common way of referring to the first four caliphs.

Al-zihar: an offense committed by Arab husbands who during the jahiliyah period punished their wives by abstaining from having sexual intercourse with them.

Amir Al-jihad: leader of jihad.

Ansar Al-Islam: supporters of Islam, a term that is used by some radical Islamic groups currently fighting in Iraq.

Ashura: the practice of observing the first ten days of the Hijri month of Muharram as days of lamentations in memory of the "absent Imam."

Asr: afternoon.

Assas: night detectives who stealthily patrol the streets.

Aurf: Islamic tradition; one of three sub-sources of Islamic jurisprudence.

Ayatollah: the "verse of God," the highest rank among Shiite Moslem clerics.

Baghi: transgression or corruption.

Bait al-Mal: the Moslem state treasury.

Berbers: ancient residents of Morocco, also known as Moors. It is possibly a derivation from German for "barbarian."

Bidaa: a human creation; an Islamic practice which is not derived from the Quran or the Sunna, and thus considered heresy.

Caliph: literally, "the successor"; leader of the Moslem Ummah.

Caliphate: the system of government used by the early Moslem rulers.

Chador: full length black veil.

Din: in Hebrew, "law," in Arabic, "religion."

Diwan: a formal meeting or a governmental office where the leader meets petitioners.

Diwan al-Mazalim: court of appeals.

Diwan of Zimam: the tax bureau.

Diya: blood money, paid by an offender instead of forgoing punishment.

Elohim: Jewish name for God.

Fadel: the title of an ethical ruler.

Fajr: dawn.

Fard: a scriptural obligation.

Fatwa: a religious statement that condones or condemns a behavior.

Fedayyin-el-Islam: martyrs of Islam, a chapter of the Egyptian Moslem Brotherhood.

Ferud: plural of fard, a scriptural obligation.

Franj: the Franks; a common reference to the Crusaders.

Hadith: statements and acts of the Prophet.

Hadd: punishment for crimes that are considered against the limitations of God.

Hajj: pilgrimage to the Kabba in Mecca. One of the five pillars of Islamic faith.

Hakimiat Allah: God's government, the unquestionable rule of God.

Haram: forbidden by commandment.

Hijrah: emigration, usually refers to Mohammed's first journey to Medina.

Hijri: Islamic calendar commemorating Mohammed's journey to Medina, based on the Jewish lunar calendar it is 11 days shorter than the Gregorian calendar (accordingly, every 34 Hijri years would equal 33 Gregorian years).

Hiraa': the cave outside Mecca which Mohammed frequented for meditation and prayer.

Hiraba: banditry, highway robbery.

Hirz: private place to store property.

Hizballah: the Party of God, initially started in Iran.

Hojat-Allah: the title of a middle-rank Shiite cleric.

Huddud: plural of Hadd meaning God's limitations. Also a category of crimes under Shariah law; crimes against the sovereignty of God.

Ibada: acts of worship.

Ibn Rushd: Islamic philosopher, known in the West as Avernos.

Ihsan: paying alms or right doing.

Ijma': consensus; the third highest source of Islamic jurisprudence, it is the consensus of the majority of ulama.

Ijtihad: doctrine of intellectual industriousness by Islamic scholars, used to handle the exigencies of interpreting the Quran. It is the fourth highest source of Islamic jurisprudence.

Ikhwan: brothers, more commonly as in Moslem Brothers and Moslem Brotherhood.

Iman: religious belief.

Imam: an Islamic religious leader or preacher.

Infidels: pagans and heathens (i.e., non-Islamic and non-Judeo-Christian).

Infitah: the opening as in economic matters.

Iqrar: confession or admission of committing a crime.

Irhab: causing immense fear; causing terror by acts of violence such as murder, using explosives or sabotage.

Isha: night.

Islam: the prominent religion originating in Arabia. The word can be interpreted two ways: "peace" as in the term "peace be with you," or "submission" as in one's wholehearted "submission to God."

Islamic Amal: Moslem hope.

Isra': Mohammed's nocturnal journey to heaven and back.

Issa: Jesus, son of Joseph.

Istihsan: preferred ideas. One of three sub-sources of Islamic jurisprudence.

Istislah: reformed ideas. One of three sub-sources of Islamic jurisprudence.

Izedaka: Hebrew for almsgiving.

Jahiliyah: the state of pre-Islamic ignorance, often in reference to matters of idolatry, ignorance, character rottenness and social decay that permeated the ancient Arabian culture. Currently used to refer to corruptness.

Jamah: community or group.

Jihad: literally, "a pursuit," "an endeavor," or "an earnest attempt." In a religious context it could mean "fighting for God's cause," or "holy war."

Jihadi: an American colloquial reference to anyone who participates in a Jihad.

Jizya: personal tax paid by zimmis in return for state protection.

Kabba: the temple of monotheism in Mecca reportedly built by Abraham.

Kafala: the voluntary sponsorship of a non-Moslem by a Moslem.

Khandaq: trench, as in warfare.

Khatim al-Anbyia: the completer of all religions, a designation given to Mohammed in regards to his status as the last prophet of God.

Khomeini: from Komein. The name of the first leader of the Islamic Republic in Iran.

Kohol: alcohol, as in drinking alcohol.

Kufr: blasphemy.

Lebensraum: (German) living space.

Maarouf: offering a service without expecting a reward.

Ma'soum: a married person, usually a female.

Madrassas: plural of madrassa, a school for children where religious commandments are taught, a derivation of the Jewish word "Midrash" which meant the same kind of teaching.

Maghrib: sunset.

Majlis: open meeting held regularly by the rulers of the state.

Majlis al shura: consultative council.

Makhzan: magazine or a public source of information.

Makruh: a characterization of an unacceptable behavior yet not punishable.

Mandub: a characterization of a matter that is meritorious or recommended.

Matrah: mattress or a specific space.

Meriam: the name of the Holy Mother, the mother of Jesus.

Miqra: Jewish scriptures at the time of Mohammed, from the root "qaraa" meaning "reading."

Mohammed: The Prophet of Islam, the name literally means "the Praised One."

Mohammedan: An older adjective, considered objectionable to both Moslems and Muslims since the Quran explicitly forbids worshiping Mohammed.

Moslem: the Islamic people from the Middle East region as well as from different parts of the world other than the United States.

Mua'zzen: a special reader who proclaims the scriptures five times a day from the rooftops of the mosques.

Mubah: a characterization of a matter that brings neither reward nor punishment.

Mujahedeen: (plural of Mujahid) those who fight for God, the warriors of God.

Mugtahid: jurisprudence consultant.

Mullah: a high ranking religious scholar, usually a Shiite.

Munzal: a message that descended from above, of divine origin.

Muslim: Used to identify converts to Islam, especially in the United States (i.e., the Nation of Islam).

Musta'min: a non-Christian or non-Jew who has entered the land of Islam pursuant to a peace treaty.

Mutawee: a lay cleric who roams the streets to watch for immoral activities.

Nakba: a major setback as in a military defeat.

Nomos: Greek for a set of norms.

Nisab: value, as in one's share.

Qadhf: defamation, usually against the chastity of women.

Qadi: judge.

Qahwa: coffee.

Qanun: the rule, also an encyclopedia of medicine written by Avicennia.

Qashar: Arabic version of the Hebrew "kosher," i.e., religiously permitted foods.

Qeryana: what the Christians called their scriptures at the time of Mohammed, possibly from the same root as the Jewish term "Miqra."

Qibla: the direction which the Moslems face during prayer.

Qissas: literally, "the equivalent," crimes against another's bodily integrity, a category of crimes under Shariah law known as "retaliation" crimes. Also refers to the penalty for such crimes.

Qiyas: analogy. The fifth highest source of Islamic jurisprudence, roughly equivalent to stare decisis in Western law.

Quran: the holy text of Islam, the name literally means "Reading." It is the highest source of Islamic jurisprudence.

Rahbah: immense fear, also awe, respect, or piety.

Rashidin: the wise, as the first four Caliphs were called.

Rasul: prophct or messenger.

Riddah: apostasy.

Rohallah: the soul of Allah, a higher ranking Shiite cleric.

Salat: prayer, one of the five pillars of Islam.

Sabt: Sabbath or Saturday.

Sadaka: almsgiving.

Salah-al-Din: more commonly known in the West as Saladin.

Sariqa: theft or larceny.

Shaheed: martyr.

Shahinshah: the king of kings, the ruler of Iran until Ayatollah Khomeini assumed control of the Iranian government.

Shariah: a pathway. Invariably used to mean "law."

Shehada: a testimony of faith. One of the five pillars of Islam.

Shiites: adherents to the fourth Caliph Ali who was murdered in Karballa in the 40th year of Hijrah during a bloody struggle over succession.

Shorb al-khamr: the crime of drinking alcohol.

Shurta: police departments.

Siyam: fasting. One of the five pillars of Islamic faith.

Sufa: sofa.

Sunna: practices of the Prophet, the basis of the Sunni sect of Islam. The second highest source of Islamic jurisprudence.

Sunni: a sect of Islam based on the Sunna.

Surat: a chapter of the Quran, probably a misreading of the Jewish word "sedra" which means a chapter of the Torah.

Taqwa: perpetual piety.

Tarifa: tariff.

Tawla: towel.

Tazir: a category of crimes under Shariah law, the punishment of which are neither prescribed in the Quran nor the Sunna.

Ulema: plural of alim, meaning religious scholar. These scholars are entrusted with extracting practical, legislative, or judicial regulations out of the Quran.

Ummah: Islamic society or nation, a community of believers.

Unzil: that which descended from Heaven.

Wahhabi: a puritanical religious and social discipline of Islam.

Wali al-Mazalim: the minister of complaints, a position equivalent to today's Attorney General.

Wazir: vizier or minister.

Zakah: religious tax, paid to the bait al-Mal.

Zakat: charity offerings, often divided into two categories: Zakat al Fitr and Zakat based on wealth. One of the five pillars of Islamic faith.

Zakat al Fitr: charity offerings paid before breaking the fast at the end of Ramadan.

Zakat based on wealth: required of all adults who possess some wealth, used to support the poor.

Zaydis: followers of Zayd, a Shiite tribe in Yemen.

Zena: adultery.

Zihar: literally, "the backside" of a person; religiously, the practice of turning one's back to his/her partner indicating a lack of interest in intimacy.

Zimmis: non-Moslems in Moslem lands; from *zimma*, meaning under the protection of others.

Zuhr: noon.

Index

A

Abbasid 61, 176
Abdullah Azzam 201, 203
Abdul Muttalib 34
Abraham 20, 21, 24, 36, 176, 178
Abu-Zahra 74, 101, 127
Abu Bakr 36, 75, 97
Abu Talib 34, 38
Adam 20, 24, 36
adultery 87, 94, 95, 102, 103, 105, 115, 136, 148, 149, 151, 153, 154
Afghanistan 13, 15, 16, 159, 199, 202, 203, 204, 205, 209, 218, 222, 227
Ahl-il-Kitab 23, 229
al-Ansar 38, 203, 229
al-Awa 98, 104, 122, 148, 153
al-Farabi 59, 216
al-li'an 94, 95, 105, 230
al-Muhajirun 38, 230
al-Quds 176
al-Razi 59
al-zihar 94, 230
Ali 54, 55
Aliya 176, 230
Al Qaeda 199, 230
Aman Writs 56
Amir al-Jihad 203, 230
Amr ibn-al-As 13, 43, 57, 176
angel 21, 26, 35, 44
Ansar al-Islam 38, 230
Anwar al-Sadat 215
apostasy 48, 54, 103, 107, 135, 140, 225
apostle 13, 15, 82, 93, 170
Arab-Israeli war 177, 179
Arab military 179
Aramaic 24, 58
Armajani 33, 34, 35, 36, 40, 56, 60, 170, 221
Ashura 35, 56, 230
Asrael 44
Assad of Syria 217
assassin 76, 158, 195
Athanasius Contra Mundum 203, 206
Atiyah 173
Avicennia 60
Ayatollah 189, 190, 191, 192, 193, 195, 197, 202, 231

B

Badr 40, 41
Baer 49, 199, 202, 207, 221, 222
Baghdad 49, 61, 76, 169
Baghi 231
Bait-al-Ansar 203
Bait al-Mal 41, 55, 231
Balfour Declaration 177
Basra 49

Bassiouni 68, 81, 82, 84, 113, 135, 147
Bebawy 27, 39, 41, 42, 43, 44, 47, 48, 54, 55, 56, 68, 97, 209, 210
Beirut 16, 163, 196
Berber 57, 58, 231
Bidaa 231
Britain 176, 177, 178
Bucallie 175
Byzantine 15, 27, 30, 55, 57, 157

C

Caliph 36, 48, 49, 55, 56, 57, 58, 59, 61, 75, 96, 97, 107, 123, 128, 129, 134, 142, 153, 154, 169, 212, 217, 221, 225, 231
Caliphate 54, 231
Caliph Ali 54
Canaan 21, 38
capitalism 162, 213
colonialism 14, 76, 173
communism 14, 160
communist 160, 178, 191
confession 102, 127, 147, 150, 151, 153
Constantinople 60, 61, 170, 206
Coptic 13, 15, 57, 77, 216
Copts 13, 14, 15, 215
crusade 45, 51, 158, 166, 169, 170, 173, 174, 175, 178, 202, 203
crusader 14, 15, 26, 45, 47, 61, 158, 169, 170, 172, 178, 194, 199, 207, 225
Cyrus 57

D

Damascus 48, 58, 61, 176
Dante 26
death penalty 115, 116
defamation 37, 95, 103, 105, 117, 154
democracy 29, 45, 70, 75, 160, 178, 210, 211, 215, 216, 217, 219, 225, 227
Divine Comedy 26
diya 86, 97, 112, 113, 114, 117
drinking alcohol 23, 65, 68, 94, 98, 102, 117, 138, 153
Druze 56, 158, 215
Durkheim 89

E

equality 30, 69, 77, 85, 96, 97, 113, 129, 211, 213, 215, 216, 217, 219
Exodus 25, 175

F

fard 71, 83, 232
ferud 26, 44, 71, 232
five pillars of Islam 24, 77
Flagellation 116
franj 58, 158, 171, 232
Franks 170
fundamentalism 11, 14, 47, 157, 159, 160, 162, 166, 173

G

Gabriel 21, 26, 44
Gadhafi 217
Gibraltar 58
Gibran 223, 225, 226, 227
Gulf War 77, 205

H

Hadd 83, 97, 103, 105, 107, 115, 117, 122, 140, 153, 154, 232
Hajj 72, 177, 232
Hanafi 76, 104, 105, 107, 128, 138, 143, 147, 148, 149, 151, 153, 154
Hanbali 76, 104, 105, 147, 149, 151, 153, 154

Hassan 67, 69, 70, 216, 220, 221, 222
Hegel 88
Hertzl 176
Hijrah 23, 25, 38, 54, 57, 70, 225, 232
Hijri 25, 40, 42, 43, 44, 56, 57, 58, 68, 194, 232
Hiraa' 35, 233
hiraba 104, 233
Hitler 45, 163, 218
Hitti 54, 57, 58, 59, 157, 158, 169, 170, 172, 176, 221
Hoffman 28, 46, 47, 49, 98
Hoveyda 190, 191, 192, 193
Huddud 25, 66, 83, 93, 102, 108, 111, 114, 116, 117, 119, 120, 121, 126, 128, 135, 137, 138, 139, 140, 148, 149, 151, 152, 233
Human Rights Convention 78
Huntington 163
Hykal 24, 26, 27, 33, 34, 35, 36, 37

I

ibada 71, 233
ibn-al-Walid 57
Ibn Khaldoun 221
Ibn Taymiah 207
ihsan 71, 233
ijma' 74, 233
ijtihad 67, 74, 233
imam 55, 56, 102, 105, 117, 121, 122, 126, 128, 143, 233
iman 71, 233
Impartial Trial 129
Incarceration 116
infidel 14, 41, 47, 49, 54, 75, 77, 157, 189, 190, 195, 203, 204, 205, 233
infitah 212, 233
Interpol 109
interrogation 123, 126, 184
intihar 186
Iqrar 150, 234
Iran 30, 56, 69, 75, 76, 159, 161, 189, 190, 191, 192, 193, 194, 196, 202, 215, 218
Iranian Revolution 189, 194
Islamic State(s) 22, 33, 40, 44, 53, 55, 67, 68, 70, 71, 75, 76, 85, 113, 122, 124, 125, 209, 213, 214, 215, 216, 217, 218, 220, 221, 225
Islam is the Solution 160
Ismailite 56, 158
Israel 14, 30, 36, 78, 159, 165, 166, 175, 177, 178, 179, 180, 182, 183, 195, 206, 225
istishhad 186

J

jahiliyah 23, 35, 54, 66, 94, 96, 119, 211, 212, 234
Jerusalem 13, 38, 39, 45, 46, 60, 169, 170, 171, 172, 175, 176, 177, 182, 196, 199, 200, 214
Jesus 20, 21, 22, 25, 27, 28, 33, 40, 46, 50, 157
jihad 14, 47, 161, 162, 185, 202, 203, 215, 234
jizya 68, 78, 235

K

Kabba 33, 37, 39, 214, 235
Karbala 55
Khadija 34, 36, 38, 45
Khalid ibn-al-Walid 55
Khandaq 41, 235
Khomeini 166, 189, 191, 196, 235
King Abdul Aziz 200
King David 38, 175

L

Lawrence of Arabia 177
League of Nations 177
Lewis 20, 29, 158, 161, 179, 221
lex talionis 89, 111

M

Maalouf 46, 171, 172
Madrassa 24, 235
Mahatma Gandhi 160
Majlis 70, 206, 235
Maliki 76, 104, 105, 107, 138, 149, 151, 154
Maronite 158
Mary 27, 46
Matthew 90
Mecca 21, 23, 25, 33, 35, 36, 37, 38, 40, 41, 42, 43, 50, 68, 72, 96, 189, 191, 199, 200, 204, 213, 220
Medina 23, 25, 38, 40, 42, 44, 46, 48, 50, 55, 57, 68, 123, 199, 200, 203, 204, 225
Mohammed ibn Abd-al-Wahhab 49
Moses 20, 22, 24, 25, 27, 35, 40, 46, 47, 157, 161
Mu'awiyah 49
mujahedeen 202, 204, 205, 210, 236
munzal 48, 50, 236
Mutawee 98, 237

N

nakba 175, 183, 196, 225, 237
Nasser 180, 197, 201, 203, 217
natural law 90
Nebuchadnezzar 38
new Islamic state 55, 225
Noah 20, 24, 36
nomos 83, 237
nullification of penalty by doubt 119, 121

O

Othman 48, 61, 75, 225
Ottoman 61, 176, 217, 225

P

Palestine 16, 30, 61, 175, 176, 177, 179, 183
Pan Arabism 197
Pan Islamism 197
Patai 158, 173
Plato 58, 59, 84
PLO 161, 193
pope 14, 25, 26, 29, 47, 69, 170
Pope Innocent 26
Pope John Paul 26
Pope Urban 170
President Assad 214
President Lincoln 216
President Mubaruk 216
presumption of innocence 119, 120, 153

Q

Qadi 66, 69, 85, 94, 114, 142, 147, 148, 154, 237
Qibla 39, 237
Qissas 89, 93, 97, 102, 111, 112, 113, 114, 116, 117, 119, 121, 126, 135, 137, 139, 140, 144, 148, 149, 151, 152, 237
Qiyas 74, 144, 237
Quran 11, 21, 22, 23, 25, 26, 28, 30, 33, 35, 41, 44, 45, 48, 49, 60, 66, 68, 69, 70, 72, 73, 74, 76, 82, 84, 85, 93, 95, 96, 98, 102, 104, 106, 107, 112, 120, 123, 129, 133, 147, 158, 165, 190, 191, 192, 194, 211, 214, 216, 217, 220, 238

R

rahbah 164, 238
Ramadan 29, 35, 40, 43, 72, 77
Rashidin Caliphs 212, 216, 225
responsible government 211, 219, 225
Richard the Lion-Hearted 45, 172

riddah 54, 55, 238

S

Saddam Hussein 172, 173, 204, 226
Sahifa Accord 39
Saint Francis 160
Saint Thomas Aquinas 26
Salah-al-Din 172
Salah al-Din al-Ayouby 61
salat 26, 72, 238
Sanad 11, 68, 78, 94, 95, 96, 101, 113, 115, 116, 120, 121, 122, 123, 125, 127, 128, 129, 133, 134, 136, 137, 139, 140, 142, 143, 148, 151, 154
Sariqa (theft) 65, 66, 82, 88, 90, 92, 97, 102, 104, 108, 111, 115, 117, 135, 238
Saudi Arabia 37, 42, 47, 49, 68, 75, 76, 98, 108, 109, 160, 161, 179, 199, 200, 201, 203, 205, 215, 217, 221, 222
search and seizure 123
secularism 161
Seljuks 170, 217
Senghass 28, 159, 215
September 11th 15, 164, 184
Shafi'i(s) 76, 104, 105, 107, 140, 147, 149, 151, 153, 154
Shah 189, 191
shaheed 41, 185, 238
shariah 29, 65, 66, 69, 73, 74, 75, 76, 82, 83, 84, 85, 86, 87, 94, 96, 99, 101, 104, 108, 112, 113, 114, 119, 122, 126, 127, 128, 142, 143, 144, 147, 151, 159, 192, 238
shehada 25, 71, 77, 194, 238
Shiism 55
Shiite 50, 54, 55, 56, 75, 190, 191, 193, 195, 202, 204, 206, 215, 225, 238
Shorb al-khamr 106, 238
shuhada 186
sine qua non 92
Siyam 72, 239
social innovation 211, 212, 213, 214, 215, 225
Socrates 160, 220
soldiers of God 196
Somalia 54, 205, 207
Souryal 65, 66, 81, 83, 84, 87, 102, 160, 162
Soviet Union 54, 163, 177, 206
St. Francis 172
Sudan 54, 201, 205
suicide 35, 163, 183, 184, 186, 194, 195, 207
Sunna 54, 73, 74, 76, 82, 85, 93, 102, 107, 120, 129, 239
Sunni 54, 225, 239

T

Tariq ibn Ziad 58
Tazir 93, 102, 103, 106, 114, 115, 117, 119, 121, 137, 139, 140, 143, 151, 152, 239
terrorism 16, 45, 76, 92, 157, 162, 163, 164, 166, 179, 183, 193, 196, 199, 209, 210, 211, 225
transgression 103, 105, 122

U

Uhud 41, 55, 70
ummah 25, 27, 39, 40, 65, 71, 78, 84, 89, 98, 178, 183, 239
Ummayad 48, 58, 61, 176, 192, 217, 225
United Nations 39, 177, 219
United States 22, 90, 108, 109, 163, 165, 177, 202, 205, 206, 216
unzil 28, 239

V

vitamin W 185

W

Wahhabi 42, 49, 75, 200, 201, 202, 222, 239
Wahhabism 50
wasta 185
wazir 59, 239
Wegner 21, 23, 24
Wright 192, 194, 195

Y

Yasir Arafat 193
Yathrib 38, 68, 70
Yom Kippur War 179, 182

Z

zakat 55, 72, 78, 102, 107, 190, 240
Zena 103, 240
zihar 94, 240
zimmi 68, 77, 78, 97, 113, 212, 240
Zionism 14, 173

Publications available from the Office of International Criminal Justice

Extremist Groups: An International Compilation of Terrorist Organizations, Violent Political Groups, and Issue-Oriented Militant Movements (2nd edition)

Senior Researcher: Sean Hill
Contributing Editor: Richard H. Ward (ISBN: 0-942511-74-3)

- Covers more than 300 terrorist organizations
- Organized by region
- Provides group history, ideology, and membership
- Details chronologies of important events
- More than 900 pages of facts and figures

Terrorism and Political Violence: An Egyptian Perspective

by Ahmed G. Ezeldin (ISBN: 0-942511-02-6)

Translated from the original Arabic edition, this book represents a unique analysis of terrorism by Egypt's leading police authority on the subject.

Policing, Security & Democracy: Theory and Practice
Policing, Security & Democracy: Special Aspects of 'Democratic Policing'

Edited by Menachem Amir & Stanley Einstein
(ISBN: 0-942511-91-3 & 0-942511-95-6)

In the second and third volumes of the series, Amir and Einstein compile a consideration of the special challenges of policing a democratic society. The wide-ranging discussions include:

- Theoretical underpinnings of the police-democracy relationship
- Protecting human and civil rights
- The challenges facing police in countries in transition including Russia, China, and South Africa
- National security considerations during interrogation presented in a framework of ethics
- Accountability for private policing